ACCESS CONTROL AND PERSONAL IDENTIFICATION SYSTEMS

ACCESS CONTROL AND PERSONAL IDENTIFICATION SYSTEMS

Dan M. Bowers

Butterworths
Boston London Singapore Sydney Toronto Wellington

Library of Congress Cataloging-in-Publication Data
Bowers, Dan M.
　Access control and personal identification systems.

　Includes index.
　1.　Computers—Access control.　2.　Identification.
I.　Title.
QA76.9.A25B68　1988　　　005.8　　　87-34220
ISBN 0-409-90083-4

British Library Cataloguing-in-Publication Data
Bowers, Dan M.
　Access control and personal identification systems.
　1.　Electronic security equipment
I.　Title
621.389'2
ISBN 0-409-90083-4

Butterworth Publishers
80 Montvale Avenue
Stoneham, MA 02180

10　9　8　7　6　5　4　3　2　1

Printed in the United States of America

To Shirley Marie,
for thirty good years past
and thirty better to come

Contents

Introduction

The material in this book had its genesis in 1973 when, after a number of years working in the security electronics field, we perceived that there was a need for a work that organized, explained, and clarified the products, techniques, technologies, applications, and vendors in the emerging business of access control and personal identification systems. We therefore created our first *Buyers' Guide and State-of-the-Art Report* on the subject, which provided both a primer on the technology and an exhaustive catalogue of vendors and the characteristics of their products. The report was well-received both by users attempting to sort through the maze to find products that solved their problems, and by vendors who wanted to find out what the competition was doing. It has been aperiodically updated through the years, and is now in its fourth edition.

In that first edition of the report, published a decade and a half ago, the complete list of vendors consisted of 29 companies, and 11 others were mentioned as having products in the development or contemplative stage. There were nine vendors of keypad access systems, 15 of card access, six of card-plus-keypad, and three vendors of what are now popularly known as biometric offerings; the majority of those early vendors have passed into oblivion. Their heirs, which now number nearly 200 companies, currently offer products which, with a few exceptions, are not markedly different in performance or technology, but are offered to a vastly more receptive marketplace.

We intend this book to serve a number of purposes. First, and primarily, it has been aimed at the needs of the businessman, executive, and manager who is using, or is investigating whether or not to use electronic and automated means to improve security provisions and system. This book provides the guidelines to carry out such an effort from start to finish. The second purpose of this book is to aid those persons in kindred fields—such as building automation, law enforcement, and physical security—to gain sufficient knowledge of electronic security that an effective melding between it and their related systems can result. The third purpose is to serve those already working in the field of access control or with other areas of electronic security such as alarm systems, closed circuit television (CCTV), and so on. This book will serve as a ready reference and refresher, and even seasoned practitioners in the field can learn a few new and useful facts. And, last but not, we hope, least, we serve those pure seekers of knowledge—students, writers, and researchers—with a source of information on the technology, applications, history, and possible future direction of access control and personal identification systems.

In that vein, let it be noted that the book includes rather more historical information than might be deemed necessary for simply an understanding of the current state-of-the-art in the field. We believe this to be useful for a number of purposes. First, because significant milestones in any technology should be recorded before those who experienced them and remember them have passed from the scene. Second, because it is important that those who have come recently into the business recognize that it did not spring full-grown into being, but has evolved—frequently painfully—over a large number of years from a very few instances in time where unique individuals were blessed with singular inspirations. And third, because the evolution of the business is a continuum, its likely future can be most accurately projected by first understanding its past history.

On the housekeeping—and peacekeeping—side, we assure our female readers that the use of masculine pronouns throughout the book is not due to chauvinism, insensitivity, or oversight, but is purely in the interests of making the material—some of which tends to become a bit abstruse on its own—more readable and not cluttered with he/she, his/hers, and so forth.

We have included, in several areas of the book, material that describes specific products, individual vendors, and the price range for equipment and systems. We do this with considerable trepidation, because in this fast-growing industry changes and advances occur by the week and month: new products are introduced, companies are acquired or go out of business, costs and economic tradeoffs become altered, and books can become obsolete before the glue is dry on their bindings. Please consider these specific references as illustrative at this particular point in time, and not as substitutes for the thorough pre-purchasing investigations which are described in Chapter 10.

We wish to acknowledge that some of the material in the book is based upon earlier work by the author which has been published in various trade magazines over the years. The methodology of vendor selection, procurement, and project management (Chapter 10) was described in various articles which appeared in *MiniMicro Systems* and *The Office* during the late 1970s and early 1980s. The description of power problems and their solutions (Chapter 9) was explored in detail in *Datamation, The Office,* and *Office Systems* during the mid-1980s. Much of the description of card access coding methods and technology (Chapter 6) appeared in *Security World* (now *Security*) in 1986, and we are indebted to them for allowing us to use the illustrations from that article. And, of course, the entire book draws from the organization and content of our own *Access Control and Personal Identification Systems: A Buyers' Guide and State-of-the-Art Report.*

As to external sources, we have drawn heavily on the published material of the manufacturers in the field for information on products and technology, tempered and augmented by our own several decades of design and applications experience with the products and their vendors and customers. We, and all other practitioners in the field, are also indebted to the trade magazines, such as *Secu-*

rity, Security Distribution and Marketing, Security Dealer, Security Management, and *Security Systems,* for a continuing flow of current information on products and applications. We also acknowledge the comprehensive source of information which is Larry Fennelly's *Handbook of Loss Prevention and Crime Prevention,* which has served as an overall source of validation and guidance, and from which we drew much of the historical material on early developments in the industry in Chapter 1.

We hope you find the book useful, interesting, and even in places entertaining as well. May your card readers never jam, your door contacts never stick, your computer never fail, your power line never have spikes, and your total security system hold you safe in the palm of its hand.

Dan M. Bowers
Allentown, Pennsylvania

Chapter 1

The Security System

In every aspect of commerce, business, and industry, automated equipment—usually a combination of mechanical, optical, and electronic technologies—has been developed to perform many functions more quickly, more efficiently, and more inexpensively than was ever possible using only people-power and manual means. In many cases, such equipment permits the accomplishment of functions which would be impossible or impractical using manual methods. Electronic computers can calculate payrolls more effectively and with fewer errors than an entire department of clerks. Process control systems can monitor and control the production of steel, glass, paper, and many other products with greater efficiency and uniformity of quality than ever before possible. Weather-forecasting computers can process volumes of meteorological data in hours, which would require days or weeks to process manually (and would then result in a hind-cast). Fire and smoke detection, surveillance of property, and control of access to facilities can now be performed using automatic, unattended, and virtually foolproof and failure-proof equipment.

Every process has a potential for error and failure. In the manual methods of operation, arithmetic errors can be made by the payroll clerk, the commodity production man can add the wrong proportions of raw materials, the guard at the gate can fail to recognize non-correspondence between a picture identification badge and a person's face. In automated systems, computer equipment failure can delay the completion of the payroll, data entry errors can result in erroneous or missing paychecks, the process control system can fail and ruin an entire batch of product, and the automated alarm system can generate so many false alarms that a real alarm is not taken seriously.

There can be weakness in an automated system, but the weakness is not usually in the mechanical or electronic mechanisms employed. In fact, redundant systems and devices can be incorporated in such a way as to virtually eliminate the possibility of failure of the equipment; whether the additional cost of such redundancy (frequently substantial) is justified must be evaluated in each case. The more common weakness is in the failure of management to understand the strengths and weaknesses of the automated system, and to consider the function to be performed as a total system entity; a total system which includes mechanisms, people, and the process which is being automated.

1

A frequent reason for the failure of management to understand the entire system and all of its ingredients is fear that the technological part of the system is too complex for the non-technical mind to understand; vital decisions are therefore abdicated to technical specialists and the proficiency of the salesman who is selling the equipment, neither of whom is in a position to appreciate the totality of the considerations which comprise the total system. But the fundamental principles of almost any technological device or system can be understood without benefit of a technical education, provided the principles are properly presented and the manager is properly motivated. To appreciate this phenomenon, one has only to view the tremendous usage of the personal computer among those who a few years ago fled at the very mention of the words "BASIC," "open file," or "modem." The manager can gain sufficient knowledge to adequately evaluate one type of equipment against another type and one vendor's offering against another vendor's. In this manner, the manager can determine what procedures and staff must be implemented along with the equipment in order that the resulting system will effectively perform its desired function. A competent manager will thoroughly attend to such details as the appearance and wording of his sales literature, the color of the walls in the cafeteria, the hiring and training of a new production manager, or the changing of a manufacturing sequence to achieve cost reduction. He can hardly afford to be less thorough in selecting automated equipment and integrating it into an effective system.

The principal intention of this book is to provide an education in the field of access control and personal identification systems, an education sufficient to enable the reader to intelligently select the appropriate equipment for his needs, to deal intelligently with vendors as he purchases the equipment, and to integrate the equipment into a total effective system.

ELEMENTS OF A TOTAL SECURITY SYSTEM

Access control devices and systems comprise an important part of almost every security system but are seldom the sole source of security; they usually work within a total security system. In order for the goals of the total system to be met, the other portions of the security system must also be well planned and executed. Even the simplest single-door access control system will include at least an electric door strike to automatically unlock the door, a timer to make certain the door doesn't stay open all day, and perhaps a bell or light to indicate that the door is open or has not closed properly. The three major ingredients of a total security system are access control systems, closed-circuit television (CCTV) systems and alarm systems. In an effectively designed security system, these three ingredients will support and complement one another, as well as providing backup and redundancy for one another. Unfortunately, all too many system designers treat these ingredients as independent entities: the access control system guards the doors, the alarm system monitors the perimeter, and the CCTV system allows the guard to view what is happening within the interior spaces. In a larger scale security system there may also be guard patrols, physical barriers and turnstyles, and a variety of other devices and systems. It is the effective interaction amongst all these elements which results in an effective total security system.

Examination in detail of all these other security devices and systems is beyond the scope of this book on access control; it is, however, important to the selection of an access control system that these other elements are understood and utilized effectively to perform their proper role in protecting the user's facility. We therefore provide a brief description of each of them, along with some advice as to their proper place in the system.

Physical Barriers

It sounds simplistic to state that in order to make certain all persons entering and leaving a facility are scrutinized by the access control equipment, they must be prevented from passing through in places where there is no access control equipment, but the design of physical barriers such as walls, fences, windows, doors, air vents (and, if you like, moats) is an important part of a security system. The need to limit the number of portals stems from the goal of making the security system of minimal complexity and of minimum cost. This must be balanced with the need for the flow of personnel for operating efficiency, the need in some business situations for the flow of outsiders such as customers and vendors, and the necessity for quick exit under emergency situations.

Portal Hardware

As mentioned above, there is usually an electrically-operated door strike to unlock the door, although there are some access control devices of the simpler kind in which unlocking is accomplished mechanically. A sensor—usually a simple contact switch or a magnetic switch—is necessary to determine that the door is open or closed. Customarily, there is a remote indicator which lights or sounds ("annunciates," in security parlance) when the door opens. In the more sophisticated systems the door sensor connects directly to the computer which manages the security system, and the computer can note the time when the door opened and who opened it, and can summon a guard if security restrictions have been violated.

There is also portal hardware for use on doors which are not protected by access control devices, but may be used in emergency situations such as fire. An example is the "panic bar" prominently labeled "Push To Open—Alarm Will Sound," which, when opened from the inside, will immediately sound an alarm and which cannot be opened from the outside.

Mantraps and Turnstiles

Once a door has been legitimately opened by a person who satisfies the requirements of the access control system, there may be a need to insure that only one person (or vehicle, in the case of a vehicular portal) enters. There are a variety of turnstiles, mantraps, parking gates, and so forth, available for this purpose.

Guards

The fact that an automated security system or some individual security device has been installed does not necessarily mean that the traditional guard force should be eliminated. Many of the most effective security systems combine the most positive attributes of guards and automated systems rather than opting for wholly one means or the other. Frequently, the number of guards required can be reduced by allowing one guard to be responsible for a number of different security points through the use of closed-circuit television and access control and alarm equipment. When the security system performs its ultimate purpose, that of detecting an attempted penetration of the premises for nefarious purposes such as a burglary or a terrorist attack, there must be people who respond, assess the situation, and apprehend the perpetrator.

Other Sensors and Annunciators

In addition to the "door open" sensor and annunciator described above, it is frequently useful to provide and monitor intrusion detectors, smoke detectors, sensors to detect that someone is attempting to tamper with the equipment, and so on. Many pure access control systems provide the capability to wire a number of such sensors into the controller of the access control equipment, and to annunciate them along with the door-open signal.

Alarm sensors in general are sufficiently important to the access control and total security system that we provide coverage of them in further depth in the next section.

Multiple Systems

Access control is also frequently combined with time-and-attendance data collection, since the data necessary for time-and-attendance—what time did the employee enter and leave the premises—is available through the access control system that allows the employee to enter and leave. It is from there a relatively small step to provide access-control-type readers at various points on the floor of a manufacturing facility, to collect data describing the time an employee began and finished a work task, thus providing input for a job-cost-accounting system.

Energy management and other forms of facility automation are frequently integrated with the access control and security system because they are very similar in concept and in the functions they are required to perform: both require communications wires to be strung to every part of a facility; both require real-time monitoring of a large number of simple (on-off) sensors and of a few points which provide numeric data (for example, employee card number and temperature); and both require that a large number of points be under simple control (for example, open the door, open a valve).

Clearly, the more functions provided by a single system the more complex become the system design and the programming of the computer equipment which provides the intelligence in the system, and also the more vital it becomes that all of the systems mesh efficiently together. Further, the ability to control this diversity of systems through a single computer-controller raises a new consideration in the design of the total system: cost-efficiency is, *prima facie,* best achieved by making a single computer system purchase serve as many purposes as possible, thus arguing for combining the systems. On the opposite side are two powerful arguments. First, most of the great computer system disasters of our time have resulted from overly complex programming which could never be made to work as its planners envisioned. Second, if the single computer which performs all your functions burns up, you are completely out of business (the all-your-eggs-in-one-basket syndrome).

Processors and Controllers

With a simple, one-portal access control device, the controller can consist of a single circuit board which can detect that the correct code was entered and can then energize the door strike. At the other end of the spectrum, a total security system with a multiplicity of access-controlled doors, alarm monitoring, and perhaps some time-and-attendance and energy management features, will require a sizeable general purpose computer and a sophisticated communications controller, along with extensive, expert computer programming. Between these extremes there are nearly an infinite number of ways in which the required control intelligence can be distributed within the system. There can be separate computer-controllers for each of the separate functions (for example, access control, alarms, time-and-attendance, energy management) that are all under the supervision of a master controller which will establish priorities among the systems, annunciate alarms and emergencies, prepare reports, and so forth. There can be local computer-controllers that control all the functions for one building or one floor of a building, again reporting to a master controller. There can be intelligent portal units that have the ability to perform local functions at a reduced level of capability if the central controller fails, or if communications with the central controller are disrupted.

The use of intelligent portal units is one means of distributing the functional eggs amongst several baskets so that a single equipment failure cannot disable an entire security system as well as other functions, such as time-and-attendance, energy management, and the like. Intelligent portal units for access control are typically capable of controlling access through one or a few portals based upon the prospective entrant's possession of the proper access code. More sophisticated features such as limiting access of particular individuals to specific time periods (work shifts, for example), or cancelling access rights on an individual basis (when an employee is fired, or has lost his access card), are usually provided by a sophisticated central computer-controller. These features will be lost if the computer or the communications with the computer fail. In the presence of such a failure, the system will operate at a lesser level of capability (known as a "degraded mode"), but at least it will not be entirely inoperative.

Another method of providing continuation of operation, even under conditions of equipment failure, is to provide redundant, (duplicate) equipment for each function. Duplicate communications channels between the remote portals and the central controller are frequently provided. For example, both a telephone connection and a radio-data channel carrying the same data will provide maximum assurance that communications will continue even if one means of communication fails. Duplicate central controllers are required in high security applications such as security systems for nuclear power plants, in order that the system will continue to operate at full capability even if one complete central computer is inoperative.

Duplicate equipment can also be provided at portals. This is seldom done, however, because failure at one portal does not seriously jeopardize the total security system; the portal can be closed or monitored by a guard until repairs are effected.

Multi-function systems, those which provide security, time-and-attendance, job cost accounting, energy management, and the like, provide the opportunity for another approach to redundant systems. Individual central controllers can be provided for each of the individual functions, with the capability for each controller to assume control of another system's functions in the event of failure of that system's controller. For example, if the controller for the security system fails, the controller for the energy management system might be used for both security and energy management temporarily. This scheme requires that each individual controller be made larger than would be necessary if it were only to be required to perform its own functions, but provides for a continuation of all functions, even under conditions of multiple failures in the controllers, without requiring that entirely superfluous equipments be included in the system.

The system design decisions regarding the distribution of the control intelligence within the system, the provision of a degraded mode, inclusion of any of the various forms of redundancy, and the relationships among the various possible multiple applications must result from a careful analysis of cost versus risk for each particular organization. Minimum *cost* is achieved by performing all operations on a single computer-controller, but this results in the dual risk that the single system may be horribly complex, and when it fails all functions are inoperative. Minimum *risk* is provided through totally redundant equipment, with a concomitant cost that will assuredly be several times that of the minimum cost.

Between these two extremes there is an infinite variety of combinations that will provide an appropriate solution for the security and other operational requirements of any organization. Any oaf can design a working system by including the maximum possible complement of equipment required, in the process spending the maximum amount of money (sometimes known as the "Government-at-Washington Approach"). It is the essence of effective system design to achieve an appropriate balance among security risks, other operational requirements, probability of failure of the system components and the probable time they will be out of service, the efficacy of fail-soft and degraded-mode solutions, the availability of alternate solutions such as guards or CCTV or shutting down a portal, and the need for the various possible degrees of redundancy. There is no single solution which fulfills the requirements of every organization, but there are guidelines and evaluation methods that can assist with the system design task, and we will discuss them as they affect the access control system, in a later chapter.

The Central Alarm Station

The monitoring of and response to burglar and other alarms at a central location was begun by Edwin Holmes in the 1870s, and continues to this day (as does the company which Holmes founded) as a major method of providing central monitoring and control of security systems. Although this form of monitoring has historically been concerned with only simple switch-closure alarm signals, the more complex functions of access control and even closed-circuit television monitoring are now offered by most central station services. Until the last decade, central stations utilized direct wires running between the central station and the location that was being protected almost exclusively. The more recent trend has been to new technologies such as telephone communications, radio transmission, and even satellite links. There are now services being offered via satellite wherein the central station may be in Detroit and the location being monitored may be in Charlotte. With the advent of more complex technologies and long-distance communication, there is an increasing trend towards installing a local processor on the customer's premises in order to provide both a reduced volume of communication with the central station, and a degraded mode of operation in the event of failure of the communications link.

There are major nationwide central station operators, such as American District Telegraph and Wells Fargo, with central stations in the principal cities. There are also independent and very capable operators in most major cities.

The Power System

Electrical power, without which the security system cannot function, is frequently taken for granted like the cabinetry, the instruction manual, and the dog wagging its tail when we get home. Electrical power, however, is subject to various vagaries. Problems which can occur fall into three basic categories: first, the electrical power utility's generating or distribution equipment can fail, leaving the user without power; second, a person who is attempting to penetrate the facility can cut the power lines, producing the same result; and third, malfunctions in the power utility's equipment or disturbances elsewhere in the power network can cause the electrical power to contain a variety of abnormalities known as noise, spikes, transients, surges, sags, frequency variations, and interruptions.

The third class, abnormalities, is easily handled by commercially-available power conditioning equipment. In fact, the better-designed electronic equipments come with such power-conditioning already incorporated. It is the total absence of power which is of primary concern in a security system; whether it occurs due to failure of the power utility or the nefarious actions of a prospective perpetrator is immaterial, the result can be an unprotected facility, regardless of how much money was spent on redundancy and degraded mode.

Again, there is a wide range of solutions which can be implemented to deal with the problem, and again, it is the responsibility of the system designer to achieve the proper balance of cost and risk. At the least-cost end in some situations, provision can be made to operate all functions manually in the absence of power. For example, protected portals can be made to fail in the "open" condition, and guards or other supervisory personnel can be summoned to serve until power is restored. At the other end of the spectrum, a complete in-house generating capability—diesel, gasoline, or battery—can be provided along with switchover equipment so that complete operation will continue as though there had been no power failure: this is the UPS, uninterruptable power system. Between these extremes is the correct solution for most facilities. For example, sufficient UPS can be provided to run in a degraded mode by operating only the intelligent portal units, allowing the central computer-controller to die until power is restored. Or UPS may be provided so that critical areas—the money vault, the reactor control room, the uncut diamond safe—will receive full protection while other less critical areas operate in a degraded mode.

A word should be said about the term "battery backup," which is a prominently-advertised feature of many computer-based equipments and systems. Battery backup is provided almost universally to only the memory portion of a computer, so that the computer will retain memory of what happened immediately before the power went off. It does not keep the entire system functioning during a power outage.

People

Frequently the last ingredient to be considered in the design of a total security system, the people who are involved with the system are probably the most important ingredient. In fact, if there were no people, there would be no need for security systems as we know them. There are several sets of people who are integral parts of the total security system. There are workers who must be admitted to the facility without delay or aggravation, and there may be different subsets of workers who must be admitted to different areas within the facility at different times of day. There are visitors and customers who must be allowed entrance but who must be restricted to certain areas. There may be classes of people who must be excluded from the facility: those carrying guns and bombs, for example. And there are the people who comprise the security force and must monitor activities, respond to alarms, and deal with any unusual situations.

A security system may be implemented with all manner of the latest sophisticated electronics, sensors, and scanners. It may incorporate the ultimate in solid-state computer-controllers. It may provide redundancy, fail-safe, and a complete UPS. But, if the system designers have failed to incorporate the needs and vagaries of all the people who will be a part of the system into the design requirements, the system cannot achieve its intended purpose.

ALARMS AND ALARM SYSTEMS

Since an understanding of the rudiments of alarm systems is necessary to the design and selection of an access control system and to the total security system, it is appropriate that we review herein those rudiments.

General and Historical

Alarms are the oldest security devices, dating back to the times when aboriginal humans stretched a thin vine fastened to a balanced rock across the cave entrances to warn them of intruders. Other early alarm systems utilized the superior senses of animals such as dogs and geese. Although it may seem specious to compare these methods with the modern intrusion detectors using microwaves, ultrasonics, and photocells, it should be observed that only the technology has changed, not the basic techniques. The light beam across the door triggers a bell or a light just as the caveman's vine brought the rock crashing down. The microwave senses the presence of an intruder and sounds an alarm just as the dog did, and perhaps no more effectively and with no fewer false alarms. The use of dogs for various security purposes is more widespread today than ever in history, although trip-wires seem to have gone out of vogue.

Modern alarm systems have followed closely on the development of electrical and electronic technology, beginning shortly after the work of Ohm and Faraday in the early 1800s, and continuing to the present-day utilization of microwaves and microprocessors. A disastrous fire in New York City in 1835 triggered the development of a citywide fire alarm signalling system, and Boston followed a decade later with fire alarm boxes annunciating to a central monitoring station by means of coded paper tape. The concepts of fire alarm boxes and the central station survive to this day. Burglar and intrusion alarms using electrical door and window contacts along with a battery (there was no centrally supplied electricity until after the invention of the electric light by Edison in the late 1800s) and a bell began to be developed in the 1850s. These alarm systems were pioneered by Edwin Holmes and by E.A. Calahan, the inventor of the stock market ticker and the founder of the American District Telegraph Company, which survives today as the largest firm totally devoted to electronic security. The combination of the local burglar alarm system connected directly to the manned central station was made by Holmes in the 1870s, and the alarm business and its technology existed then substantially as we know it today.*

Layers of Protection

Modern alarm systems and techniques can be conveniently divided into categories by the kind of protection that they provide; this in turn is determined by where in the physical premises they are to be used. It is useful to consider the various layers which constitute a physical premises from the outermost edge of the facility to its interior.

Perimeter Protection

The perimeter of a facility is defined as the area surrounding the physical buildings which contain items of value; for a warehouse or nuclear power plant the perimeter would comprise the fence around the property and the clear area of ground between the fence and the buildings; for a downtown bank the perimeter might be the city sidewalk, over which the bank has no control. Alarming at the perimeter provides early warning of an intrusion or attempt at intrusion, thus allowing greater time for an appropriate response.

Portal Protection

Portals are openings through which intruders can enter the physical premises: doors, windows, skylights, air vents, sewers, electrical cable conduits, and so forth. One must also consider the possibility that the intruders may attempt to create a new portal for their own purposes, by such means as cutting or blasting a hole in the wall.

Space Protection

Once past the perimeter and through the portal, the intruder enters the interior space of the premises. Since this space is larger than a portal, there is a different group of alarm systems which are capable of detecting the presence of a person therein.

---

*We are indebted for much of the historical material to William Greer's "The History of Electric Alarm Protection," from the *Handbook of Loss Prevention and Crime Prevention,* Lawrence J. Fennelly, published by Butterworth Publishers, 1982.

Object Protection

Even if the intruder passes through all the external layers of the alarm system and reaches the object for which he has taken all the previous risks, there are alarms which can detect the proximity of a person to an object, or an attempt to move or remove an object (such as a cash box, safe, art object, gold bar, negotiable securities, etc.) from the premises.

Manual Alarms

At any point in the facility where there exist in-house staff, such as tellers, stock-boys, guards, or supervisors, they can act as sensors of trouble and can activate manual alarms. The manual system is the only resort, for example, in a banking office during regular business hours, since anyone can walk in during these hours, and the alarm systems that are provided for the hours when the bank is closed will not be in use.

Monitor and Control

Alarms must be monitored, detected, processed, identified, and acted upon, and there are two different means of accomplishing these functions. In the **Central Station System,** described earlier, alarms are transmitted from the protected premises to a central monitoring station. Security personnel at the central station determine and initiate the appropriate response, such as calling the security personnel at the protected facility, sending out their own patrols, or calling in the police or fire department. The second means of monitoring alarms is through use of a **Proprietary System.** In this system, the alarms are monitored and responded to by local personnel using a locally-installed system. In both cases, the monitoring system is most usually a computer-controller which monitors and prioritizes the alarms, and presents a display of their status on a computer terminal, and prepares a printed log of all events which occur. There are still surviving systems in which alarms are displayed using large arrays of lights, called annunciator panels. There are also combination systems in which alarms are monitored locally during business hours and at a central station at all other times.

Many of these systems also have the capability to simultaneously control other functions, such as card access control and energy management.

Alarm Products

Alarm products fall into the general categories described above, since each kind of alarm is usually most suitable for use in a particular layer of the physical premises. They can be divided into the following groups.

Fence Alarms

There are two basic means for detecting intrusion at the outer perimeter, or the fence. The first is to detect that a person has approached to within a certain distance from the fence. This is known as a proximity detector. The second is to detect that contact has been made with the fence, and that it is being climbed, cut, or torn down. This is known as a contact sensor.

Proximity Sensors.   Proximity sensors, otherwise known as E-Field sensors, incorporate the fence as part of a radio-frequency tuned circuit. When a human body approaches, the capacitance of the circuit is altered, changing the amplitude and phase of the signal in the tuned circuit, and causing an alarm.

Contact Sensors.   Contact sensors are of several varieties. The simplest utilizes a mercury switch suspended by one end so that motion of the fence will move the switch and cause an alarm; unfortunately, a good stiff breeze will frequently do the same. The taut-wire method utilizes tightly stretched wires across the fence, with tension sensors at each end to detect either less tension (the wire has been cut) or more tension (it is being climbed upon). A third method utilizes the panels of the wire of the fence, which must be specially insulated, as two legs of an electrical Wheatstone bridge, and detects the voltage difference caused by tension on the wire when it is being climbed upon or cut.

Vibration and Seismic Detectors

Vibration and seismic detectors are utilized for a number of purposes. One popular use is to bury the detector underground where it will detect the passage of vehicles or people on the surface above, tunnelling under a protected fence, or someone digging to gain access to a buried communications cable. There are magnetic devices which report disturbances in the surrounding magnetic field; some facilities use geophones which detect acoustic vibrations; others use tubes filled with pressurized gas or liquid which sense the change in pressure due to the weight of a vehicle or person. Taut-wires similar to those attached to fences are also used; these detect increased tension due to the weight of a vehicle or person. Piezoelectric sensors, which are solid-state crystals, generate a voltage when the crystal is deformed, for example, by weight above.

All of these sensors are used in buried applications, and some are used elsewhere as well. Piezoelectric sensors are used in home and business applications because they can be attached to the underside of a floor joist to detect the weight of a person walking on the floor above. Geophones in the basement can perform the same function. Floor mats with tension-wires or pressurized-tube detectors incorporated within them can detect the weight of a person treading upon them.

Simple Switches and Switch-Equivalents

The simplest alarm detector is a switch that opens or closes when a door is opened or other intrusive action takes place, like the switch which turns on the light in your refrigerator or automobile when the door is opened. This and many of the other simple alarm switches were invented by Edwin Holmes more than a century ago and they are still the most widely used because they are the cheapest alarm on the market and yet they provide effective protection in many situations. The more modern switches are magnetically-activated, that is, opening the door moves a magnet affixed to the door away from the switch contacts that are affixed to the jamb, allowing the contacts to open. Metallic foil used as window tape acts as a switch: when the window is broken and the foil parts, the circuit is opened. There are also glass-break detectors which sonically sense the sound of breaking glass and create an alarm. Other window-entry detectors utilize the window screen as a carrier for fine wires. These wires, when cut, interrupt a circuit thus causing an alarm to sound. Photocell detectors can also serve as a form of switch, sounding an alarm when, for example, the beam of light across a doorway is interrupted by a person entering; the light beam need not be visible, since there are infrared versions available, and complex laser systems are used by the military and offered for home use for the man who has almost everything else.

Space Intrusion Alarms

The most popular forms of space protection today are volumetric in principle; that is, they fill the entire volume of a room with sensing waves and detect any disturbance to those waves made by an intruding body. The two kinds of waves used for this purpose are ultrasound waves and microwaves. Passive infrared sensors also cover a large volume, but they work on a reverse principle: the intruding warm body emits infrared radiation that is detected optically by a wide-angle sensor. There are also sonic sensors which will alarm if the sound level within a space rises above a preset threshold, and some of the more popular central monitoring services can listen to the activity within a space after having been alerted by such an alarm that there is activity there. Invisible-laser systems are also offered which fill a space with laser beams reflected from a series of mirrors and end at a photocell detector which alarms if the beam is interrupted at any point.

Object Disturbance Alarms

Object disturbance alarms operate either on the proximity principle that an approaching body will disturb a field that is generated around the object, or on the vibration-sonic detection method. Vibration detectors can be tuned to detect specific noises such as sawing or drilling, and have been used for decades to protect bank vaults. There are also simple switch-type object disturbance alarms which will alarm if an object is moved from its customary place.

Miscellaneous Alarm Devices

A number of alarm devices have been devised for specialized purposes. Video cameras exist that can detect any motion within their field of view, or within particular areas of their field of view. There are sonar systems for use in detecting underwater motion, which have application in protecting military facilities and are also used in the water-intake areas of nuclear power plants.

Features and System Considerations

In addition to the type of alarm that is chosen for use at each point in the security system for a facility, there are a number of features and system-level considerations which must be addressed in an alarm system.

Supervised Alarm Devices

A simple switch that closes to initiate an alarm is easily circumvented by cutting the wire leading to the switch. The reverse, a switch that is normally closed and opens to initiate an alarm, is just as easily circumvented by shunting the switch. Early-on, the alarm industry recognized the need for alarm devices that not only sounded the alarm when appropriate, but which could also indicate that they were alive and well and functioning properly: these are "supervised" alarms. Simple burglar alarms since the last century have been simply supervised by allowing a low level of current to pass through them during their alert-but-not-alarmed state, and a higher level of current to pass through them during their alarmed or shunted state; no current at all means either tampering or a malfunction. The means of providing supervision varies according to the type of alarm. In a microwave system, for example, an independent detector might be provided to detect that the proper level of microwave energy is indeed filling the room; a contact-fence alarm might require that the fence be rattled periodically.

Failsafe or Failsoft

One of the more interesting challenges in the design of any system is to provide for an orderly transition to an alternate mode of operation when the system or any of its parts ceases to operate in the required manner. The first rule is that a failure cannot be allowed to have deleterious or disastrous effects, such as locking persons irretrievably in or out of the vault, or automatically calling in every police force in the county: this is **FAILSAFE.** The second rule is that those parts of the system which are not intimately associated with the failure should continue to operate, even if at a reduced level of speed or convenience. A short-circuit in the fence alarm, for example, should not bring the alarm processor to its knees and prevent it from recognizing an alarm from the vault vibration detector: this is **FAILSOFT.**

Tamper Alarms

Even though an alarm is supervised, there may be a means of circumventing its operation if the perpetrator can gain access to its internal mechanisms. For this reason, the alarm mechanism is usually protected by a sturdy housing, and a separate alarm is provided to signal if someone attempts to penetrate the box—an alarm to protect the alarm, as it were.

Alarm Logging

Any adequate alarm system controller will automatically log all alarms, the time of their occurrence, and the response taken to them, for later reconstruction in the event of a crime, and for insuring the efficiency of the alarm monitoring staff.

Multiple and Combination Alarms

Two alarm systems working in combination are at least four times more difficult to defeat than either is singly, and three systems may provide more than ten times the security of one. The systems may be layered such that they are encountered in succession by the prospective perpetrator (for example, fence-portal-space-object). Or they may be in combination, such as providing both passive infrared and sonic protection for a space. Some vendors now offer combination sensors within a single package. The vexing false-alarm problem caused by a malfunctioning or over-sensitive sensor can be greatly reduced by majority-voting among a multiplicity of sensors, each monitoring a different physical manifestation of intrusion.

Protection of Communications

The wiring between the alarm sensors and the central monitoring location within the facility, or the location at which the signals are consolidated for sending to the commercial central station, is a vital part of the security system and must be protected both physically and with tamper or space alarms. Additionally, if the commercial central station is used, there is the further exposure of the communications link to the central station.* An attack upon the communications can render the alarm system helpless without requiring the perpetrator to enter the protected facility. Careful application of supervision methods must be used to insure the integrity of communications; the use of redundant communications (for example, both radio communications and a direct wire) is frequently deemed desirable.

CLOSED-CIRCUIT TELEVISION EQUIPMENT AND SYSTEMS

A second of the three major ingredients of a total security system (access central systems, CCTV-systems and alarm systems) is made up of closed-circuit television equipment, CCTV. CCTV systems perform two basic functions: first, they

---

*The communications link to the central station can take any of several forms: ordinary dial-up telephone lines; direct wires, including direct telephone lines, cable-TV lines, and real wires; radio signals direct to the central station; or radio signals via satellite relay to the central station (which in this case does not even have to be in the same city as the monitored premises).

allow a person to observe a scene without being present at the scene; second, they allow an activity to be recorded for future viewing without the viewer or any other person necessarily having to be present at the time the activity took place. These functions are no different from the functions that commercial television equipment performs for its viewers: television allows the viewer to enjoy a Celtics game without actually being present in Boston Garden (which has been sold out since the time of Holmes anyway), and the video recorder allows him to play golf on Sunday afternoon and watch the game later at his own convenience.

The first function of CCTV is useful to business and industry in several ways. Remote and unattended areas, such as storerooms, can be monitored from a central location for fire or intruders. Areas where the environment is hazardous to the health of a human, such as nuclear reactors, chemical processors, and outer space, can be observed from the safety of a separate location. A guard, seated at a console receiving pictures from a multiplicity of CCTV cameras, can monitor a large number of different areas within the facility.

The second function is useful for recording an experiment or process and playing it back later in slow-motion or stop-action to analyze it. This is done in the archival recording of events which are of historical importance or legal significance—such as activities during the commission of a bank robbery. By far the most important applications of CCTV have been in the field of surveillance for security purposes.

Principal Attributes

The effectiveness of CCTV in helping to protect both people and property is due in large part to the following three principal attributes.

Deterrence

The visible presence of CCTV equipment warns the person who is contemplating perpetration of a nefarious act that he is being observed and possibly recorded, and that swift response is probable, along with photographic proof that he committed the act. The mere installation of CCTV equipment results in a decrease in criminal activity on the protected premises: for this reason, "dummy" CCTV cameras, which are vastly cheaper than real cameras, are sometimes installed. (This is similar to the installation of signs at automobile toll-collecting facilities which warn that "Your License Plate Will Be Photographed If You Pass Through Without Paying the Toll," accompanied by a strobe light which flashes if you ignore the sign—almost none of these facilities are actually equipped with cameras.) In practice, a combination of real CCTV cameras and dummies is quite frequently used with excellent results.

Response

The ability to remotely monitor a scene whether on a continuous basis, scanned periodically on a monitor that switches among several scenes, or on-demand (for example, the sounding of a silent alarm by a bank teller will cause that teller station to be immediately displayed at the guard console), enables the security force to determine precisely the nature and cause of the problem, and to implement exactly the correct response: different actions are appropriate for a bad-check passer, an armed robber, an obnoxious drunk, a bomb threat, and a gang of machine-gun-waving men taking hostages.

Evidence

Whether the crime is recognized at the time it is taking place (armed robbery) or is not discovered until later (a bad-check passer), CCTV recording can provide moving-pictures of the crime which will help both in identifying the perpetrator so that he can be apprehended, and in proving in court that the crime actually took place and was committed by the suspect.

CCTV Versus Film

Two of the same attributes which make CCTV a valuable security tool also apply to film-camera equipment: the deterrence attributes of the two are equal, and the evidence-gathering capabilities of film are at least equal to those of CCTV. There is, however, no remote-monitoring and response-determining capability with film cameras. Some of the factors which should be considered when making the decision between the two methods are as follows.

Clarity. In general, better resolution, and therefore clearer pictures, can be obtained with film than with CCTV.

Cost. CCTV systems are more expensive to install, but cost less per-picture on a continuing basis because the video cassettes can be re-used when there is no further need for the images they contain. Film systems make up for their lower initial cost with the continued cost of the film and its processing.

Lifetime of Equipment. CCTV equipment will serve for approximately seven years, film equipment for twice that, depending upon volume of use, maintenance discipline, and so forth.

Addition of Equipment. Additional CCTV cameras can usually be added to an existing system without adding monitors, recorders, communications equipment, and the like, by means of an existing switcher. New film cameras are roughly the same cost regardless of how many cameras are already installed.

Motion. CCTV can provide motion-pictures, which may be valuable in certain situations, such as identifying a suspect from his gait or other mannerisms. Almost no one uses motion-picture film cameras for security purposes.

Other Benefits

CCTV equipment is frequently used for other purposes in addition to security monitoring, for example, customer traffic analyses and employee training and monitoring.

CCTV Components and Equipment

There is a wide variety of CCTV equipment available for use in a wide variety of environments and for a wide variety of applications. Cameras can have a wide-angle view of an entire room, or be focused for a close-up view of a particular work station, depending upon the lens which is used. There are cameras for use in bright daylight conditions and cameras which will function under nearly-dark conditions. There are camera housings which can provide operation in environmentally severe and even hazardous conditions. There are mechanisms which can cause the camera to scan a scene, zoom in on a particular area, or travel over an area on a track. There are installation packages which can conceal the camera, make it look like part of the furniture, or hide it under an opaque dome so no one can see where it is scanning. There are switchers to enable one monitor to select its picture from among several cameras sequentially or at random, and there are monitors which can display pictures from several cameras at once, using a divided single screen.

CCTV systems are made up in a building-block fashion from a selection of sub-units, each of which is useful in a particular situation. The building-block components represent the products sold in the CCTV business; these products are integrated by systems houses and alarm installers to form a CCTV system customized to the user's needs. The component building-blocks of CCTV systems can be grouped into the following categories.

Cameras

For ordinary, run-of-the-mill situations where there is adequate and controlled lighting and no special requirements, there are two choices of cameras.

The venerable antimony trisulphide *vidicon tube* has excellent picture clarity and is usable over a rather remarkable range of lighting conditions from bright sunlight to dim indoor lighting, a ratio of about 100,000 to one; it is cheap, available, and proven. On the downside, it is subject to damage from bright spots, and will burn in fixed patterns (such as when it is fixed on the same scene for days and months on end).

Solid-state cameras were introduced about a half-dozen years ago, and have begun to find their way into security applications. They are smaller, consume less power, and are lighter than tube cameras, but they do not currently have the sensitivity or ability to operate under a wide range of lighting conditions. Following the pattern which has occurred in other areas of solid-state technology, we expect that these cameras will, within the decade, provide performance equal to that of the tube, and at lower price.

There are also cameras available for applications where the lighting level is below that which would be acceptable to a standard vidicon tube. These cameras use vidicons made from silicon or cadmium selenide, and are called low-light-level-silicon, or Newvicon and Ultracon tubes, respectively. There is also an extremely-low-light-level, silicon-intensified-target tube which can see on an overcast night.

There is also the choice as to whether to use a monochrome (black-and-white) or a color CCTV camera and system. Because the cost of color is significantly higher than that of monochrome, and because there are seldom significant benefits from the use of color in a security situation, and because there is not the range of equipment performance available in color (for example, low-light-level cameras), there is very little use of color in security and surveillance CCTV applications. This is markedly different from the trend in the computer and controls business, where color monitors are *de rigueur* whether or not they are needed for the application. We consider the development of a similar trend in the security industry to be unlikely before the 1990s, when the cost of color equipment may become more comparable to that of monochrome, and the decision will be a coin-toss.

Lenses

Selection of the appropriate lens for a CCTV camera depends upon the optical characteristics of the particular situation being viewed, i.e., the level of illumination in the scene, the distance of the camera from the scene, the size of the area being viewed, and the kind of camera being used.

The various calculations (focal length, lens opening, etc.) required to design a camera-and-lens system for a particular operation requires a technical education in the field of optical physics. Fortunately, people trained in this field have reduced these calculations to cookbook nomographs which enable those with considerably less training to assemble a system.

There are wide-angle lenses which enable a camera to view an entire scene, such as a company parking lot. There are telephoto lenses which enable the camera to concentrate upon only one small portion of a large scene, such as the company president's automobile. There are zoom lenses which, depending upon their setting, can view wide-angle or telephoto or anywhere between, and the zoom function can be remotely controlled from the security officer's console. There are side-looking lenses for looking around corners or for difficult mounting situations, such as when the camera must be mounted flat to the ceiling. There are split-image lenses, using lenses and mirrors combined, which can present two views using the same camera; these may be two different views from the same camera, or they may be a wide-angle and a close-up view of the same scene. There are also three-view lenses. Lenses exist which are made for looking through very small openings (such as mounting the camera behind a wall and poking the lens through the eye of the founder's portrait on the other side); some of these use fiber optics for conveying the image to the camera.

Monitors and Monitoring Consoles

The scene viewed by a CCTV camera through its lens must be viewed using a monitor, which is merely an ordinary TV set without channel controls and fancy woodwork. The monitor can be directly connected to the camera, which allows remote viewing of one scene per monitor, and in some industrial applications, such as using CCTV to view an operation being performed in a hazardous environment, this is appropriate.

In most security applications, however, one monitor is used to view the scenes from more than one camera, for two reasons. The first reason is that it is cheaper, since fewer monitors are required. The second is that the security guard at the monitoring console cannot humanly attend to more than four to six monitors, and in a typical security installation there are usually more than this number of scenes to be covered by CCTV. Further, it is not necessary that every scene be observed 100 percent of the time, since events of interest take at least a number of seconds or minutes to transpire; also, there are frequently alarms in the same area (such as a teller holdup alarm) which will automatically direct the security officer's attention to the scene needing it. For these reasons, the scenes on a monitor are usually switched from one camera to another on a programmed basis, with each scene being presented for a sufficient length of time to allow the security guard to make an adequate observation. When an event worthy of more extensive viewing is noted, the guard can halt the switching process and devote the monitor to a single camera; electronic alarms will usually perform this function automatically.

Controls and Switches

These devices provide for remote, and in some cases automatic, control of CCTV cameras and their accessories in order to present the desired view to the security guard at the monitor. There are the switching equipments described above which will automatically present the views from different cameras, and which can be overriden by the operator or by an automatic alarm; there are also manual switchers with which the guard must manually select one scene after another, but these are almost never used in modern systems. There is also remote control of pan and tilt (moving the camera across a scene either horizontally or vertically), and this function can be programmed for automatic operation in most systems, in addition to being controllable manually. The modern control consoles are computer-controlled, providing a great amount of flexibility of control of the CCTV system.

Communications Equipment

The simplest, cheapest, and most common means of transmitting the television picture from the camera to the monitor, or to the switching equipment that governs which picture will be displayed on the monitor, is direct connection of the camera to the monitor or switcher using coaxial cable. There are several kinds of coax for use at various distances, and they can be relied upon up to distances of 1000 to 1500 feet. Beyond those distances, other means are needed. One such means is to add booster amplifiers at the camera end, or along the intervening cable run. There are expensive measures for providing picture transmission over any distance required, such as microwave systems and infrared lasers. Fiber optic transmission is coming into use for long-distance applications; distances of up to five miles without intervening amplification have been claimed. There are also amplifiers advertised which are claimed to transmit the picture over one-half mile using an ordinary pair of wires.

Two other aspects of the communications portion of the CCTV system should be noted. First, using a broadband channel such as any of those described above, it is possible to send more than one signal over the wire at a time; these multiple signals can be from different CCTV cameras, they can be a combination of television pictures and control signals (for example, pan-tilt-zoom commands); they can even be voice conversations, or can even be going in opposite directions simultaneously.

Second, there is a means for sending CCTV pictures over ordinary telephone lines, called slo-scan TV. The telephone line has far too little bandwidth to carry the picture as it is captured, by a factor of a thousand or so. Therefore, slo-scan sends only every thousandth picture, which results in a new picture about every thirty seconds, that is, it is a series of snapshots. This may seem inadequate, but consider that it is not dramatically different in the presentation to the guard at the monitor from the sequential scanning of ten different cameras with three seconds devoted to each.

Clearly, the design of the communications portion of a CCTV system requires the analysis of and tradeoff among a large number of possible options, and must be closely tailored to the degree of security which is required, the number and location of the spaces to be observed, the physical geography of the facility, and the other security functions such as alarm monitoring and access control which are part of the total security system.

Recording and Playback Equipment

Videotape (reel-to-reel) and video cassette recorders are the means by which pictures captured by the CCTV camera are preserved for later use as evidence or for other analysis. Since the vast majority of the pictures taken by security cameras are mundane and of no subsequent use, it does not make sense to exhaustively record all events from all cameras, and a number of control systems are available which can reduce the number of recorders required. Some systems record on a time-sampling basis, similar to the switchers which are used to present one picture at a time on the monitor; and, again similar to the monitor-switcher, an alarm or manual command can cause the recorder to be devoted to a particular camera and record continuously from it. There are also controls which, during later viewing, can automatically locate the place on the tape where the alarm occurred, so that attention can be directed to the appropriate spot without having to scan the entire tape. Some systems record on demand, for example, recording a single snapshot of every customer at a teller window, triggered by an action on the part of the teller. The tapes themselves can be erased and re-used after their contents have been determined to be no longer of value.

Accessories

There are housings for cameras that are weatherproof, vandal-proof, and explosion-proof; there are housings that are made to be relatively attractive additions to the decor; there are housings that camouflage the camera by making it look like something else . . . a potted plant, for example. There are also mounting arrangements in which the camera travels over an area on a ceiling-mounted track, and opaque domes within which the camera scans without being seen. On the electronic side, there are time-date generators which will add printed time and date to the picture, and there are screen-splitters which allow one monitor to display pictures from more than one camera at once (at reduced size and quality).

Special-Purpose Systems

There are a number of security systems and devices which utilize CCTV as the basis of their operation, but which are not strictly CCTV systems as we have defined and discussed them in this section. One such system is a motion detector which detects motion within its field of view, or within a definable portion of its field of view, by observing that successive images differ, and therefore something must have moved. We consider these to be alarm systems in the same way that microwave and sonic motion detection systems are alarm systems. Another system, aimed principally at apartment houses, allows the dweller to view the face of a caller in the lobby by having a CCTV camera and monitor built in to the telephone equipment: we consider this to be an access control system. Another CCTV-based access control system allows a guard to view the face of a person requesting admission at a portal alongside his picture-badge, which is also presented via CCTV, or alongside a file photograph that is retrieved from an internal microfilm or video file.

DESIGNING THE TOTAL SECURITY SYSTEM

The process of designing a total security system does not begin with an analysis of the varied, wondrous products of the technological revolution such as card access control, solid-state CCTV equipment, and the latest dual-alarm sensors. It does not begin with a study of whether to use an in-house proprietary system or the services of a central monitoring station, or of whether or not to combine the access control system with data collection for time-and-attendance. Most importantly, it does not begin with a stroll through the aisles of the ASIS show, beginning discussions with a plethora of highly-motivated (on commission) salesmen for the various kinds of security equipment, who will immediately vastly confuse the process by offering premature and time-consuming proposals and sales presentations.

The process of designing a total security system begins by understanding the eight distinct phases in the security process, and continues by understanding the threats and risks present in the organization in which the total security system is to be installed. Only then should one consider how the various tools of the security trade, including but not limited to those based upon electronics and other technology, can be best combined to provide appropriate protection at the most attractive cost.

The Eight Phases of the Security Process

There are eight phases of the security process. These phases are described in Table 1-1 and on the following pages.

Anticipation

Anticipation of the kinds of possible threats against the facility and which are likely to happen is the first phase in the security process. What are the risks? What items are likely to be stolen, copied, destroyed or disabled? What are the motivations of the likely perpetrators? Are there items which are easier and cheaper to repair or replace than to protect? What are the possible access routes to the items which are to be protected? Can the items which are to be protected be consolidated into one area so as to reduce the amount of protective measures required? What are the requirements for normal people-flow: employees, vendors, contractors, visitors, customers?

Such an analysis of the risks and threats is the professional specialty of a number of security consulting and planning firms. The analysis will lead to a total security plan encompassing the physical design of the facility, the flow and control of the people moving within it, and the proper interrelationship of the sixteen kinds of products and services which will comprise the final system.

Deterrence

A primary goal of the total security system is to deter prospective perpetrators from even attempting to commit unwanted acts upon or within the facility. The most effective means of accomplishing this is to prominently advertise the fact that a total security system is in place, that gaining unauthorized entrance is unlikely, and that even if such entrance is accomplished, apprehension and punishment will swiftly follow. An armed guard at the gate, or an unpleasant Doberman pinscher behind the chain-link fence are deterrents, as are visible CCTV cameras (real or dummy), and signs which say "Protected by the Sam Spade Security Agency," "Push to Open—Alarm Will Sound," or "Your License Plate Will Be Photographed If You Pass Through Without Paying The Toll."

Prevention

If the perpetrator is not deterred from attempting to commit an unwanted act, then the next phase—probably the most important of all the active measures—is to prevent him from doing so even if he tries. Walls, doors, bars on windows, safes and vaults, fences and barbed wire are physical preventive measures, as are guards and roving patrols. Access control equipment, including old-fashioned locks, are electronic and mechanical preventive measures which are used in conjunction with the physical preventive measures. Data encryption is a preventive measure against those who would attempt to listen-in to a data communications line, or retrieve stored data from a computer file.

Table 1-1. Phases of Security and the Supplier Groups Which Service Them

	Anticipate	Deter	Prevent	Detect	Respond	Apprehend	Recover	Punish
Security consultants and planners	X							
Personal profiling and screening	X					X	X	
Investigations	X					X	X	
Guards and patrols		X	X	X		X		
Armored cars		X	X					
Central alarm stations		X		X	X			
Fixed fences, barriers, safes		X	X					
Security lighting		X						
Access control equipment		X	X			X		
Alarm and intrusion equipment		X		X				
Closed-circuit television equipment		X		X		X		
Electronic article surveillance equipment				X				
Data encryption		X	X					
Police forces	X	X	X	X	X	X	X	
Courts and legal system							X	X
Insurance companies							X	X

Detection

If, despite the provisions for deterrence and prevention, the perpetrator succeeds in penetrating the facility, the next phase of security is to detect him either within the facility or in the act of penetrating the perimeter. Alarm systems and CCTV equipment serve this purpose, in conjunction with guards and patrols.

Response

Once an intruder has been detected, there must be people who can be summoned to the appropriate location, both to prevent him from committing further theft or damage and to apprehend him. Local guards and the police force of the municipality within which the facility is located perform this function.

Apprehension

Apprehension of the perpetrator by the response force serves to provide further deterrence to future attempts to penetrate the facility, to recover any goods the perpetrator may already have stolen, to remove that particular perpetrator from circulation by incarcerating him, and to punish him for his misdeeds.

Recovery

Recovery of stolen property, or repair of damage done, can be through apprehension of the perpetrator and recovery of the goods, through payment by the perpetrator for damage done, or through reimbursement from the insurance underwriter who has insured the premises.

Punishment

Punishment of the criminal is accomplished through the courts and legal system, and is made possible by evidence which has been collected during the several stages of the crime: logs of activity in the alarm and access control systems; photographic records from the CCTV system; observations of the responding guards and police force; and results of investigatory work, interviews, and psychological testing done after the crime.

The Sixteen Groups of Security Resources

The resources which are applied to these eight phases of the security process can be conveniently divided into sixteen different groups. Some of these groups are physical means of preventing entry such as walls and barriers; some are electronic and mechanical devices and systems such as locks, alarms, CCTV, and access control; some are personal services such as guards and investigators; and some are institutional services such as municipal police forces, insurance companies, and the courts. Following is a summary of the constitution, roles and missions of these resource groups.

Security Consultants and Planners

Security consultants and planners are the backbone of the **anticipation** phase of the security process. Their role is to analyze the risks and potential threats against the facility, and then to recommend the most efficient blending of the other security resources so as to provide an effective total security system.

Personal Profiling, Screening, and Interviewing

These are psychological-personnel specialties that can be of great value in identifying potential problem employees before they are hired. This is one of the prime tools in the **prevention** phase. These services can also be useful in the **apprehension** and **recovery** phases through examination and evaluation of suspects, witnesses, and other possibly related persons.

Investigations

Investigations into the backgrounds of prospective employees, contractors, etc., are another valuable tool in the **prevention** phase, and are the backbone of the evidence-gathering activity during **apprehension, recovery,** and **punishment.**

Guards and Patrols

Guards and patrols can be useful across much of the spectrum of security requirements. Before the advent of modern technological devices and equipment, of course, virtually the total capability to **deter-prevent-detect-respond-apprehend** resided in combinations of guards with physical barriers such as fences and vaults. Guards and patrols are still a valuable resource in these phases, usually in combination with the modern equipment.

Armored Cars

Armored cars are a specialty service, provided by a limited number of specialty vendors. They **deter** and **prevent** theft of money and other valuables while they are being transported from one place to another, and of course are always used in conjunction with guards.

Central Alarm Stations

Central alarm stations are a **deterrent** when it is well-publicized that they are being used to protect a facility, and they can **prevent** if they are used to control the access control system within the facility, but their primary purpose is to **detect** an attempted penetration through monitoring of the alarm system within the facility.

Fixed Security: Fences, Barriers, Safes and Vaults

These are the front-line of **deterrence** and **prevention.**

Security Lighting

Lighting is a frequently overlooked but valuable means of **deterrence.** Properly designed and placed lighting can motivate the criminal to take his business elsewhere, and is especially effective when combined with monitoring through a CCTV system.

Access Control Equipment

Access control equipment includes mechanical locks, electronic locks, card and pushbutton equipment, and systems which can recognize an individual by his face, voice, or fingerprint. They are a **deterrent** when the prospective perpetrator knows that they are in place and that they work effectively; they are **preventive** because the portal will not open unless they are satisfied as to the credentials of the prospective entrant; and they can aid in **apprehension** if they include the proper logging capability.

Intrusion Detection

Intrusion detection and other alarm equipment and systems are, like the central stations that are frequently used to monitor them, **deterrents** because of their known presence, but their primary purpose is to **detect** penetration or an attempt at penetration.

Closed-Circuit Television

Closed-circuit television equipment is also a **deterrent** when the cameras are visibly displayed, is an effective **detector** when properly monitored or when the motion-detector versions are used, and provides valuable evidentiary records for use in **apprehension** and subsequent conviction.

Electronic Article Surveillance

Electronic article surveillance (EAS) is, like an armored car, a specialty area with a specific application and served by a limited number of specialty vendors. EAS tags, which are from postage-stamp to luggage-tag size, are attached firmly to merchandise in a retail store, and can only be removed using special equipment at the cashier's counter and after the item is paid for. An attempt to remove the merchandise from the premises with the tag still attached will result in an alarm being sounded by tag-detector equipment located at the exitway. They have considerable **deterrent** value even though their **detection** capabilities are generally less than that of conventional alarm systems.

Data Encryption

Data encryption, which is discussed in some detail in Chapter 3, is a means for scrambling digital information (that is, computer data) so that it cannot be understood by anyone not having the proper code-key and translating equipment, even if he succeeds in obtaining the data, or a copy thereof, through nefarious means. It is both a **deterrent** and a **preventive** in the security system which protects the computer and its data, and is used in conjunction with other security means tailored to the special parameters of computer systems, such as access control, physical means, alarms, and logging.

Police Forces

Police forces are an adjunct to the in-house guard and patrol force, and are sometimes relied upon to replace them entirely. They serve in the **deter-prevent-detect-respond-apprehend** phases as do the in-house guards, but they also provide assistance in the **anticipation** phase because of their wider law-enforcement duties and experience with the community within which the protected facility is located. Police forces also have mandated duties in the phases of **recovery** and **punishment.**

Courts

Courts and the legal system are, of course, the duly-constituted means through which **punishment** is applied; they also assist in **recovery** in cases where restitution can be effected.

Insurance Companies

Insurance companies provide restitution and reimbursement for damage and loss due to criminal activity; proper insurance coverage is an important part of a total security plan. But it is unfortunate that in many cases, the certainty of **recovery** from the insurance company is used to reduce the expenditure for the security system, thereby leading to increased insurance premiums. Overall, money is merely transferred from one kind of expenditure to another: there is no such thing as a free lunch.

The Design Process

Every total security system requires that there be a complementary balance among the available security resources. While armored cars and data encryption apply only in particular situations, all of the other security measures should be at least considered. The perimeter can be protected by alarms, guards, CCTV, or a combination thereof. Portals can be guarded by guards or access control systems. Space protection can be guards, CCTV, and alarms. Objects can be protected by guards, alarms, CCTV or EAS equipment. While virtually any combination of the possible techniques can be construed to comprise a security system, the true total security system must be designed around the particular combination of risks and threats present in the facility. For example, CCTV cameras covering every space and monitored by a single guard at a console may be adequate for some situations, but will not provide the immediate response capability that, for example, the guard who stands at your elbow when you view the Mona Lisa in the Louvre provides.

While it is beyond the scope of this volume to provide a complete education in the field of risk and threat analysis and total security system design, following are highlights of the analysis process which must be accomplished.

Identify the most serious threats and risks. If you have a Mona Lisa, a pile of gold bars, a sack full of diamonds, or a store of nuclear fuel, it is certain that you will need a high-level security system, not just a padlock on the door. Frequently, after the decisions are made as to what security measures must be provided for the maximum-security portions of an installation, the other areas can be provided for as by-products and extensions of these basic provisions. A storage room containing iron bars requires far different security than a storage room containing gold bars; and after one has provided a sophisticated alarm system, probably with CCTV, access control, and guards for the gold, the iron bars can probably be protected by a single additional intrusion alarm point.

Who and how many are the authorized entrants to the various areas? All employees must be allowed within the premises, but only senior management should be allowed to visit the gold bars, and perhaps even senior management should only be allowed near the gold during certain hours. There also must be provisions for admitting and controlling vendors, contractors, visitors, and customers. Additionally, the security system should not inhibit the legitimate activities of any of these classes of people, so that the basic work of the facility will not be rendered inefficient. Further, different equipment, and perhaps even different system design, is indicated depending upon whether the number of persons to be controlled are tens, hundreds, thousands, or tens of thousands.

What is the geography of the facility? Different security systems are required for a one-room branch bank, a single-building plant containing offices, manufacturing, and warehousing, the several highly-sensitive structures within the single perimeter of a nuclear power plant, and a multi-plant corporation that is dispersed among several locations within a city. The question of a single central system versus individual dispersed systems must be addressed for the more complex of these situations, as must communications problems which are not relevant to the smaller problems.

Should the various elements be independent or combined? In every security system which encompasses a multiplicity of security technologies—alarms, access control, CCTV, EAS—a decision must be made between the efficiency of placing the systems under a single central controller, and the dangers of the "all-the-eggs-in-one-basket" syndrome which results from doing so.

Should the security system be combined with other functions? A similar risk-versus-efficiency determination must be made with respect to combining the security system and other facility-serving systems such as time-and-attendance, energy management, and job-cost management under central control.

Local control versus a commercial central station. Whether control, monitoring, and response-initiation will utilize in-house personnel and facilities or will be contracted out to a central station is a two-stage decision process. If the response requirement is for greater immediacy than a central station can provide—as in the case of the Mona Lisa—then in-house capabilities must be provided. If it is not, then either method will provide completely adequate service, and the decision can be a cost-based one. Frequently, however, it is based upon management style and psychology: management may prefer everything under its own wing, or prefer to hire-out for services rather than create new in-house departments and bureaucracies. Either way can be made to work satisfactorily.

The Project Management Function

Another fundamental decision that the management of the facility must make is who will assume the role of system integrator, that is, who will be the general contractor for installing and implementing the total security system. As can be seen by perusing the sixteen different elements of the security supply-side, there is a wide range of disciplines which must be understood and managed by the system integrator. Even eliminating the outside, governmental, and management disciplines such as the courts and police, insurance and initial planners, the system integrator will still be responsible for the smooth integration of the following kinds of diverse tasks.

- *Mechanical:* doors, walls, windows, vaults, bars, locks, turnstiles, automotive barriers, security lighting.
- *Electronic:* door strikes, automobile gates, access card readers, installation of alarms of all types, CCTV equipment.
- *Computer hardware and software:* ranging from microcomputers to large-scale computers, from digital logic design to assembly-level programming to compiler-level and operating-system programming.
- *Construction and construction trades:* installation of electrical conduit, mechanical alterations to the building to mount card readers, CCTV cameras, and door strikes, installation of fences and buried sensors, etc.
- *People management:* from engineers and programmers to tradesmen, laborers, and guards, from company management to vendor salesmen, technicians, and installers.

Responsibility for this project management task can be assigned in any of several ways, or in combinations thereof, as follows.

In-House

The user can act as his own general contractor, buying each of the security subsystems from a vendor, having the wiring and construction modifications designed by an architectural-engineering firm, hiring the electrical and mechanical contractors, conducting the final test of the system, and so forth.

The A & E as Project Manager

Most architect-and-engineering firms have the capability to take on responsibility for the project management, in addition to their design duties on the project. There are also capable project management consulting firms who are not A & Es.

The System House

Many security systems are sold by system integration companies, system houses for short, who manufacture none of the components used in the security system, but gather the appropriate components from a variety of manufacturers and provide a complete working system to the user. The system house may provide the computer programs which cause this assemblage of components to function as a security system. Many system houses are capable of assuming the role of project manager.

The Electrical Contractor

In some instances the electrical contractor can assume the role of project manager, and in rare instances the mechanical contractor has the capability to do so. Since these organizations are less high technology oriented than, for example, the A & E system house, they will generally require very strong support from the subcontractor who supplies the central control system and its software.

THE ACCESS CONTROL SYSTEM AS PART OF THE TOTAL SECURITY SYSTEM

In reviewing the discussion in this chapter regarding the total security system, it is appropriate to extract those comments which describe the appropriate role of the access control system within the total security system, an example of which is shown in Figure 1-1. Such a summarization follows.

1. The access control system operates as one element in the total security system, and must function smoothly in conjunction with the other elements of the system, which are: physical barriers; mantraps and turnstiles; sensors

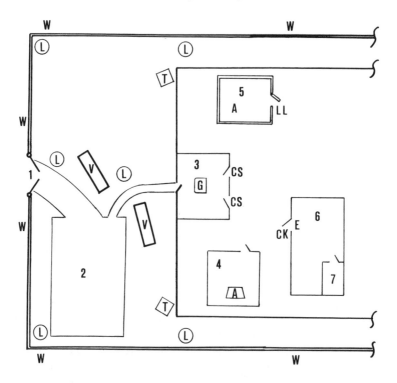

Figure 1–1   *Functional design of a total security system.* **W:** *wall or fence around perimeter of property;* **1:** *main gate, can be closed and locked at night;* **2:** *parking area separate from building, enforced by vehicle barriers* **(V)**; **L:** *lighting for clear area between wall and building;* **T:** *CCTV surveillance cameras cover gate, parking area, and clear area;* **3:** *main lobby with guard post* **(G)**; *entry into interior of building controlled by card-access doors with turnstiles* **(CS)**; **4:** *office area with object disturbance alarm* **(A)** *affixed to personal computer;* **5:** *vault with heavy metal and concrete construction, intrusion alarm* **(A)**, *and time-lock with dual-combination* **(LL)**; **6:** *computer room with card-plus-keypad access control* **(CK)**; **7:** *tape data storage room with article-surveillance tags built into tape cartridges, and detector* **(E)** *to prevent removal from computer room.*

and annunciators; processors and controllers; the power system; portal hardware; guards; other specialized security systems; central alarm stations; and people.

2.   One of the major elements of any total security system will be alarms and the alarm system, and another frequent major element will be a closed-circuit television system. The most effective total security system will be one which smoothly integrates the three major components of alarms, CCTV, and access control, along with the other elements listed above, taking advantage of the best features of each.

3.   Protection of a facility can be planned by considering the measures which are appropriate for each of the layers of the perimeter, the portals, the inner

space, and the objects of value within the inner space. The usual role of the access control system is at the portal layer.

4. The design of a total security system should provide proper protective facilities for each of the eight phases of the security process, which are: anticipation of the risks and threats to be expected; deterrence of prospective criminal activity upon the premises; prevention of criminal activity upon the premises; detection of criminal activity within the premises; response to penetration of the premises; apprehension of perpetrators; recovery of stolen property or repair of damage done; and punishment of those who commit criminal acts upon the premises

Access control systems constitute one of the sixteen groups of resources which are used to satisfy the requirements of these eight phases of the security process. Access control systems are used in the deterrence and prevention phases, and can contribute to the apprehension phase.

5. The essence of effective design of the total security system is to analyze the threats and risks, the requirements for access and movement of people, and the geographical characteristics of the facility to be protected; to design the security system which is responsive to the most critical needs; to then add functions which satisfy the less critical requirements; and to then decide upon the details of the control system and the brand of equipment that will be required. The functions required from the access control equipment and the specifications for the purchase thereof, will flow naturally from this process.

Chapter 2

Applications of Access Control Systems

Functioning within the framework of the total security system, access control systems and devices assume the responsibility for insuring that only authorized persons are permitted to pass through the portals which have been designed into the system. A portal may provide access through the perimeter fence, it may provide entry into a building, or entry into the various spaces, rooms, storage areas, etc., within the building. Smaller portals are the accessways to safes, vaults, and files.

It is the function of physical barriers and the alarms protecting them to channel all prospective entrants to the portals where they can be screened by the access control system. It is the responsibility of guards, CCTV, and intrusion detectors to detect and prevent any attempts to circumvent the barriers or the access control system, and any nefarious acts by persons who were admitted to the facility legitimately. And it is the duty of the access control system to stand guard at the portals.

Access control equipment ranges from a simple $3.98 padlock to multi-million-dollar systems which control hundreds of portals using redundant computer systems, and operate on a range of technical principles from the simple metal key to the optical-electronic analysis of a person's fingerprint. Conceptually, however dissimilar these systems may seem, they all perform the simple function of permitting passage through a portal to only those persons who satisfy the criteria which were established by the system designers. This criteria may be as simple as the correctly-notched metal key or as advanced as having the biometric characteristic of particular fingerprint pattern. The decision as to whether to utilize the padlock or the fingerprint system to protect a particular portal is made by the system designer pursuant to the total security requirement analysis which was described in the preceding chapter.

There is, of course, more function to be obtained from an access control system than merely releasing the bolt on a door when the proper key or fingerprint appears. Time-period control can be exercised, to admit persons during certain times and exclude them at other times. Master-keying is possible, allowing lower-level persons through only certain doors, while management can pass through all doors. In-out control covers both entry and exit, making it possible to keep a list of those persons who are inside a particular area at any time. Logging can provide a history of who went through each door and at what time, and has a variety of uses. We shall discuss each of these capabilities in greater depth in later chapters.

In this chapter we present a few examples of the use of access control systems in industry, government, and institutions, and some brief insights into the motivations which lead to the installation of these systems. On the surface, it may seem that applications are generic: one warehouse, manufacturing plant, office, or research-and-development laboratory looks much like any other. But the warehouse at Fort Knox presents a vastly different security problem from the warehouse at the Ajax Cement Block Company. We shall examine a sampling of access control problems and solutions from a diverse group of enterprises.

ACCESS CONTROL SYSTEMS IN INDUSTRIAL FACILITIES

The increasing incidence of criminal and violent activity within and against industrial facilities has mandated that security system planning and design be raised to a level of importance at least equal to the other criteria which are the principal purposes of the facility: production efficiency; convenient, ready, and inexpensive storage of raw materials and finished goods; employee safety, convenience, and well-being; and community image. Within the facility there are a number of valuable commodities which tempt the thief, there may be a valuable store of data and records which are vital to the company's continued ability to operate, and there is increasing reason to protect the facility against vandalism and sabotage. A newly increased level of attention is being focused upon security within the plant environment, and there is an increasing utilization of the kinds of electronic security systems which were previously in common use only in such environments as computer rooms, research laboratories, sensitive defense installations, and nuclear power plants. An example of such a system is shown in Figure 2–1.

Risks

Following are a few of the risk factors that must be analyzed by the facility planner, security analyst, and management during the process of determining what level of security, and what level of expenditure for that security, is justified for the various elements of the operation.

Raw Materials

Exposure of raw materials to potential theft varies greatly depending upon the intrinsic worth of the material, its bulk and ease of handling, and its concealabil-

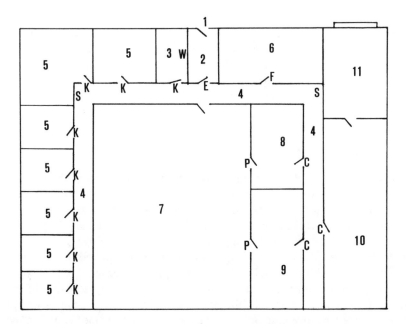

Figure 2-1 *Example of an access control system in an industrial facility. 1: main entrance into lobby (2), which is overlooked by a window (W) from the security-reception room (3); passage from lobby into main corridor (4) is controlled by electrically operated lock (E) from security-reception room, and is left open during shift changes; 4: main corridor is entirely in view of CCTV surveillance cameras (S); 5: office entrances are secured by lock-and-key (K); 6: research and development laboratory, with entrance controlled by fingerprint-recognition system (F); 7: main manufacturing area is open-door within the plant; 8: finished-goods storage area is accessed through pushbutton-keypad lock (L) from manufacturing, card-access controlled (C) from the corridor; 9: incoming-materials storage area is also controlled by keypad (L) from inside and card (C) from outside; 10: shipping and receiving area is card-access controlled (C); 11: loading area and dock can only be opened from within the shipping and receiving area.*

ity; here again we have the gold-bar versus iron-bar syndrome. For bulky material with a low value per pound, such as coal, cement blocks, and iron bars, protection can be limited to a sturdy fence, adequate lighting, a simple lock on the gate, and a roving guard patrol. For processes utilizing precious metals and stones, the most sophisticated of security systems is required. The majority of manufacturing and industrial processes utilize raw materials which require a relatively low level of protection during their warehousing and transportation.

Finished Products

Since finished goods are presumably worth selling, they are *ipso facto* worth stealing. Like raw materials, their attractiveness to a potential thief depends upon the value per pound and per cubic foot. This attractiveness ratio, however, is much greater for a finished television set, for example, than for the components that went into it and that have nearly equal size and weight. As a class, therefore, finished products will require a higher level of security than the raw materials used to make them. The security requirements for the products continues after they leave the factory and must be observed during the transportation and retailing processes.

Tools, Machinery, and Equipment

Pilfering of tools has always been a problem in manufacturing facilities; other machinery and equipment used in the factory may not be portable or concealable, except in their component parts. Since the majority of the theft of these items is committed by employees of the company, access control systems play little part in the protective measures used: one cannot exclude employees from passing through the portals, or from having access to the tools needed to do their jobs. Strict accountability for all tools is the most common measure applied, although electronic article surveillance systems such as those used to deter shoplifting are beginning to be used. Tools, machinery and equipment as well as finished goods must be guarded against not only the outside, truck-full thief, but against the insider who takes only a tool, a pocket-sized product, or a portion of a product or a machine at intervals of a day or a week. In the immortal words of Johnny Cash, "I got it one piece at a time, and it didn't cost me a dime . . . ."

Office Equipment. Typewriters, adding machines, and the like are particularly vulnerable to theft in an industrial complex where mini-offices may be located throughout the facility. This is a particular case of the machinery and equipment category.

Data Files

There is a danger that adequate security may not be provided in the various areas of the plant where limited individual data elements—such as shipping orders and personnel records—are used. If the total data base can be obtained one section at a time from loosely-secured individual locations, there is no need for the industrial thief to attempt to penetrate the security of the main office.

Proprietary Processes. Proprietary processes are a special case of data files. Production processes which form the foundation of a company's business must be protected against outsiders by denying them access to the data base, and against insiders, where possible, by dividing the critical elements of the process among a number of persons or departments and then protecting each of the elements. The formula for Coca-Cola remains a deep company secret because it is protected every bit as assiduously as the gold which it generates for its company's vaults.

Research and Development Laboratories

Research and development laboratories are obvious candidates for extensive security systems because they create the proprietary processes which will become the bases of the company's future products. Many are protected by perimeter and access control systems and need-to-know spaces within, to an extent worthy of a top-secret military base. In addition to the obvious need to protect the data, there is usually an extensive array of laboratory equipment, electronics and computers, and there may be valuable raw materials as well. Recent trends have created a need for protection from mob and terrorist kinds of activities, as presumably civilized persons and organized groups physically demonstrate their disapproval of research on nuclear fuels, new weapons, or testing on animals.

It is patently obvious that one cannot describe a generalized total security system, or even a generalized access control subunit, for an industrial facility because of the diversity of the sizes and kinds of operations which occur. There are different levels of risk for each operation, and for each physical and operational area of each operation. The design of a total security system must efficiently integrate the individual requirements of the manufacturing areas, the office spaces, the computer rooms, the storage areas for high-value goods, the shipping and receiving area, the building maintenance center, and so forth.

ACCESS CONTROL SYSTEMS IN THE OFFICE

The day of the open, walk-in office environment has come to an end with the increasing incidence of industrial crime, vandalism, terrorism, violent protests, and physical violence against individuals. Within the office there are now numerous items of considerable value to tempt the thief. Only a few years ago the major loss from an office theft would be some $800 typewriters and adding machines, now the office is populated by equally-portable personal computers, computer terminals, and other electronic machinery valued at up to $10,000 per item. These trends are causing new attention to be focused upon the provision of modern security within the office environment, rather than relying upon the receptionist to deter unwanted intruders.

Risks

Following are some areas of risk that must be considered when designing the office portion of the total security system.

Office Equipment

Typewriters and adding machines have always been targets for both the casual and the professional thief, but their value is exceeded many times by that of the personal computers, computer terminals, word processors, facsimile machines, and so forth, that populate the modern office. There are a number of manufacturers who offer physical locking pads and cables to secure these equipments, but the most certain protection is to exclude all but authorized persons from the office by means of an access control system.

Data Files

Data files tend to be concentrated in the office area in the form of both paper files and computer data banks which can be accessed using terminals within the office. Customer lists, personnel files, product design data, and other valuable information may find its way to a competitor if it is stolen. In addition, if valuable information—receivables, prospect lists, orders pending, and the like—is destroyed, the company may be unable to operate. The protection of computer-based data is discussed at length in the following chapter.

Computer Terminals

Computer terminals and personal computers are not only valuable items of equipment, they are also repositories of the data files discussed above. There is an increasing need to provide control of access to computer terminals in addition to the access control which is provided to the office itself, since not all persons who are to be admitted to the office should have access to the computer. Further, access to the computer is now beginning to be provided by the same physical means (such as keypads and card) that are used to control access control to the premises, since the efficacy of the traditional password-control has been cast into serious doubt by the successful adventures of computer "hackers."

Employee Safety

Regrettably, a portion of the increased number of violent crimes against persons have occurred in the office and plant environment. The presence of a receptionist at a desk is no match for an unbalanced person with a gun. Unlike the industrial facility, it is possible to describe a generic type of office environment and therefore to provide a generalized plan for protection within an office. The sophistication of the system will depend upon the nature of the business being conducted and the value of its products and processes, but the following essential elements will be the same.

General access control is required to ensure that only authorized persons enter the office.

Control of paper data files using locked cabinets or separately-access-controlled rooms is necessary.

Control of distribution, copying, and disposition of paper data must be done through implementing controlled procedures, including limiting access to the copying machine.

Protection of physical equipment through strict accountability, locking devices, electronic article surveillance equipment, and marking so that they can be identified if stolen, is necessary.

Limiting access to computer terminals and personal computers, using the techniques described in the following chapter, is essential in any modern office.

ACCESS CONTROL SYSTEMS IN FINANCIAL INSTITUTIONS

Control of access to vital areas was a concern to banks and other financial institutions long before the invention of the systems that comprise modern access control. Therefore, adequate physical means were developed to meet this need: vaults, combination locks and time-locks, buzzer-gates, dual-key systems, mantraps, pneumatic transport systems, and human guards. With these adequate and proven systems already in place, financial institutions have not rushed to replace them with new electronic marvels, but, steady inroads are being made by new technologies such as computer facilities, automatic teller machines, and paperless by-wire transactions.

Vaults and teller working areas continue to rely on heavy metal, personal presence, and combination and time locks for access control rather than upon electronic systems. Although there have been some noteworthy card access systems installed in central and Federal Reserve banks, these have been in addition to, not in place of, personnel-control systems using human guards. Office areas are frequently unprotected except for the traditional and casual control of a receptionist at the front desk: the comments in the earlier section of this book regarding security in the office apply to offices in banks as well as offices in commercial and industrial facilities. Storage areas for office or other supplies occasionally have keypad or card access control, but more often than not they are simply under lock-and-key or the supposedly watchful eye of a person at a nearby desk. Drive-up and walk-up teller windows are easily protected by heavy metal, bulletproof glass, offset drawers and hydraulic tubes, since they do not allow access to the innermost parts of the bank where, as Willie Sutton said, "the money is."

Areas of Exposure

Because they play a unique role in the activities of all people, companies, institutions, and governments, financial institutions have a number of unique security problems. And because their business is centered upon a uniquely valuable, negotiable, transferrable and transportable commodity, they are highly visible targets with tempting branches on almost every city block. Following are some of the areas of exposure which must be considered when creating a total security system for a financial institution. For many of these areas, protection is, at least in part, provided by access control systems and devices, most frequently in combination with other types of security resources.

Computer Facilities

Over the past twenty-five years, computer facilities in financial institutions have run the gamut from being showcased to the world in glass-fronted rooms, to being placed in a non-public but non-hidden areas of the building, to being located in separate, anonymous, innocuous, and well-protected buildings. This has been the result of both the increasing amount of business transactions and records which have been entrusted to the computer system, and the increasing tendency of this visible and valuable resource to come under attack. Card access systems began to appear on the locked doors of computer rooms about a decade ago, and they have become standard equipment. Some facilities augment the card access system with CCTV surveillance; however, since there is a limited number of persons who require access to a computer room, there is a natural secondary security check since everyone in the room knows by sight everyone else who works there. A more complete discussion of the security requirements for a computer facility appears in the following chapter.

Automatic Teller Machines

Automatic teller machines (ATMs) are one of the more innovative—and one of the most popular—new facilities to be offered by banks in recent times. They are also, by nature of being unattended and frequently remotely located, the most vulnerable to attack by unauthorized persons. A primary concern is limiting access to the ATM (thereby limiting access to individual bank accounts) to only the depositor who owns the account. This is accomplished by using the bank card, which is a plastic card with magnetic-stripe encoding, along with a keypad or keyboard into which the customer's unique number (Personal Identification Number or PIN) must be entered. The fact that this card-plus-keypad system has proven adequate in the ATM application, where there exist both a prime motivation (there is real money in the box) and an ideal opportunity (unattended, frequently remote, and available 24 hours a day), provides a powerful endorsement for the level of security provided by this combination of two simple security systems. In the early days of ATMs there were frequent instances of "jackpotting" through manipulation of the access cards and codes, but the card-plus-PIN technique has now been well-proven.

Having thus adequately secured access to the ATM terminal, the remaining electronic exposure in this facility is the telephone wire which carries transaction information to the bank's computer and returns the authorization signal. (In their early days, ATMs were self-contained units which did not have the capability to communicate with the central computer; this eliminated the communications security problem, while raising a number of other problems.) Some institutions have incorporated rudimentary encryption of the information on these lines, but such codes are relatively easily broken or mimicked (the perpetrator listens-in on the line for a long enough time to determine what code opens the cash box), and a more sophisticated rolling-key cryptographic system is expensive. There is no such thing as a free lunch.

Many of the risks associated with ATMs are not amenable to solution by electronic security systems. For example, unauthorized and fraudulent use of bankcards is the number one source of loss through the ATMs, and 95 percent of such unauthorized use is by family and friends (some friends) of the cardholder. There is no electronic system which can ascertain that a person does or does not have the permission of the cardholder to make a withdrawal. Further, a substantial amount of such fraudulent use is by the cardholder himself. Personal identification systems such as those using fingerprint recognition and other biometric characteristics, which are discussed at length in a later chapter, could be used to limit ATM transactions to the cardholder himself, but they have thus far proven too expensive. Within the next decade such protection may become routine.

The second most common form of ATM fraud is committed by bank employees who are adept at creating fictitious accounts and running cash into them, learning the PINs of actual accounts and making duplicate cards to access them, and other time-tested means which have been used on bank accounts since long before the ATM appeared. These methods of fraud and embezzlement can be prevented by proper systems and procedures within the banking system, and can be detected by use of an effective auditing software product; this subject is discussed at length in the next chapter.

The primary security need of an ATM installation, however, is the physical protection of the machine itself, since the ATM is located outside of any physically protected area, and may in fact be in a remote or even high-crime location (in New York City several years ago, a group of residents successfully brought discrimination proceedings against a bank which was planning to install an extensive network of ATMs throughout the city but excluding certain high-crime areas). The ATMs must resist physical assault by those who may have a relatively long time to work on the assault unobserved: the same heavy-metal construction and alarm systems which have proven effective on vaults and night depositories are used. The customer and the cash that he obtains from the ATM must be protected: a secure and lockable enclosure, CCTV monitoring, adequate lighting, and a call-for-help intercom are usually provided. Finally, the personnel who replenish the cash box and remove the deposits must also be protected: two-person deliveries, radio communications, and other means which are standard within the armored-car industry are used (the provisions for protecting the customer are also useful in protecting the servicing personnel).

Computer Terminals

Computer terminals are located throughout a bank, and not all terminals are necessarily located in access-controlled areas. Some of the terminals have access to and can execute financial transactions, and these are generally well-protected. Others are connected to non-money data bases, but with a little ingenuity they can frequently be subverted to achieve financial gain for a clever criminal. In the following paragraphs, we divide the computer terminals according to the kinds of operations which they can perform.

Local Item Transaction Processing.   We define this category as including those transactions that are processed within the bank's own facilities, and therefore on terminal equipment owned and controlled by the bank. Examples are transactions performed over the teller window, transactions received through the mail such as deposits and loan payments, and bulk mail operations such as lock boxes (which are used, for example, to handle incoming payments for charge cards). Security provisions for these operations consist of limiting access to the terminals using physical rather than electronic means, since all of the persons working in that area of the facility should be known to each other and are under close supervision; limiting access to the computer programs through software sign-on procedures and passwords is also routine. Auditing software, discussed in the following chapter, is also valuable for these kinds of operations, as are procedural regulations limiting the size of transaction which operators can perform, requiring two signatures or manager's approval for large amounts, and so forth.

Bank-to-Bank Transactions.   Because bank-to-bank transactions usually involve large amounts of money, because they have been performed in one way or another since banks existed, and because they are usually performed through a sophisticated computer on each end, they are in most cases well-secured. On both ends they have the benefit of the security provisions in place for the bank's terminals, computer, and communications systems. Because they are neither voluminous nor involve a large number of terminals (as, for example, does the ATM network) they can be treated with great individual care, such as being encrypted with a sophisticated algorithm. And they are balanced through well-established clearing and auditing processes. Nonetheless, their very size represents an instant jackpot, unlike skimming-type schemes which require a long time period to achieve a satisfactory illicit return. They are therefore a continuing temptation to the technically-expert criminal. The major facilities for effecting these transfers are the Federal Reserve Wire Transfer and Electronic Funds Transfer (EFT) networks. These facilities are fully encrypted using the Data Encryption Standard (DES), a combination hardware-software method developed and blessed by both IBM and the National Bureau of Standards, which represents the current state-of-the-art in commercial-grade encryption.

Dial-Up Transactions.   As banks search for new means of attracting new customers by providing expanded financial services to them, an important segment of services is being provided at remote locations through communicating terminals. The first kind of such service provides the ability for a retail establishment to directly communicate with the bank's computer for processing of credit card or debit-card purchases, using a Point-of-Sale (POS) terminal (a computerized, communicating cash register) at the retail establishment. The second enables the customer to perform banking, bill-paying, or money-transferring functions from home using the touch-tone telephone as a data terminal (a concept which was first attempted in the early 1960s by a now-forgotten company in Massachusetts, using the old rotary telephone with a keypad and strip printer: the bleached bones of pioneers lie in the sands of technology's past). Both of these "new" services are actually more automated versions of services that have been offered for many years: credit card purchases in which the retail clerk dials the telephone for credit authorization, and bill-paying and money-transfer by telephone with the customer verbally communicating with a bank clerk and validating the trans- action by using a "secret code." The more modern methods utilize card-reading and key-entry (from the POS terminal) or pure key-entry (from the home tele- phone) digital communication directly with the bank's computer, rather than voice communication with a bank clerk who then enters the information into a conventional computer terminal.

From a security point of view, these two forms of transactions-by-wire have the following common characteristics: the bank has no control over the physical premises within which the terminals are located; there can be a very large number of transactions but there are generally few per originating terminal; and the average transaction amounts are not large. Security provisions therefore cannot take the form of physical measures, encryption, call-back, and the like, although some POS terminals are connected to their own computer systems and can be subjected to the usual measures associated with captive terminals. The security of these retail transactions depends to a large extent upon the association of the "secret code" (a PIN) with the account, and upon systems, procedures, and auditing software similar to those needed for the ATMs. Since these services have existed in their less automated form for many years, proven systems for control- ling and auditing them have been developed.

Charge Card Operations.   From a transaction-processing standpoint, charge cards (which include both credit cards and debit-cards, the difference being how fast the money is deducted from your account) are part of two previously dis- cussed subjects: they come in by wire from a POS terminal, or they come in mailed batches for local item processing. There is some potential for fraud in the credit-authorization process: the amount of available credit as stored in the com- puter can be fraudulently inflated for a legitimate account, so that excessive pur- chases can be made. This has not been a large problem, and proper procedures can prevent it.

The bulk of charge-card fraud, and therefore the bulk of preventive mea- sures, has been in the area of counterfeit cards. Since there is no PIN associated with the charge card to provide identification such as is done so effectively with the ATM card, the possessor of a legitimate-appearing card with a legitimate account number can use the card for purchases. Measures currently taken to make counterfeiting difficult include using hard-to-duplicate graphics such as holograms, flourescent printing, multi-colored graphics, engraving, hidden micro-printing, and non-erasable signature panels with special background inks. Techniques that are used for access-control cards, such as special magnetics for magnetic-stripe encoding, and the "smart card" which embodies coded information in a self-contained microcomputer, are being tested for use in charge-cards; a key to their usefulness will be the development of inexpensive reading equipment for the retail establishments.

Portfolio and Access Management.   Data on the assets of these accounts, posting of dividends and interest, buying, selling, and trading, are all usually stored within the computer and manipulated through local captive terminals. These accounts present no unusual security problems that cannot be addressed through those measures already in place for the general computerized applications, such as control of access to the terminals and through them to the appropriate computer files, proper systems and procedures, and effective auditing programs.

Administration and Office Management.   Although this area encompasses mostly non-financial activity, there are a number of opportunities for fraudulent activity which can result in financial loss: false letters of credit; false credit reports; falsification of information within the process of loan origination and authorization, which itself is frequently automated on a small, self-contained computer system which is separate from the main electronic data processing (EDP) department. The payroll process and personnel records should also be considered a part of this category, although payroll, as a financial process, is subject to well-proven checks and balances. Control of access to the appropriate computer system is the first obvious safeguard, but it is difficult to protect against malfeasance by insiders upon data which is susceptible to neither numerical balancing nor auditing by sampling. Effective paperwork procedures and dual-signature controls are effective. Audit trails, both on the computer and on the manual side, necessitate that all changes to files, preparation and release of reports, and so forth, are traceable to a date, a time, and a person. End-to-end audits, routinely performed, provide both deterrence and occasional apprehension.

Banks and other financial institutions represent a unique applications area for security systems, practices, services, and equipment, and they also represent nearly a third of the non-governmental consumption of these security goods and services. As such, security for financial institutions constitutes an industry in itself, and there are a number of important companies who serve that industry almost exclusively. Notwithstanding all that, the process through which an effective total security system is created for a bank is no different from the process for any other institution, organization, or facility, and the equipment used to provide security for a bank is, with rare exception such as signature verification equipment, the same equipment that serves industry in general.

ACCESS CONTROL SYSTEMS IN HOTELS

Hotels and motels present some interesting security problems. They are filled with hundreds or even thousands of people in the course of a single day: employees, guests, persons attending banquets and meetings, droppers-in to the bar or restaurant, and persons wandering in from the street to use the telephone or the rest room. With the exception of the employees, most of these people will be within the facility for a time ranging from a few minutes to several days; many will never be seen again, just as many were never expected in the first place. The lodging industry has the usual security problems with respect to safeguarding valuables—both its own money and the valuables of guests—and protecting property such as the television sets in the rooms, linens, liquor, and the like; but it represents a unique problem in access control.

The Security Problem

A paying customer (the term "guest" has never seemed quite appropriate) rents a room for the night and has in his possession, for a number of hours or days, a key which opens the lock to that room. When he departs, another customer rents the same room and is given the same key. If Customer #1 has made a copy of the key, given that there is no restriction upon who can wander the corridors, he has the ability to enter the room and pilfer whatever valuables Customer #2 has stored in the room (although hotel managements always advise us to leave our valuables in the hotel safe, who among us has ever bothered to do so?). The ultimate solution to this problem is to re-key the locks every time the room changes occupancy, but the cost of doing so with traditional mechanical locks is unacceptable.

Historical and Modern Solutions

Attempts to provide electronically re-keyable locks for the lodging industry go back two decades. The first serious attempt at marketing a finished, complete system was Cardgard from American District Telegraph Company, in the early 1970s. It operated as follows. When a customer checked in, an identical pair of simple plastic cards was automatically punched with holes representing a code chosen at random from among 2.5 million possible codes. One card was given to the customer to be used as the room key; it was inserted into a reader at the room door. The second card was placed in a slot corresponding to the room number at a console located at the front desk, and the room door could be opened only if the two cards corresponded exactly; if the control card was removed, no card could be used to open the door. Insertion of an incorrect card at the room signalled a "tamper" alarm at the front desk. When the customer departed, the cards were destroyed and a new "key" was made for the next occupant. The system was also used for controlling access to storage areas for food, linen, silverware, and so forth, by employees, and for controlled access to rooms by housekeeping personnel.

Cardgard was an effective solution to the access control problem for the lodging industry, but it required extensive and expensive installation and modification: there needed to be an electronic reader with automatic electric door strike at every room, and this equipment had to be connected by wire with the central console. It was not widely accepted, and a decade passed before new systems embodying new concepts were introduced. Substantial inroads are now being made with these new systems.

The first of these new systems operates similarly to ADT's old Cardgard system, in that two plastic cards are punched at random each time the room changes hands. In the newer system, one card is placed within the lock, thus instantly recoding it, and the second card is the customer's key as before; this eliminates the necessity to run wires from each room to a central console at the front desk.

The second kind of system also eliminates any need to run wires to the front desk, but it operates on an entirely different principle. As in the other systems, a random code is generated for each new customer, but it is embedded onto only one card which becomes the customer's key; in one manufacturer's system, the card is plastic with punched holes, in another's it is a metal card with invisible magnetic coding, and there are also those that use conventional magnetic-stripe-encoded plastic cards. The lock on each room contains a card reader and a microprocessor with its own battery power. When the room is vacant the microprocessor is placed into a "ready" state by the housekeeping department, and the next card which is inserted will determine the code which the microprocessor will recognize until it is told to do otherwise. The customer thus codes his own lock using the random code which he was assigned at the front desk.

The systems provide master-keying so that housekeeping and security personnel can enter the room, and one system stores data on the last 13 entries, including master-card entries, for aid in post-burglary investigation.

Protecting valuables within the room is another interesting lodging-industry application of access control equipment. In one such application, the customer is issued a lock with a key already in it when he checks in. A safe is securely fastened within the room, and the customer inserts the lock-and-key into the safe and removes the key. This eliminates any correspondence between a room number and the key which fits the lock on the safe.

OTHER APPLICATIONS OF ACCESS CONTROL

We could obviously go on indefinitely describing the problems and solutions of security systems, and access control in particular, in various industries and applications, but we shall close this chapter with brief comments on a few additional areas where there are interesting or unique applications, and a few where attention to access control problems is long overdue.

Nuclear Power Plants

Nuclear power plants represent the epitome of security systems in general and electronic security in particular, a distinction they share with a few ultra-high-security military installations. Nuclear power plants are highly visible targets for a variety of people and groups, including saboteurs, protestors against nuclear power, and terrorists who would like to obtain the nuclear material so as to build a bomb. For this reason, nuclear power plants are protected by a multiplicity of the most sophisticated electronic security systems and devices, with overlapped areas of protection and a high degree of redundancy. The perimeter, including the intakes for the massive amount of cooling water that the reactor requires, is protected by cleared areas and fences, which in turn are protected by intrusion sensors and CCTV surveillance. Entrance to the facility is controlled by guards and access control equipment, aided by metal detectors, CCTV, and bomb-sniffing dogs. Within the facility there are individually-controlled areas, all protected by access control equipment, alarms, guards, and CCTV. In control of this array of electronics is a completely-redundant pair of computers, either of which is completely capable of running the show. In addition to all of this, the ultimate in response capability is instantly available in the form of an impressively-armed "SWAT-type" team.

The equipment and systems which comprise these security systems are no more exotic than those which are used in other industries and applications; it is the sheer magnitude and complexity of the total security system into which they have been combined that is of special interest.

Home Security

Home security is at the other end of the security spectrum from the nuclear power plant in size, cost, and complexity, but here again the systems, devices, and technology are the same as in other applications. Most home security systems depend upon either or both of two kinds of protection: at the perimeter and within the space. Perimeter protection consists of window and door tapes, switches and photocells, and space protection is provided by microwave, infrared, or sonic listening devices. Access control is effected by several means.

Arming-disarming controls utilize keypads or keys that are provided at the control unit of the system for arming and disarming the system, with a time-delay built-in so that the homeowner can open the front door and get to the disarm facility before the system alarms; this can be considered a form of keypad access control.

At a modest cost increase, *mechanical pushbutton switches* can be used to replace the conventional lock-and-key, but they are not widely used in residential applications despite widespread use in industry.

Electronic pushbutton switches, to which we devote a complete chapter later, are an important element in the array of access control resources. They are also priced appropriately for use in residences, but they have achieved virtually no acceptance in that marketplace.

Garage door openers are a form of proximity access control, to which we also devote an entire later chapter. They are not commonly tied in with the security system, therefore one must still run to the disarm switch in order to beat the alarm timer; similar devices are beginning to be offered for controlling the front door.

As the prices of electronic access control devices continue to decrease, we expect greater home usage of cards, pens and other access tokens, but none of us will live long enough to see them make substantial inroads against the familiar metal key and the lock that solidly goes "clunk."

Multi-Tenant Office Buildings

Multi-tenant office buildings and shared industrial-park kinds of facilities also present a unique problem in access control, since different tenants will establish different levels of security due to their differing risks and threats, and all employees (and vendors and visitors) must be allowed access to the building. Lobby guards and intercoms (sometimes incorporating CCTV) are frequently the first (and frequently ineffective) line of security. Elevators can be access-controlled, refusing to stop at a particular floor unless proper credentials have been presented (but are subject to the piggyback problem: if anyone on the elevator has the credentials, everyone can get off on the floor). As a tenant in such a situation, part of the analysis of risks and threats must deal with those presented by the presence of all the other tenants. Each tenant's own area must be made secure by an individualized total security system, working in concert with—or, if necessary, substantially in addition to—the overall building security. High-security requirements frequently require that another facility be found.

Vehicles

Vehicles, including boats, are the target of a number of access control products which have been introduced in recent years. Most offerings are simple pushbutton locks; in fact, they can now be ordered as original factory equipment on some luxury automobiles. There are also remote-control devices, similar to the garage-door-opener and therefore falling under our category of proximity access control devices, that start the motor, unlock the door, and turn on the lights from a block or so away (these are useful to a very small segment of the population who have reason to suspect that someone may have wired a bomb to the ignition). Keypads are also being used to allow the ignition switch to be energized, and include versions that can detect that the prospective operator is so inebriated as to be unable to properly depress the keys and will therefore refuse to start the engine: sometimes machines do have more sense than humans.

Hospitals

Hospitals are another case of facilities wherein the general population is permitted to wander about, and where there is a continuing flow of new faces who do not linger long. They therefore represent another difficult case for security in general and access control in particular. Attention to security in hospitals is primarily directed at the thievery of supplies such as linens or drugs. The thievery problem is not to be belittled because it is enormous, but one is forced to wonder how many more newborn babies must be stolen before hospitals begin to work with the security profession to create appropriate access control.

Schools and Universities

Schools and universities also have a free flow of a large population, and an effective solution for public schools has yet to be suggested. In universities with a resident population, conventional access control and other security techniques are being installed in dormitories.

Chapter 3

Access Control in Computer and Communications Security

We choose to treat the subject of computer and communications security separate from the applications discussed in the preceding chapter because these technologies have become important tools of every trade and business: as important to the manufacturer as his metal-bending machinery, as important to the banker as his vault, as important to the retailer as his January White Sale. Computer and communications technology has a life of its own. Regardless of what industry it serves, it is an industry of its own, and from a security point of view it needs to be studied as a separate entity.

We choose to treat the subjects of computer security and communications security together because the communicated information that is of the most value, and therefore most frequently requires protective measures, is digital data rather than voice conversation, the same digital data which is generated by the computer and communicated between the computer and other computers or input-output terminals of various sorts, including ATMs, facsimile machines, and ordinary CRT terminals. Further, one of the principal means of penetrating a computer system for nefarious purposes is through its communications channels; even further, and for the same reasons, there is overlap and in many cases coincidence between products intended for computer security and those designed for protection of communications links.

REASONS FOR LOSSES TO COMPUTER CRIME

In terms of actual loss, theft through the route of the computer and its communications channels ranks far ahead of the more visible and the more physical means of illicit activity. In banks, for example, the average holdup nets just under $6,000, while the average computer bank theft amounts to about $1.5 million;

there have been single computer crimes reported in the $65 million range, which alone is twice the yearly amount lost due to all holdups. There are several reasons for this seemingly greater exposure to criminal activity through electronic rather than physical means.

1. Physical protective measures—heavy metal, electrical alarms, and guards— have been developed over a hundred years or so of trial and error, and are proven and well-understood. Computer and communications security has, on the other hand, emerged as an area of risk only within the past couple of decades, and the security measures for coping with these risks are still being developed.
2. In a robbery there is time-pressure on the perpetrator and an intentionally limited amount of cash which can be transferred into his possession within a short time; the robber is also in physical danger of being immediately and perhaps violently apprehended. Computer crime takes place by remote control and usually over a comparatively long period of time, with access to much more substantial sums of money; identification of the perpetrator is usually a time-consuming auditing process, and his apprehension (presuming he has not utilized the intervening time to flee the country) is in the genteel fashion befitting the executive criminal.
3. Computerization of the processes and procedures of business and industry has proceeded at a breakneck pace for twenty years. The pressure upon the EDP department is to provide the capability to offer more goods and services to more customers at more locations at a lower price. The priority of security provisions is low when it comes to allocating scarce EDP resources, in some cases through ignorance, inattention, or bad management, in other cases pursuant to a conscious management decision that it is better business to risk loss through computer crime than through loss of customers by not offering more and better goods and services.
4. Computer people have not understood security and the need for it, and security people have not understood computers, in fact, have shared the fear of the computer held by the general population (including a substantial portion of company managements). This situation is changing due both to the increasing computer literacy of the population in general, and the fact that the increasing size and number of computer crimes have at last begun to capture the attention of computer people, security people, and management.

Motivation

The principal motivation for computer crime has traditionally been considered to be theft and embezzlement ("that's where the money is") but there are equally damaging results of computer crime that is not committed for direct or immediate monetary gain. The motive of malice or revenge by disgruntled employees or crusading outsiders can result in destruction of computer data files that are vital to the operation of the organization. Theft of data, which can be accomplished from a computer without disturbing the original data or, frequently, even leaving behind any indication that it has been copied, can be damaging: customer lists and product secrets can enable a competitor to make serious inroads into a company's business; employee lists are of value both to competitors and to unscrupulous headhunters. Modification of payment records, credit data, and so forth, within the computer files can bring gain to the perpetrator. And there are the well-publicized "hackers" who, like mountain climbers, penetrate computer files "because they are there."

Systems and Procedures

As we examine the various security products and methods which are now burgeoning upon the computer and communications equipment and software market, we should observe that a large percentage of security problems can be solved with commonsense measures in physical protection and systems-and-procedures areas. Most theft of data from EDP installations is accomplished by purloining extra or uncontrolled or obsolete copies of computer printouts (the customer list which was printed last week is just as useful as this week's updated version), or by retrieving the perfectly readable carbon copies from the trash. Another convenient means is to copy a file onto a blank, uncontrolled magnetic tape and carry it out the door. Programmers' working files, source decks, and test programs are usually (and casually) controlled only by the programmers themselves, and can be useful to an outsider in working up a means to access the computer. Programmers' and operators' access to the computer system is frequently controlled loosely or not at all; they therefore have both the skill and the opportunity for criminal activity, and it cannot be presumed that none of them has the motivation and lack of character. A comprehensive fail-soft and disaster-recovery plan and procedure, although not strictly speaking a security matter, is all-too-frequently last on the EDP priority list. No amount of sophisticated electronic security can reduce the exposure of an organization which has not tended to these fundamental operations matters.

RISKS AND EXPOSURES IN COMPUTER AND COMMUNICATIONS OPERATIONS

The tremendous rush to automate the operations of every kind of business, industry and institution has had two important results. The good news is that more EDP services can be offered more efficiently, and more economically, and these services are based upon current, up-to-the-second data. The bad news is that there is often no time-proven methodology for these new operations, or for insuring their security, impenetrability, and auditability. In the competitive rush to offer ever new products, services, and facilities, a great burden is placed upon the

EDP facility to install operable equipment and software; security provisions are nearly always a subsequent task, deferred like leaving the barn door open until after an unacceptable number of horses have been stolen. One result of this inattention to security matters is that only recently has there been an adequate number of products offered by the vendor community, and we are therefore in a stage where the computer products and operations and the security products are all being tested together to determine whether they adequately serve the purpose for which they were developed.

Since there is virtually no area of the operation of a business which is not now heavily dependent upon the computer system, it is useful to group the operations into categories which relate somewhat to the kinds of security risks that they create.

Computer-Internal Transactions

Substantial business and financial transactions take place without any interaction with people outside the company, controlled only by the computer and those who are intimate with it: programmers, operators, and data input clerks. Among these transactions are posting of interest to bank accounts, calculations of overhead, shipping, late charges, preparation of invoices and posting of payments. Although they are frequently individually small amounts, when multiplied by hundreds or thousands of accounts they can amount to considerable sums. All the resources of computer security products and methods must be in place in order to prevent the perpetration of fraud through the use of the internal workings of the computer. A considerable number of schemes have been concocted by authorized computer-users. There is the round-off scheme, where the rounded-off fractions of cents are skimmed to the perpetrator's account. There is the pure skim, where a few unnoticed cents from each of many accounts is purloined. There is the flow-through scheme, where money resides for a day or two in an account belonging to the criminal en route to its legitimate destination, creating a large average balance on which interest is collected (interest on an average balance of a million dollars can be ten grand a month). And there are new schemes being hatched in the fertile brains of a hundred modern-day grifters even as we write these words.

Control of access to the computer facility and to the computer itself are an obvious first line of defense, but the most likely perpetrators of fraud within the computer are those who work daily with the computer, its operations, its programs, and its data files, and who understand the computer's innermost workings. Since these persons cannot be excluded access to the computer, security provisions must assume both of two forms: first, effective systems and procedures for operations and programming people, such as dual-person access to the computer, detailed documentation of operating programs, and strict control over alterations to the programs; second, an effective auditing program under the control of an auditing department which is computer-literate, separate from the

EDP department, and populated by a bunch of hard-nosed and thick-skinned employees.

Computer Terminals

The proliferation of computer terminals within the ordinary working spaces throughout a company makes possible the commission of computer-crime without it being necessary for the perpetrator to be anywhere near the EDP installation. Like any assets, the data bank information can range from that which no one is likely to go to much trouble to steal (for example, the word-processing files for the text of a sales brochure, or the mailing list for the company Christmas party) to items of considerable value (names and addresses of sales prospects, bank account balances, production process formulae). Therefore, as in any security problem, the amount and sophistication of security measures which should be put in place will vary.

Several methods are in use for access control to computer data through the computer terminal. The longstanding approach is to provide passwords within the computer operating system and applications programs, and to segment the data and programs and allow access to them based upon individual passwords; this is much like segmenting a physical plant using doors guarded by card access equipment, and allowing persons access to only specific areas based upon specific codes in their cards. The efficacy of the pure-password protection has been shown in the exploits of the "hackers": a determined expert can penetrate most password systems.

The most widespread application of access control technology to protect very important data stored in computer data bases is the card-plus-PIN system used in the automatic teller machines. Card and token access control systems for computer terminals have been in use for some years, although their market penetration is limited to a very small percentage of the terminals in use, and they have generally been custom installations for particular large computer systems (and have usually been installed after a major penetration has captured management's attention). There are now standard products being offered for this purpose.

Transactions by Wire

Access to the computer through the conventional telephone network has become commonplace only within the last decade, and presents its own new set of security problems. The ATM accesses valuable data by wire, but the terminal, its environs, and the communications line are all under the control of the bank which owns the ATM; access to any such captive terminal can be readily controlled. Other forms of communication may be from portable or general purpose terminals at a variety of locations, or even from another computer. Security measures against unauthorized access using these routes take the general forms of validating that the calling terminal or computer is an authorized entity (using callbacks or encryption) and that the active operator of the terminal is an authorized person (using passwords, PINs, and cards). Specific product categories for these uses are discussed in the next section.

The Personal Computer

The tremendous popularity of the professional version of the personal computer gives rise to an entirely new security concern. After decades of extensive use of the conventional computer system within all areas of commerce and industry, we have yet to adequately impress computer professionals with the need for access control, safeguarding of data, backup and disaster recovery provisions, and the like. We are now confronted with a profusion of computer-amateurs at the executive level, who are in many cases using the same or more critical data, and who in most cases are under none of the security restrictions which apply to the EDP department. A proper security plan must insure that personal computers are considered part of the information processing function, and must provide for the same degree of control and security that applies to other areas where equivalently important data is processed and stored. (For nearly two decades useful and voluminous data have been accessible through the millions of ordinary computer terminals connected to large computer systems. Yet until the personal computer hype began to focus interest on the subject, only scattered attempts to physically control access to these terminals were made: a case of the right result finally happening, even if for the wrong reasons.)

PRODUCTS FOR COMPUTER AND COMMUNICATIONS SECURITY

The products that are offered for protecting the equipment and data within the EDP facility and upon the communications lines and terminal equipments connected to it fall into four general categories, according to the kind of protection which they offer:

1. Control of physical access to the equipment
2. Control of electronic access to the computer system
3. Prevention of physical removal of equipment and data
4. After-the-fact discovery of criminal activity

Specific products and their functions are described in the following paragraphs.

Control of Physical Access to the Computer Facility

This has been a longstanding application of the conventional products that are used for general physical access control, that is, card readers, keypads, and the like, along with physical means (walls and doors) to make certain that the facility cannot be entered except through the protected portals. CCTV and alarm systems are frequently also used as additional protection. All of these products are fully discussed in other chapters, since they have broader application than the purely computer and communications security products discussed here.

Control of Access to the Computer System

Presuming that one has gained access to the computer facility, there are products which control access to the computer itself and to the data contained within its files. Within this class of products there are those which will allow or prevent access on a wholesale basis, and others which will allow access to portions of the computer and data but not to other portions, based upon the need-to-access of the particular person. These products operate on one or more of the following principles.

Hardware Control. Physical devices similar to those used for general purpose access control—cards and keypads—protect terminals and other equipment within the computer room, so that not all persons who have gained access to the computer room may have access to the computer. It follows, of course, that the card-and-code which opened the door to the computer room must be different from the card-and-code which allows one to operate a terminal.

Software Control. A person is allowed access to the computer system, usually through his having knowledge of a correct password which is recognized by the computer software, but also possibly using hardware control as described above. The operating system within the computer determines which files and applications he may use, modify, or read, nearly always based upon a password.

File Encryption. Data within the computer files may be stored in encrypted form, therefore even a person who has been granted access to the computer and the data files cannot use or even read the files unless he also possesses the encryption algorithm and the key to the code.

Control of Access by Wire

Although the "hackers" have caused great consternation, some financial loss, and perhaps a little damage, by their well-publicized penetrations of major and supposedly well-secured computer systems, they have actually done a great service by demonstrating the ease with which such penetrations can be accomplished when security relies upon the venerable yet often ineffective password. They have triggered substantial new product offerings by vendors of computer and communications security products, driven in turn by a substantial new interest on the part of users in incorporating them into their operations.

Communication with a computer over telephone lines can be from a wired-in terminal device, such as an ATM, which is always hard-connected to the same telephone line; it can be from a portable or general purpose terminal which must dial-up the computer on the public telephone network; it can be from another computer, including personal computers, which also usually accesses on a dial-up basis. Protection against unauthorized access over these routes takes four forms.

Physical Access Control. If the terminal is hard-wired to the computer, then physical means such as card access and keypads can be used to insure that only authorized persons gain access to the terminal, and anyone communicating with the computer from such a terminal can be deemed to be authorized. ATM terminals are a prime example of this method.

Call-Back Devices. For terminals and other computers that are communicating over dial-up lines from fixed locations, the computer can ask for their identity, and then disconnect the call and originate a new call to the telephone number which is in the computer's file for the calling terminal. This limits access to known terminals at specific locations, and is an effective defense against the "hacker" problem.

Passwords. Although passwords have long been used within computer operating systems and applications software to control access to programs and data files, they are now also appearing in communications controllers to validate the credentials of a caller before letting him through the communications link into the computer. Although the password as a sole security device is relatively ineffective, the combination of passwords with other techniques can comprise an effective system; as witness, the combination of the PIN (which is actually a password) and card in the ATM. Several recently announced devices employ smart cards on tokens carried by the user, and provide pseudorandom passwords.

Encryption. Encryption of the data before it is sent over the telephone line and decrypting it at the receiving end serves two purposes: the data can be sent and received only by a terminal equipped with the appropriate cryptoequipment and by a person who possesses the correct key; and data obtained by wiretapping the actual telephone line is useless without the same cryptoequipment and key.

Electronic Article Surveillance

EAS devices and systems have been used for more than a decade to prevent shoplifting in retail stores by means of an electronic tag that is attached to an item of merchandise, that can be sensed by the system if it passes through the exit of the store, and that will therefore cause an alarm to be sounded if the merchandise is removed from the store without the tag having been removed or deactivated by store personnel. Such systems are also widely used in libraries to prevent purloining of books, and they are also beginning to see some usage in grocery stores. Products are now beginning to be offered for similar protection of valuable materials and data in the computer room: there are tape reels and tape and disk cartridges which have EAS tags built into them, tags which can be attached to personal computers and other large items (and which have been available for years to protect office equipment such as typewriters and adding machines), and tags which can be embedded into paper sheets to protect printed materials as well.

Auditing Software

Computer programs can process data at rates of tens of thousands of transactions per day, far beyond the ability of any corps of mere humans to monitor or cross-check. Further, errors or misappropriations of relatively small amounts of money per transaction can, over a period of time, result in substantial losses. And finally, tracing such illicit operations to verify that they have occurred, how they have occurred, and at whose hands they have occurred, would be an enormous task if done by humans. Auditing software operates within the computer, and therefore at computer speeds, to enable this vast amount of financial or other data to be monitored, cross-checked, balanced, and, if necessary, tracked from end-to-end. Short of re-processing all the individual transactions, there are several very effective means of auditing.

Sampling. Random or directed samples of the transactions and accounts are selected and exhaustively validated; the probability of detecting errors or malfeasance is directly related to the number of samples which are processed.

End-to-End Totals. Processes or sub-processes can be batch-checked, for example, the number of transactions and the amount of money coming into and leaving the process, regardless of redistribution or consolidation into other accounts.

Statistical Analysis. Unusual kinds or levels of activity in particular accounts, or by particular persons or companies, or from particular terminal locations, may indicate illicit actions. Statistical analysis programs can identify such activity for further scrutiny through either computer-checking, human investigation, or both. We have for many years recommended to our computer-system clients that statistical analyses be a routine ingredient in their data processing.

Access to the Personal Computer

With the recognition that important data frequently resides in the executive personal computer, and that the personal computer does not fall under the protective measures which have been put in place for the EDP facility, there have come a number of recent products intended to supply protection for and control of access to this new and all-pervasive form of data processing: an example is shown in Figure 3-1. There are physical anchoring devices which prevent the perpetrator from simply picking up the machine and carrying it off. There are electrical devices which will not allow electrical power to be applied to the personal computer until one has unlocked them with a key, or with a conventional access control means such as card, PIN, proximity device, or pen. And there are systems which become a part of the personal computer by means of being contained on a circuit card which is inserted into the PC and connects to its data bus, and which exerts internal control over the PC based upon its own access control means of card or sophisticated password, or combination thereof.

VENDORS OF COMPUTER AND COMMUNICATIONS SECURITY PRODUCTS

There are several categories of vendors who offer computer and communications security products; they range from entrepreneurial start-ups to the largest company in the computer business, and include vendors of both equipment and software. The four major categories of vendors are as follows.

Mainframe Software Vendors

Three basic product groups are offered by these vendors: computer access control software; data file encryption software; and auditing software. The supplier structures vary considerably among these three applications, and with a few exceptions the vendors each offer one kind of product but not the others.

Computer Access Control Software. Nearly half of the two dozen products currently offered are designed for the large IBM mainframes—370, 30xx, 4300; there are a handful which operate on the smaller IBMs (34, 36, 38, S/1), and one or two each for DEC VAX and PDP, Wang VS, Four-Phase, Sperry, and Prime. With the exception of IBM and its Resource Access Control Facility which was introduced in the mid-1970s, there are no large, established vendors and all of the products have been introduced in the mid-1980s. Since the products are applicable only to specific computer systems, marketing can be targeted to the owners of such systems through direct mail, user-group publications, and by cooperative arrangements with the computer manufacturers. It should be noted that nearly all operating systems which are supplied with large computer systems have basic user-ID and/or password access control capability; the separate software systems provide additional features such as violation logs and remote alarms, time-period control by person, remote monitoring of the user's screen, user profile analyses, and so forth.

Figure 3-1 *Access control system for the personal computer. (Courtesy of Datakey, Inc., Burnsville, Minnesota)*

Data File Encryption Software. IBM offers its DES for this purpose, and there are half a dozen small-to-unknown independent software companies also offering products which are almost exclusively for use on IBM mainframes.

Auditing Software. This is a mature product area which has been populated for more than a decade by such well-muscled independent software companies as Applied Data Research, Cullinet, and Pansophic Systems. There are also half a dozen or so of the smaller independents beginning to participate. The established companies market through an extensive network of local and regional offices, and have a well-established clientele.

Microcomputer Software Vendors

The advent of the microcomputer has brought tens of thousands of new people into what is broadly known as the computer programming industry, which was formerly a rather exclusive community. In the early days, the microcomputer, or personal computer as it has come to be known, was foisted upon the world by hardware vendors with very little in the form of accompanying useful software (they believed that all the world, including Joe Sixpack and his wife Mary Mahjongg, was consummately interested in becoming BASIC programmers and writing their own software rather than watching Monday Night Football, the Soaps, and the other mind-numbing offerings of the 23'' hypnotic eye). The door was thus open for anyone who developed a program which worked to sell it by mail or through advertisements in the popular magazines to other amateurs, and thousands did so. A few built successful businesses, most went back to their basements, but the syndrome remains that wherever two programmers are gathered together a business is born. Thus it is in the field of security software packages for the microcomputer: fifty-odd companies offer products, and after one passes beyond the name IBM on the list they are all small or start-up companies. A very few also offer products for the larger mainframes, and a few are crossovers from the vendors of physical access control technology.

Communications Hardware Vendors

The need for encryption and access control on data communications lines has attracted several of the major long-time vendors of modems and communications controllers to this market, which has been populated for twenty years with a few lonely and unprosperous black-box vendors: Milgo, Codex-Motorola, Paradyne, Penril, Anderson-Jacobsen, Racal, and NEC have all entered products. There is also IBM, and there are two dozen smaller contenders, some of which specialize in specific-industry products such as banking communications. Some offer data communications with cryptographic capability, some have communications controllers with passwords and callback, a few offer encryption of both data and voice communications.

Hardware Specialists in Cryptographics

A smaller handful of vendors, the heirs of those who labored in the data security wilderness two decades ago, offers only the cryptographic boxes: the user plugs one into the data path on each end of his communications link, which must be equipped separately with modems and other strictly communications equipment, and the data on the line is encrypted. This method will be useful only in specialized applications once the coming mature generation of integrated communications-and-security products is in place.

Chapter 4

Principles of Access Control and Personal Identification Systems

We have devoted the first three chapters of this book to the understanding of the environment within which access control and personal identification systems work. We have emphasized that access control is only one of many subsystems that comprise the total security system, and that unless the total security system is properly designed to cope with the risks and threats of the operation that it is to protect, the security of the facility will be inadequate no matter how sophisticated is the access control or the CCTV system, no matter how well-trained and armed are the guards. In this and the following chapters we shall be dealing only with the access control systems and the other elements which are usually contiguous with it, such as physical barriers, mantraps and turnstiles, portal hardware, and in some instances guards. We urge the reader to at no time lose sight of the total security system into which the access control system is smoothly blended.

We would also remind the reader that of the eight phases of the security process, access control systems are useful in only the deterrence and prevention phases, and can contribute to the apprehension phase if certain usually optional features are incorporated. As one studies the myriad forms and options available in the technology and products of the access control field, one must keep firmly in mind the purpose of the access control subsystem in his own operation, so as to select a system and options which satisfy all of one's requirements but do not go beyond those requirements and thus expend money and add complexity to no useful purpose.

In addition to the necessity for the access control system to blend in with the other elements of the total security system from a security point of view, there is also frequently a physical connection and commonality of equipment and devices among the access control system and the other ingredients of the system. The most frequent manifestation of such commonality is the control of the total security system using a single central computer that contains the authorization list for the access control system, monitors the alarm system and reports alarms, controls camera selection and pan and zoom for the CCTV system, and manages the guard tour. Other forms of commonality might be the sharing of communications links among several systems, and the dual use of alarms such as door-open sensors between the access control and alarm systems. Thus, even when it has been well-defined as a subunit, selection of the access control system can seldom proceed in isolation from the other system elements. The ultimate commonality of all subsystems, of course, is that they must interface with the security and guard force who must manage them, and the employees, visitors, and potential perpetrators whom they must manage.

These principles apply regardless of the application to which the system is applied. The purest access control system, from an equipment point of view, is the hotel system: there are no other subsystems such as CCTV or alarms to which it must connect, but it must operate in consummate harmony with that ultimate of critics, the person who rented the room, and it must also accommodate the hotel workers such as the housekeeping staff, desk clerks, and security force. Computer-room access control systems may be simple door-locks, or may be required to operate in conjunction with alarm and CCTV systems. Computer-terminal access control may be merely a complicated power-on switch, or may be required to operate in conjunction with the internal workings of the computer. As one progresses to larger and more complex operations such as industrial plants and financial institutions, the access control system is certain to be only one element within a complex total security system.

We can and shall discuss access control as an independent entity so as to gain a proper grasp of its principles, tradeoffs, and possibilities, but we must be ever mindful that there is no single solution which is appropriate to all, or even a substantial portion, of the applications and security requirements.

THE TECHNIQUES OF ACCESS CONTROL

All of the products, models, features, and options notwithstanding, all access control systems are based upon three simple techniques for insuring that a person is authorized to pass through a portal. We define them in terms of the manner in which they have been used for access control during most of this century, since the techniques themselves predate all that we know as modern technology. The three fundamental forms of access control are: the combination lock; the portable key; and the physical attribute. Others have described these three kinds of access control as being based upon (1) something a person knows (that is, the combination to the combination lock), (2) something a person has (that is, the portable key), and (3) something a person is or does (that is, the physical attribute). The following paragraphs describe how the entire world of access control is encompassed in these three principles.

The Combination Lock

The combination lock, also called a stored-code system, operates upon the principle that the prospective admittee knows the code (it is stored in his brain, hence "stored-code") which, when entered into the access control equipment, will match with the code stored in the equipment, thus certifying to the access control equipment that the prospective entrant qualifies to be admitted. The simplest and most venerable such access control device is the combination lock itself: a three- or four-digit code is set into the tumblers of the lock, and the person rotates the dial successively to each of the numbers (remembering to rotate in the correct direction and for the correct number of times before stopping at the number, else the innards of the lock become hopelessly confused and one must begin again); when the operation has been done satisfactorily, the lock may be manually opened and the person has access to the door, locker, safe, or vault.

Modern combination lock access control systems nearly always replace the rotary dial of the conventional combination lock with a set of pushbuttons, usually ten in number; they are thus usually called keypad access control systems. The combination is still three or four digits which must be depressed in the proper sequence, and the code is recognized, in most cases electronically, but in a few cases mechanically, within the device. Anyone who knows the right sequence of code numbers may enter. The pushbutton system is much more convenient and easy to operate than the rotary dial, but note an important difference in the security provided: a ten-key pad will provide 1,000 different combinations if a three-digit code is used, and 10,000 different combinations for a four-digit code; the ordinary combination lock found on most bicycle chains uses a three-digit code and the dial has 40 numbers, which provides 64,000 combinations. The average home safe has a 100-number dial and a four-digit code, for 100 million combinations. Advanced technology does not necessarily confer greater security.

Another form of stored-code system is embodied in the key-questions technique frequently used by banks. Personal information that is unlikely to be forgotten (for example, your mother's maiden name) but is also unlikely to be known to an outsider, is stored in the data base with your bank account, and can be called up by the bank teller and asked of you as supplementary verification of your identity.

The Portable Key

The portable key operates on the principle that if the prospective admittee has in his possession an object which contains the code that has been preset into the access control system, that person is qualified to be admitted. The simplest and most venerable form of this kind of access control is the ordinary metal key which most of us use to open the front door to our house, operate the ignition on our automobile, or secure our most treasured possessions whether they are contained in the gun locker or the liquor cabinet. The ordinary metal key with notches and grooves is easily duplicated at your corner hardware store, but there are also metal keys coded using dimples, holes, and other means that provide greater protection against duplication, primarily because of the fact that they are less common. The codes in metal keys are sensed by matching mechanical fingers or slots in the lock, and the positioning of these mechanical parts defines the key-coding which will be accepted.

Modern portable key access control systems utilize many different forms of keys. The most common is the plastic card, identical to the credit cards which bulge temptingly in our wallets. There are also plastic, key-shaped tokens which are substantially larger than an ordinary metal key, but that still fit conveniently into the pocket or even onto a keyring. There exist plastic and metal cards which are smaller than a credit card, coded pens, and intelligent portable keys which can be as large as a pack of cigarettes. Without exception, these devices provide greater coding capacities than the metal keys, and than the keypad systems. Even the simpler ones will provide tens of thousands of code combinations, and a magnetic-stripe card offers a billion.

If it appears specious to discuss an everyday lock-and-key in the same context as a sophisticated card access system, be advised that there are lock-and-key systems which are every bit the equal of some electronic access control systems in both the level of security provided and in price. Consider also that both your post office box and your safe deposit box are opened with metal keys. And consider well that in both of these latter instances, the portable-key access control system is combined with other security measures to comprise an effective total security system. Technology does not confer security, the total system does.

As with the ordinary metal lock-and-key, the portable key of the modern access control system is inserted into a slot, hole, or groove, so that the code which is contained in the key can be sensed by the lock (known as a reader because it reads the code using the appropriate one of a variety of means which are discussed in a later chapter). An exception to this procedure is made in a new form of portable-key which has achieved a considerable market share just within the past five years: these are known as proximity access control systems, because their key-devices need not be inserted into a reader, but will be recognized when they are in the immediate vicinity (some at a few inches, some at several feet) of the reader. In these devices, the code contained within the key is read by radio-frequency interrogation and response rather than by intimate contact such as in a conventional insertion reader. Here again, the concept and technology are not new, only the application of the concept to identification of humans with intent to control access. For many years, radio interrogation and coded response have been used to identify aircraft to the air traffic controller, and there have been a number of experimental installations to identify automobiles, for example to collect tolls without the need for an automobile to stop at a toll booth, using RF identification and later billing.

Another form of portable-key access control token is the disposable cardboard ticket that one buys from the movie theater cashier and uses for entry to the theater to see the movie (which, if he were patient for a few months, he could see for free on cable TV without taking a shower and getting dressed to go out). The movie ticket may be only a $5 item, but the same means of access control is used for a $40 Broadway play, and for rock concerts and the Super Bowl, where scalpers' prices can be in the hundreds of dollars. Airplane tickets and boarding passes are similar manifestations of this simple form of access control. Similar disposable passes are frequently used for visitors in conventional industrial access control situations.

The Physical Attribute

This form of access control has become popularly known as biometric access control because most of the techniques now used rely on measurements of a biological characteristic of the person to be identified. Physical attribute systems differ fundamentally from the combination lock and portable key techniques, since there is no code to be memorized or embedded into a device. A physical attribute system uniquely identifies a particular individual person, and the criterion for granting access is whether or not that person is listed in the system's files as being qualified for access.

From time immemorial, the physical attribute used for access control has been the human face, since Og let Moog into the cave because he recognized Moog's face as being one of his tribe. In more civilized times, Og became a security guard who recognized the faces of everyone who worked at the plant whose portal he guarded. When that system became impractical because of the number of people, the employees were given a picture-badge so that Og's descendant could compare the face on the badge with the face on the card. This is still the most widely used form of personal attribute access control system today.

A number of semi-automatic systems have been developed to assist a human in comparing an actual face or other physical attribute with the one on file for that employee, but the glamour has been in the development of fully automatic systems that recognize an individual by comparing the characteristics recorded in the data base for that person, with an instant machine-scanned reading of the characteristics of a person attempting to pass through the portal. Fingerprints, the geometry of the hand, voiceprints, signatures, and the patterns of the blood vessels on the retina of the eye are all physical attributes which form the basis of one or more of the systems that are currently offered for access control purposes.

COMBINATIONS AND MISCELLANEOUS FEATURES

These three fundamental techniques for access control have been in use for many decades through the combination lock, the lock-and-key, and the guard-recognizes-face. Automatic access control systems merely apply the most current technology to these concepts, providing systems that can be more difficult to defeat, and require less high-cost human help.

Weaknesses in the Techniques

There are basic weaknesses in all of these techniques, however, which no amount of automation and technology can change. A code can be told to an accomplice, or observed while an authorized person enters it into the lock or keypad; a key can be lost, stolen, copied, or loaned, and so can an access card or token. These facts are true regardless of whether the code and key are meant to open $1.98 locks, or $100,000 computer systems. Physical attribute systems have inherent false-accept and false-reject errors, because there are similarities among faces, fingerprints, voices, and all other biological characteristics. "Doubles" have been used effectively by movie stars and heads of state, for similar reasons having to do with personal risk, for many years.

Code-Plus-Key Systems

Combinations of techniques can greatly increase the security of an access control system. A code-plus-key system, for example, provides both a keypad and a card reader, and the prospective entrant must both enter a valid access card into the card reader, and depress the correct pushbuttons; the bank ATM is a shining example of such a system. The code-plus-key system eliminates the weaknesses of the two simple systems: if the code is observed it is useless without the card, and if the card is stolen it cannot be used without knowledge of the code. (Unfortunately, authorized users all-too-frequently record the code number on the card so that they will not forget it, or record it on a slip of paper which resides in their wallet next to the card so that both can be easily stolen together; proper training and indoctrination are required to prevent this, but there will still be some lapses.) The code-plus-key system, of course, costs substantially more than a keypad-alone system, and somewhat more than a card-alone system: there is no free lunch. The risk and threat analysis will guide the user in determining whether or not the additional security of a dual system is required, and whether or not it is worth the additional cost.

Code-plus-key systems are in widespread use in industrial and commercial security systems, and are also implicit in the home security system where a keypad must be used to disable the alarm system after a conventional key has been used to open the door. They have also been a boon to the physical attribute systems, which have been around for nearly two decades, and have been widely predicted to become the dominant form of access control for nearly all of that time. That they have not done so is primarily due to the much higher cost per portal which the manufacturers have not been able to overcome, but also due to their unacceptably high rate of errors, both of the false-accept and false-reject kind.

The addition of a keypad or a card reader to the physical attribute system allows the person to identify himself to the system, which then needs only to compare the observed physical attribute with that on file for that person. The earlier systems were required to compare the person's attribute with the attributes of the entire file of authorized persons, with a consequently large probability of a false cross-match.

There are other combinations which can increase the security of an access control system, combinations which draw from alarm system technology, system design philosophy, systems and procedures, and other areas. Some that should be considered in the design of any access control system are the following.

Tamper Alarms

If a sophisticated and determined perpetrator can gain access by smashing or disassembling the access control mechanism and tinkering with its insides, the security that the system provides is obviously diminished. A well-designed access control system will be impossible to dismantle from the outside of the portal. For additional security, the access control system should incorporate a sensor that can detect that the box is being attacked and sound an alarm.

Power Fail Protection

Some units have internal batteries so that the access control device will continue to perform its function even if the power utility fails. At the very least, the device should have the acceptable code stored in some means which will not be lost if power fails, and therefore have to be reprogrammed into each unit. Static semiconductor memory, jumpers, and switches are frequently used; battery backup that protects only the memory is also a means of accomplishing retention of memory of the code. The battery required to preserve memory is very small and long-lasting, similar to the battery in a pocket calculator, whereas the battery required to keep the entire unit operating is much larger and more expensive.

Fail-Safe or Fail-Soft

The total security plan and the system design created in response to it must consider that power will fail occasionally, and that equipment will also fail. When failure occurs, should the portal be made permanently-open or permanently-closed? Should there be a conventional-key bypass or other means to allow access under failure conditions? There are different answers to these questions for different security requirements and system designs, and there may be different decisions made for different physical areas within the same facility.

Code Changes

Part of the security plan may require changing the access codes occasionally, frequently, periodically, or aperiodically and at random. We recommend changing the codes for cheaply gained additional security in any system. This requires the ability to change both the code which each person has or knows (for example, the set of numbers to be entered into the pushbutton or the code contained on the card), and also the code stored within the access control equipment which will be compared with the code entered by the person. In most systems, changing the code within the access control system is made easy for the user. In some systems, a serviceperson must make the rounds of each portal device and change the positions of a set of switches and jumpers, or enter the new code electronically using a programming device. In most centrally controlled systems, the new code can be sent electronically from the central control to all portal devices; in some centrally controlled systems all comparisons are made at the central control and therefore the code need only be changed there.

Changing each person's code is simple in a combination lock system: the personnel are simply informed as to what the new code numbers are. Changing the code in a portable key system is frequently not so simple. First, there will be at least hundreds, perhaps thousands, and in some cases tens of thousands of cards or other devices on which the codes must be changed. Second, replacement of all cards is not usually an option since they cost anywhere from $1 to $10, depending upon what technology they use and whether they have been printed with company logos, employee pictures, affixed with pocket clips, and so forth. In some card systems, for example, magnetic stripe and sandwich systems, the coded data can be rewritten easily; however, in order to do so each card must be passed through a reprogramming device. Other card systems, such as Wiegand, magnetic slug, and bar code systems, have the code permanently embedded into them at the time of their manufacture, and changing the code requires that new cards be procured and issued. This is never considered a practical process, and therefore the same cards are used for many years. If changing the code is an important part of the security plan, selection of the access card or token must be made with that object in mind.

There are systems being developed that will provide code-changing capability using the same equipment that is used for card-reading to permit access. In fact, some will automatically change the code on a daily or random basis without the card-holder being aware that it is happening. None of these systems has reached the marketplace yet.

Derived-Code Systems

While we are on the subject of codes and code-changing, we should consider a few varieties of the combination portable key and combination lock systems, that is, card-plus-keypad. Some such systems are simple combinations of the two techniques: all authorized persons know the same code numbers to enter into the keypad, and all have a card that contains a separate and unrelated access code. There are systems, however, in which the two codes are related, resulting in different code numbers which different persons must enter into the keypad. In its simplest form, the card could contain a different number for each individual to enter into the keypad, thus providing individual PINs and preventing an outsider who has stolen a card and observed entry of a code number from using the stolen card to gain entry. There are a number of methods in which these card-related numbers can be used, including some that relate the PIN to today's date. Very complicated schemes, however, run the risk of confusing the authorized entrants, and backing up traffic at the portals, therefore they are seldom used except in high-security situations where relatively few persons are allowed access. In nearly all cases, sufficient security can be provided without resort to exotic, confusing, or complicated methods.

ACCESS CONTROL SYSTEMS VERSUS PERSONAL IDENTIFICATION SYSTEMS

We have not defined as yet the distinction between an access control system and a personal identification system, and have in fact been using the terms as if they meant the same thing, which they do not. An access control system is not necessarily a personal identification system, and a personal identification system need not necessarily be used as an access control system.

An access control system allows or denies access through a portal based upon whether or not a person satisfies the criteria which have been established for access. These criteria can be of several kinds.

Universal Code or Card

Everyone who is to be admitted knows the same code or carries a card containing the same code, and the access control system opens the portal without further ado or discrimination when it recognizes the code.

Group Coding

In addition to the common access code, a card may contain an additional coded number that defines a group to which the cardholder belongs. This group code may be used by the access control system for such purposes as excluding the cardholder from certain areas or at certain times. For example, one group may be the production workers who are to be admitted only to the assembly line during the first shift, a second group may be the second shift workers on the same assembly line, a third group may be the cleaning staff who work in the offices from 6 P.M.

to midnight, and a fourth group may be executives who may enter where they please at any time they please. This is still an access control system.

Personal Identification Systems

Personal identification systems uniquely identify an individual; when used for access control, these systems base the decision of whether or not to admit a person upon the knowledge of who the person is and whether or not he is to be permitted access to that particular area at that particular time. There are two basic means of providing personal identification. The first is to add a personal ID number to the code on the card (group coding and personal identification are seldom used with pure combination lock systems, because of the problem of memorizing lengthy numbers, the time required to enter them, and the simplicity and low cost of most keypad-only systems); the second is to utilize a physical attribute recognition system (which usually uses a card-ID for primary identification and the physical attribute comparison for verification of the identity only). Once personal identification is established, access control can be based upon groups, areas, or time-of-day by reference to data in the memory of the controller. Individual access privileges can be cancelled if a person leaves the company. If his card is lost or stolen the old ID can be voided and a new one issued. Personal identification systems can, of course, be used for many more purposes than access control: time-and-attendance; job-cost-accounting; chargeout of tools, equipment, books, and the like; or cafeteria charges. Many systems that are sold primarily for access control also provide some or all of these other features.

ERRORS IN ACCESS CONTROL OR PERSONAL IDENTIFICATION SYSTEMS

An access control system can fail to perform its assigned function in either of two ways: it can admit a person who should not have been admitted (a false-accept error), or it can deny admittance to a person who should have been admitted (a false-reject error). The cognoscenti have always referred to these as Class I and Class II errors, but since most of us have always had trouble remembering which was Class I and which Class II, the false-accept and false-reject definitions facilitate much more accurate communication.

The principle purpose of any access control system is to prevent false-accept errors, that is, to keep the bad guys out. But it will not be acceptable to accomplish this while having a high number of false-reject errors. A solid brick wall will allow no unauthorized entries, but it will not allow the legitimate workers to get into the plant either. When an authorized person is false-rejected, the usual procedure is that he immediately tries again to enter the code or have the card read. If the false-reject was due to a card-reading error or some other temporary abberation, chances are that the second reading will be successful. If the card is damaged so it cannot be read, or the code has been changed, no number of re-readings will result in the person being admitted. In such a case there must be a means of providing human intervention to solve the problem, such as a means to call the guard. Most systems automatically place a limit on the number of re-tries that can be attempted, so as to eliminate the possibility that an unauthorized person can stand at the portal and try a large number of different codes until he gets to the correct one. A high percentage of false-reject errors results in annoying delays at the portal while the legitimate people try again, and is undesirable in an access control system.

The performance of automatic access control systems with respect to false-accept and false-reject errors varies with the technology being used. Barring equipment failure, a combination lock system will have neither kind of error: either the correct number has been entered or it has not. From there on it goes downhill. A card can become dirty, bent, scratched, or demagnetized, and therefore become difficult to read. Such damaged card will give false-reject errors if the card reader cannot detect all the correct code-bits on the card. It is extremely unlikely that a non-valid card would become altered in such a way as to create the proper bits in a well-conceived card access system, and therefore card access systems—and other forms of portable-key systems—should not have false-accept errors.

Personal attribute systems represent a different class of problem. In these systems, identification is based on the probability that certain measured characteristics are unique to a particular person. The problems are twofold: first, there are limitations to the accuracy and repeatability of the physical measurements of the characteristics; second, these physical characteristics themselves may vary somewhat from time to time. For example, a fingerprint can be both different physically and be more difficult to measure on a Monday morning after the person has spent the weekend working on an automobile engine (grease in the grooves of the finger), laying brick (the ridges are worn down), or clearing the back forty (cuts and scratches which may look like grooves).

Personal attribute systems, therefore, have the inherent potential for both false-accept and false-reject errors. Further, there is always a dependence between the two. If the system is adjusted so that it must be absolutely certain of the identification, and therefore have virtually no false-accept errors, then an unacceptably high level of false-reject errors nearly always results. Reducing the acceptable threshold so as not to delay the authorized workforce in getting to their tasks, and therefore having a minimal level of false-reject errors, could cause a false-accept rate in the range of 10% or higher. If, however, the means are in place to apprehend the attempted penetrators, even a 10% false-accept rate will result in nine out of every ten attempts being foiled and punished. In many cases this deterrent effect will be sufficient to make the system viable.

As always, the risk analysis and total system design are the key elements, not a blind reliance upon high technology and automatic devices. The most effective solution will be a combination of several security devices, systems, procedures, and people, carefully designed to function together as a total security system.

Chapter 5

Keypad Access Control Systems

Keypads are the embodiment of the combination lock technique of access control. While it is certainly possible to contrive devices which utilize other forms of the combination lock or stored code principle, keypads are universally used because they are easy to operate and therefore cause minimum delay and confusion to the prospective entrant. Also, keypads are both mechanically and electronically simple to create from the manufacturer's point of view.

Keypads access controls are available in four basic forms, as follows.

Mechanical keypad devices usually have four or five keys (but can have as many as ten) which operate a mechanism that is similar in concept to the tumblers in a rotary combination lock. When the mechanical interposers have been properly aligned by depression of the correct sequence of pushbuttons, the door bolt may be manually opened. A mechanical keypad device is shown in Figure 5-1.

Electric-Mechanical Keypad Devices may have the mechanical mechanism described above for insuring that the correct code has been entered. This mechanism then closes a switch that electrically causes the door bolt to be opened. There are also versions in which the pushbuttons operate a set of electrical relays which, when activated in the correct sequence, electrically open the door bolt.

Electronic keypad devices are the most popular form of keypad access control. The keys themselves are simple pushbutton switches, and the sequence in which the keys are depressed is decoded by digital logic circuits. If the sequence is correct, an electrical solenoid is energized, thus unlocking the door. As in all digital logic operations nowadays, the intelligence is frequently conferred by a microprocessor rather than discrete logic chips.

Computer-controlled keypad devices come in two forms, a local-and-intelligent unit, and a central computer-controlled device. The local intelligent unit contains its own microcomputer (which is little more than the microprocessor used

Figure 5–1   *Mechanical keypad access control unit. (Courtesy of Simplex Security Systems, Inc., Collinsville, Connecticut)*

for decoding purposes), to which has been added additional functions such as increased memory and perhaps some input-output capability. In addition, this microcomputer can perform some more extensive functions—such as personal identification, zoning, and digit scrambling—than merely opening the door. The centrally controlled device is connected to a conventional computer, which can range from personal-computer-size up to the largest of real-time computers used for building automation control. When so connected, the simple keypad can become part of a sophisticated security and facility management system which provides all of the features of which access control technology is capable.

KEYPAD ACCESS CODES AND THEIR SECURITY

All keypad access control devices require that the correct sequence of numbers be depressed on a set of pushbuttons in order to open a door or other mechanism. As in all combination lock kinds of devices, the level of security which is provided is considerably dependent upon the number of combinations that are available. If there are ten keys and the prospective entrant is required to depress only one to gain entrance, he has one chance in ten of getting in even if he doesn't know the correct number; if two keys are required his chances are required to one in a hundred, and if three keys are required he is down to a one-in-a-thousand shot.

Number of Code Combinations

The number of possible combinations provided by a keypad system depends upon several parameters: the number of keys provided; the number of key-depressions required to enter the code; whether a key may be used more than once in the code sequence; and whether or not multiple keys may be depressed at once. The following examples provide an insight into the effect which these parameters have upon the number of combinations available in a keypad system.

Number of keys:
- on a 5-key pad, using a 2-digit code, there are 25 combinations;
- on a 10-key pad, using a 2-digit code, there are 100 combinations;
- on a 5-key pad, using a 3-digit code, there are 125 combinations; and
- on a 10-key pad, using a 3-digit code, there are 1,000 combinations.

Number of key-depressions required:
- on a 10-key pad, using a 2-digit code, there are 100 combinations;
- on a 10-key pad, using a 3-digit code, there are 1,000 combinations; and
- on a 10-key pad, using a 4-digit code, there are 10,000 combinations.

Whether a key may be used more than once (repeat):
- on a 10-key pad, 2-digit code, no repeats, there are 90 combinations;
- on a 10-key pad, 3-digit code, no repeats, there are 720 combinations; and
- on a 10-key pad, 4-digit code, no repeats, there are 5,040 combinations.

Whether or not two keys may be depressed at once (multiples):
- a 10-key pad, 2-digit code, with multiples, gives 2,025 combinations;
- a 10-key pad, 3-digit code, with multiples, gives 91,125 combinations; and
- a 10-key pad, 4-digit code, with multiples, gives 4,100,625 combinations.

Selection of the appropriate keypad, therefore, may not be as straightforward and simple as it may seem, since a 5-key pad with a 3-digit multiple code will provide more combinations than a 10-key pad with a no-repeat no-multiple 3-digit code.

Defense Methods Against Code-Breakers

The simplest method of attacking a keypad access control system is to try all of the possible numerical combinations. This can be done all at once if the keypad is located in an unattended area where no one is likely to take note of a person standing at the keypad for a long period of time; or it can be done piecemeal, trying a hundred or so combinations at a time over the span of a few days or even weeks. As a measure of the effort and time required, if the attempted penetrator can enter a code every three seconds, less than an hour will be required to enter all of the possible codes in a 1,000-combination system, and the probability is that the correct code will be found in about one-half hour. There are a number of defenses which have been developed to deal with this weakness.

Number of Combinations

Obviously, the more possible combinations provided, the less attractive and feasible is the approach of trying all of the combinations. 10,000 combinations will require 8 1/2 hours at 3 seconds per combination; 100,000 would need 3 1/2 days of round-the-clock effort.

Frequent Code Changes

Frequent code changes are another defense means, and are particularly effective against those who attempt to find the correct code by trying a few hundred combinations at a time over a long period. By the time the prospective penetrator has tried a significant portion of the possible codes, the code has been changed and he must start over. Of course there is a non-zero probability that he will hit the correct code on the first day, just at there are those who win the lottery and hit big on the slot machines without having played every number or turned up every combination of cherries and oranges. One of the difficulties with frequent code changes is that all of the authorized entrants must be informed each time the code is changed.

Time Penalty

A feature available with many keypad access control systems is time penalty. It deactivates the system for an amount of time, which is usually adjustable, after an unsuccessful attempt has been made to enter a code. This can greatly increase the amount of time required to enter a large number of codes, while penalizing the authorized entrant who has simply made a mistake, only a few seconds. If the time penalty were set, for example, at seven seconds, this would raise the time required to try 1,000 combinations from less than one hour to nearly three hours, and for 100,000 combinations from 3 1/2 continuous days to a week and a half.

Combination Time

Another feature which is available with many keypad systems is combination time. It allows a fixed amount of time, usually adjustable, for the code to be entered. The theory behind this is that authorized persons have the number memorized and can readily enter it, whereas anyone taking excessive time is probably up to no good, and may be, for example, reading numbers from a list of those he has not yet tried, and checking them off.

Error Alarms

Error alarms are a more forceful form of dissuasion of the interloper. In its simplest form, an alarm is sounded whenever there is an incorrect entry of the code sequence. The alarm can be a local bell, siren, or light to call attention to the portal, or it can annunciate within the protected premises or at a guard station. Because even authorized entrants can sometimes make a mistake and enter the code incorrectly, single alarms are not usually annunciated, although they may inobtrusively light a bulb or appear on a log or as a line on a CRT, simply as cautionary indicators. Sounding of an alarm is usually made to follow two or more successive wrong entries, and eliminates the try-all-the-codes attack, provided, of course, that a means of responding to the alarm has been incorporated into the total security system.

Methods of Code Storage

The code or codes which are to be recognized as correct by the keypad access control system must be stored within the system, and this is accomplished in a number of different ways, depending upon the kind of keypad system and the proclivities of its designers. The more common methods are as follows.

Mechanical Units

Mechanical units store the code in portions of their internal mechanism, such as detents, rotating cylinders, and interposers. Some mechanical units utilize replaceable sheets of metal or composition board with holes or notches in the appropriate positions for each code: a mechanical read-only memory. Changing of the code requires access to the interior of the mechanism, usually from the side of the unit that is inside the secured area, but sometimes from the front with special tools and a knowledge of the current code. None requires more than a few minutes to change the code.

Electrical Units

Electrical units usually store the code in the position of a set of switches or jumper wires. When the code punched into the buttons matches the positions of the switches or jumpers, current flows to the relay which allows the bolt to be removed and the door to be opened. To change the code, one merely changes the position of the switches, or moves the jumper wires, having first obtained access to the interior of the unit, usually from inside the protected premises. The entire operation should take less than a minute.

Electronic and Computerized Units

Electronic and computerized units sometimes use the switch or jumper method simply because they are easy to perform and provide visible indication of the code to the serviceperson. Most often, however, these more sophisticated systems utilize the more sophisticated methods of code storage appropriate to their high station in the hierarchy of keypad devices, solid-state memory being the most common. There is read-only memory (ROM), the solid-state equivalent to a template, which must be physically replaced every time there is to be a code change. There is EAROM (eletrically-alterable read-only memory) and its kinfolk, which act like ROM for code storage but can be reprogrammed (re-coded) electrically without having to be removed from the unit. There is conventional computer memory storage for the local microcomputer that is contained in the portal unit. There is also the ability, in centrally-controlled systems, to store the code only in the central computer itself.

Changing of the code in most of these equipments is done from the keypad itself; a master code allows access to the memory, and the new code is entered through the keypad. The unit need not be physically opened, and the operation can be accomplished in seconds. The ROM version requires that the unit be opened (from the secure side) and the ROM replaced: for this reason, ROM-coded units are not usually used in situations where frequent code changes are anticipated. In the centrally-controlled systems, the new code is entered once into the computer console—using, one hopes, the strictest of security procedures and precautions—and is immediately in force for all keypads in the system, either because it is sent downline for storage in each unit, or because the individual keypads must refer to central each time they are comparing an entered code. There are also, of course, systems in which the individual keypads may have different codes and all may be entered at the central computer console.

Changing of the Code

Selection of a keypad device should be affected by whether or not one plans to make code-changes an important part of the security process. It does not make sense to never change the code, any more than one should never change conventional locks. After a sufficient period of time one must presume that everyone except the hobo who just rolled in on the 8:04 has learned the combination in one way or another. On the other end of the spectrum, too-frequent changes of the code will tend to confuse the good guys, and lead to the use of undesirable memory techniques such as writing the code down in a very accessible location. The logistics of informing everyone that the code has changed can also be unwieldy. However, in situations where only a few—for example, the partners in the firm— have access, frequent code changes can be very workable. The bottom line, as always: first the security system must be designed, and then the devices which might be used to implement the system should be evaluated. Ease of code-changing varies among the different kinds of keypad access control systems, and should be evaluated with these differences in mind as well as their other attributes.

Another consideration relative to code storage is its permanency: jumpers and switches, unless physically disturbed, will retain the code stored into them until the physical material from which they are made returns to its primordial state some eons hence. Computer memories, on the other hand, become afflicted with permanent and incurable amnesia after having been subjected to only a few millionths of a second of absent or unstable power. Remedies such as EAROM, static chips, battery backup and the like exist, but this is an important area which must be examined with respect to one's total security system needs when one is contemplating buying keypad access control. It may be no bother to occasionally reprogram one keypad at the entrance to the computer room. But if 5,000 employees are jammed at the 50 entrances of an industrial plant every time there is a thunderstorm, heads will roll.

FEATURES, FUNCTIONS, AND CONSIDERATIONS

A pushbutton access control system is, for all practical purposes*, free of both false-accept and false-reject errors. Either the code is entered correctly or it is not, and there is no possibility of incorrect interpretation unless the controller logic unit has failed (presuming, of course, that the designers have paid proper attention to potential causes of erratic operation such as power line fluctuations and electromagnetic noise). One must, however, deal in advance with the possibility of equipment failure, and determine what mode of failure will be acceptable or desirable, since there are well-known means for designing systems which, when they fail, will do so in predictable fashion. Should the access control system fail in such a way that the door cannot be opened? If so, how does one get inside to fix it? If, on the other hand, there are always people on the secure side, the door can be manually opened. Each security situation must be analyzed in terms of its own particular requirements and parameters, and the available products must be measured against those requirements.

Master-Keying

Master-keying is a common feature in keypad access control. It usually takes the form of a master code that will be recognized as such when it is entered into the keypad and will cause the portal to be opened regardless of what the code-of-the-

---

*Our favorite mathematical definition of "for all practical purposes" is that of a sailor and a woman who assume initial positions at opposite ends of a football field. Each, in turn, moves half the distance towards the other. Theoretically they will never meet, but they can get close enough "for all practical purposes."

day is for the ordinary peasants. In mechanical keypad systems, and also in some of the electric and electronic versions, master-keying takes the form of an ordinary metal key inserted into a conventional key-slot and opening the door. Unfortunately, although such master-keying has its uses, it results in a weaker system from a security point of view. A penetrator now has two ways to compromise the system: learn the code or obtain a copy of the metal key (or pick the metal lock as if the keypad were not even there). We have seen examples where combinations of security devices or techniques could be used to provide greatly increased security, but those were in all cases the AND-combination of two techniques: in a card-plus PIN system, for example, one must possess both the card AND know the PIN. In the master-key situations we have an either/or situation: one may know the code OR have the key.

Because keypad access control devices are relatively simple and inexpensive, they are frequently used as replacements for the conventional lock-and-key in the stand-alone, one keypad to one portal, configuration. All the intelligence required to perform the access control function must be contained within the keypad and its local electronics; therefore, these units are usually simple combination locks without frills or sophisticated features.

There are also keypad access control devices that operate under a central control or a computer to which are connected a multiplicity of keypads. Using central control, a multi-portal keypad system may provide individual ID and lockout, event logging, and other sophisticated access control features.

It is unusual, however, to find a sophisticated and extensive access control system which is based entirely upon keypads. One frequently finds a centrally-controlled system that controls portals which are protected by a mixture of card-alone, card-plus-keypad, and keypad-alone devices. The two most common uses for keypads in access control are as stand-alone, single-door protection, and as adjuncts in card-plus-keypad systems, which are usually centrally controlled.

Conventional burglar and intrusion alarm systems for both home and commercial-industrial use frequently utilize keypads for arming and disarming the system. In some cases the system must be disarmed before the premises can be entered, in others there is a fixed time allowed for one to get to the keyboard and disarm the system after having entered the premises using a conventional key. Both of these operations constitute access control using keypads, and comprise the third most numerous use of keypads in access control.

Features and Options

There are a number of features and options which can enhance the security provided by keypad access control, or which make it more suitable for specific situations. Following are descriptions of them and the situations in which they can be useful.

Door Delay

In most units there is an adjustable timer which controls the length of time the door remains unlocked. This prevents piggybacking, an unauthorized person following closely upon the heels of one who has opened the door legitimately. There are other ways to solve this problem, such as turnstiles and mantraps. Also, there must be positive closure of the door and a door-ajar sensor and annunciator if door delay is to be an effective preventive measure.

Remote Indication

There may be remote electrical indication (lamp, bell, etc.) at a guard station or central logging facility, that the door was opened or is still open.

Visitor's Call

Many keypad systems provide one pushbutton that can be used by those not possessing the code to request entry. This is also useful for employees who have forgotten the code, or who were absent yesterday when the code was changed.

Hostage Alarm

In the event that an authorized entrant is being physically coerced into opening a portal, an alarm can secretly and silently be created by pressing a designated extra or alternate digit, also known as a duress alarm. To the person holding a gun in the employee's back, everything appears to be happening in the normal way: the buttons were depressed and the door opened; however, the alarm was created and appropriate response is underway.

Multiple Zones or Times

Some of the more sophisticated keypad systems have the ability to relate several acceptable codes to various times of day, so that, for example, those on different work shifts will have different access codes. Restricted access to particular areas of a facility can be accomplished by proper distribution of keypad controls, with master-codes that allow specific people (for example, management, maintenance, and security personnel) to enter all areas.

Individual Identification

Most keypad access control systems allow entry to any person who possesses the correct code, and if they have logging, can record only that the portal was opened by an authorized person, and at what time. A few keypad systems provide individual codes for each authorized person, and can therefore identify the particular person who opened the portal. This is a common capability of most card access systems, but is uncommon in keypad systems.

Anti-Passback

To prevent a person who has already passed through a portal from passing-back the ability to enter to another person using the same code, a few keypad-access systems have the ability to remember that a particular person (code) has entered. These systems will then not allow another entry using that code until an exit has first been made. This has been a common feature of card access systems for many years, but its incorporation into keypad-access systems is a relatively recent development.

Weatherproof Units

Since many portals which are to be protected are located in the exterior perimeter of a building, and by the nature of their function are outside, most manufacturers offer units that can withstand and operate under adverse weather conditions such as snow, ice, rain, or heat. On the other end of the scale, there are units fashioned of brass, brushed aluminum, or woodgrains made to attractively complement the interior decor.

MANUFACTURERS AND THEIR OFFERINGS

There are nearly forty manufacturers offering keypad access control products at the time of this writing. The products can be categorized as follows.

- Simple stand-alone keypad access control products   46%
- Keypads offered as part of a sophisticated access control system   25%
- Keypads offered as part of the alarm system   25%
- Special-purpose keypads (car, boat, etc.)   4%

The mechanism of control and code-recognition is distributed as follows among the manufacturers.

- Mechanical   4%
- Electrical and Electronic   41%
- Microcomputer and Microprocessor   52%
- Full-Scale Computer   2%

The number of keys which are used to enter the code (not counting keys that are used for other purposes such as "enter" and visitor's call) is overwhelmingly ten.

- 14 keys   2%
- 10 keys   77%
- 8–9 keys   10%
- 6–7 keys   6%
- 5 keys   6%

The stated number of possible combinations varies from 63 to one million, with the majority falling in the 1,000–10,000 range, as shown in the following distribution.

- Under 1,000 combinations   16%
- 1,000–5,000 combinations   26%
- 5,000–10,000 combinations   23%
- 10,000–50,000 combinations   5%
- 50,000–100,000 combinations   16%
- 100,000–500,000 combinations   2%
- 500,000–1 million combinations   9%
- Over 1 million combinations   2%

The frequency with which the various options and features are offered by manufacturers on their products is also of interest, since it provides some insight into the level of demand for security attributes beyond the basic combination-lock-level of capability. Following are the percentage of manufacturers that offer each feature with their keypad access control systems.

- Remote Indication   81%
- Door Delay   70%
- Multiple Zones or Times   58%
- Multiple Doors per Controller   56%
- Central Control or Logging   56%
- Hostage Alarm   47%
- Weatherproof Unit   40%
- Error Alarm   38%
- Time Penalty   32%
- Individual Identification   28%
- Combination Time   20%
- Visitor's Call   13%
- Antipassback   10%

It is interesting, considering our earlier discussion on the defensive measures that are most appropriate for use with keypad access control systems, to find "error alarm," "time penalty," and "combination time" very low on the hit parade, proving once again that the tastes of the masses can be a very poor indicator of merit.

PRODUCT FEATURES AND COSTS

There are a number of novel or unique features which are offered by only one or a few manufacturers, or which may be the *raison d'être* of a manufacturer's product. Following is a group of semi-random descriptions and comments on products for for keypad access control.

Hiding the Pushbuttons

Several manufacturers provide a sort of privacy panel for the pushbuttons, on the theory that one of the possible means of penetrating a keypad access control is to watch an authorized person enter the number; the privacy panel prevents the potential penetrator from seeing the keys as the number is entered.

Scrambling the Pushbuttons

Even with the privacy panel, one line of reasoning goes, the sequence of numbers can be deduced from observing the positions of the keys as they are depressed. In order to prevent this, one vendor, Hirsch Electronics, has developed a scrambled keypad that is widely OEM'd by others. The engraved numbers on the keypad are replaced by an electronic LED (light-emitting-diode) display of the numbers. The positions of the numbers can then be varied randomly by the electronics of the keypad, so that the same number does not always appear in the same position, preventing an outsider from deducing the code by observing the positions pressed. The price paid for this (since there is no such thing as a free lunch) is a somewhat longer time taken to enter the numbers and a somewhat higher wrong-number rate, since the human brain is accustomed to storing positional patterns corresponding to the numbers, as on a telephone or calculator keypad.

Commercial Computer as Controller

Computer-controllers have always been commercially-available minicomputers that the manufacturer has purchased in bulk and customized to perform the particular functions that are required in the system he is providing. An interesting departure from this process—standard since computer-based systems first began to emerge in the early 1960s—is to design the system around an unmodified standard-issue computer which is readily available to all, and to sell the computer software and the specialized equipment for the customer to attach to his own computer. Two companies—Applied Realtime Systems and Northern Computers—have pioneered this approach in the access control field, utilizing commercially-available complete computer systems as the controllers for their access control systems. The increasing presence of the personal computer is resulting in its being used as the controller for all varieties of electronic access control and other varieties of security systems.

Specialized Systems

Specialized systems have been developed by some manufacturers for particular applications. There are systems for controlling access to boats (by Boat Sentry, Inc.), to automobiles (by Crimestopper Security Products, Inc.), to mini-storage modules (by Mini-Storage Alarm Company), to parking garages and lots (by Federal APD and Parking Products, Inc.). We have already described the home security systems which include access control capabilities, along with fire and burglary protection. One company, Securtec, has a simple keypad access control system which interfaces with the home garage door opener.

Expanded Keypad and Display

Within the past year or two, there have been an increasing number of manufacturers offering keypads with fourteen keys instead of the usual ten (which is actually twelve like your telephone dial, if one counts the * and #) (Figure 5-2). Displays have also been enhanced, with the red and green lights labeled "enter code," "try again," and so forth, being replaced by one-line alphanumeric displays that spell out the messages. Diebold, Inc., one of the leading companies in the sale of security equipment to the banking industry, and also a leader in the point-of-sale and electronic credit card sale business, has offered these features for a number of years. Rusco Electronic Systems and Matrix Systems (which

Figure 5-2 *Fourteen-key keypad with LCD readout. (Courtesy of Matrix Systems, Inc., Dayton, Ohio)*

makes the units for Diebold) now also offer such keypad-displays, and other manufacturers are beginning to follow suit.

Telephone Access Control

It might be argued that voice recognition over the telephone from an apartment lobby constitutes a form of access control. We shall see in a later chapter that video identification is now possible using CCTV in the same scenario. There are also systems that use the keypad on the telephone in the lobby to provide true keypad access control in this application. Select Engineered Systems, Inc., is one of the leaders in this marketplace.

Automatic Reprogramming

Radionics provides their total security system with a bar code wand; reprogramming, including the access codes, is done by passing the wand over a bar-coded menu rather than manually keying in codes.

Remote Inquiry

Moose Products, Inc., offers a total security alarm system, including access control, with two unique features. One is a temporary access code that automatically becomes invalid after a preprogrammed number of uses. The other is the ability to interrogate the system and determine the status of the home or plant using a remote touch-tone telephone pad, and over the standard direct-dial network.

Variable-Length Access Codes

Variable-length access codes are allowed in the keypad system from SecuraKey, as part of a relatively sophisticated keypad access control system.

Glow-In-The-Dark

Glow-in-the-dark keys are offered as a keypad option by Security Sciences Corporation of America.

Mechanical Keypads

Mechanical keypads are offered by only two vendors, Simplex Security Systems, and Preso-Matic Lock Company. Both companies have credentials that go back two decades in the business. They can supply keypad access which can be added to current locks whether they are made by Schlage, Medico, Sargent, or others. They are installed by the user just like regular keyed locks, and are available with or without conventional-key bypass. These systems are approved for D.O.D. Restricted Areas.

Expected Cost Range of Keypad Systems

The cost of a simple, single-door keypad access control device begins in the $30–$50 range with simple electrical and electronic keypads. The keypad, with all necessary electronics, can be bought for as low as $20, but one must then add door strikes, batteries, and other such goodies to make it a working door system. For pure electronic combination-lock level of access control, without penalties and remote gadgetry, these units are an attractive buy. Electronic single-portal units are available with greater features at increasing prices up to the $300–$500 range, wherein one can obtain an intelligent unit with considerable features and the ability to be connected to a central controller.

Mechanical keypad units begin at about $90 and run to the $250 range with all features or including electrical drives and strikes. They are always single-portal units and have no capability to be centrally controlled, although the units having electric-strike output can be centrally monitored.

In summary, single-portal keypad access control can range in cost from $50 to $500, but a satisfactory installation should be possible in most cases for about $100; with a few added features this cost could easily double.

If sophisticated features, multiple portals with central control, logging, annunciation, and the like, are required, intelligent portal units and/or a central controller will be required. Intelligent stand-alone units will run in the range of $300–$500, incorporating most of the useful features. A complete centrally-controlled, multiple-portal system can cost anywhere from $100–$1,000 per portal. However, a completely satisfactory installation should be possible in most situations for under $400 per portal.

Chapter 6

Card and Other Portable-Key Systems

A portable-key access control system admits the holder of a device (usually a plastic card but embodied in other forms as well) which contains a pre-recorded code which the access control system has been programmed to recognize; the device is inserted into a reader, and if it contains the required code, the portal is unlocked. This process is no different in concept from the ordinary metal key and lock which have been in use for centuries: the metal key is machined with grooves and notches that represent the code, and the lock has been mechanically set so that only a key having the proper grooves may be inserted, and only one having the proper notches will allow the bolt to be turned.

The modern electronic access control system offers a number of advantages over the venerable lock-and-key. First, the ordinary lock-and-key is limited to a few thousands of different combinations (tens of thousands in the industrial-grade versions), whereas the electronic version has millions of possible combinations. Second, the majority of metal keys can be duplicated by the part-time high-school worker at the corner hardware store, whereas the electronic keys require higher technology to duplicate. Third, the electronic systems can provide complex logic, control, personal identification, and logging functions which the simple keys do not. However, it should be recognized that there are relatively sophisticated versions of the lock-and-key which provide more security than the simplest electronic devices at about the same cost, and they should not be ignored as the user designs his access control system.

The plastic, wallet-size, credit card type of card has become the most popular device used for access control systems; it forms the basis of over 75% of the systems offered, although some manufacturers offer both the plastic card and other forms of portable-key. The second most popular form is a key-shaped token, usually of plastic, with some versions being small enough to fit an ordinary key ring. There are also metal cards of various sizes, and a number of other metal and plastic tokens in use (see Figure 6–1). With the exception of the "standard" plastic card, the other forms of portable-key are unique to one manufacturer and can be used only in that manufacturer's system. Many (but not

93

Figure 6–1   *An access control token. (Courtesy of Corkey Control Systems, Torrance, California)*

all) embodiments of the plastic card are standard in size and coding, therefore some degree of interchangeability and second-sourcing is possible.

The form of the portable-key is not high on the list of considerations that are important in choosing an access control system. As a general rule, the larger the device (in flat surface area), the more different codes can be stored upon it; the exception is portable-keys which contain coding in self-contained microchips, where the code capacity has no relationship to the size or form of the portable-key. In some applications it may be useful to adopt a "standard" portable-key such as the plastic card, so that it can be used for other applications (such as a standard charge-card) in addition to access control. The choice of a "standard" technology can also be a sound business decision since it makes the user less dependent upon one particular vendor if things go awry or the vendor goes out of business.

Various forms of portable-keys for access control have been marketed since the 1960s, and most of them have taken, however roughly, the form of the plastic card. By the mid-1970s, the plastic card containing magnetic-slug coding (which is further described later in this chapter) was the preferred form. During that time period, the new breed of credit and banking cards was being perfected, and this gave great impetus to the use not only of the plastic card itself, but of the magnetic-stripe method of encoding computer-readable data onto the card (which is also further described later in this chapter). Today, more than half of the portable-key access control systems offered are based upon the plastic card using magnetic-stripe encoding.

Banking and credit card systems are really a form of access control: they control access to money rather than to a physical premises. They are encoded by the same means used in 40% of access control systems; they are read by the same card readers; they are controlled by the same computers and communications equipment; and in a few cases they are purveyed by the same vendors. Although it is not the purpose of this book to cover the features, applications, and manufacturers of these financial systems, the technology which we cover will enable the reader to understand their workings.

CODES IN PORTABLE-KEY SYSTEMS

There is a variety of technologies that are used to store the code upon or within a portable-key, and these are described in detail in the following section. Owing to the wide variety of both the coding technology and the form—and therefore the available encoding area—of the portable-key, there is also a wide range of encoding combinations available: devices are offered which range from fewer than one thousand to more than one billion* combinations. Devices with imbedded microchips and cards with laser-encoding can offer many times these amounts of coding, but such additional capacity—as we shall discuss—is superfluous for access control purposes and intended for other applications, perhaps in addition to access control.

The number of combinations provided by a portable-key system depends wholly upon the amount of code (measured in binary digits, also known as "bits," which is the base-2 number system used by all computing systems: either a spot is magnetized or it is not, either there is a notch at a particular spot on a metal key or there is not) that the device can contain. There is no adjustment to be made as there is in the keypad systems, according to whether a key can be used twice. The following list illustrates some important relationships with respect to coding of a portable-key device.

- 1 bit provides 2 combinations.
- 5 bits provide 32 combinations and require 5 times the area of 1 bit.
- 10 bits provide 1,000 combinations and require 10 times the area.
- 15 bits provide 32,000 combinations and require 15 times the area.
- 20 bits provide one million combinations and require 20 times the area.
- 30 bits provide one billion combinations and require 30 times the area.

If we consider that 1,000 combinations is the practical minimum for access control purposes, then we see that using the same coding technology, we can obtain 1,000 times more coding capacity for every time we double the area that can be encoded. On the other hand, the commonly used encoding techniques require an

---

*"Billion" is one of the words in the language—we hesitate to say "English language" for the following reason—which is unusually imprecise for a quantitative term. We mean here the usual American (and also French) quantity of one thousand millions. The British (and German) billion is one million millions. And my Webster's Collegiate Dictionary (publ. 1969) hedges with "a very large number," which is a definition few can dispute.

encoding area per bit which ranges from 0.25 to 0.01 square inches; this means that, for example, all the encoding on a slug-coded device could be contained on a small spot of a magnetic-stripe card. As a practical matter, the conventional plastic cards contain sufficient encoding area for any access control requirement, regardless of the coding technique used; the same is true of all other portable-keys which are in common use.

In a simple access control system, all cards will contain identical coding, and all portal readers will be programmed to recognize the same code, much the same as a metal-key system. In such a system, a few thousand possible code combinations are sufficient to provide all the security of which the system is capable: 10 to 15 bits will be sufficient. The same system can be used to provide segregation such that different portals will require different codes. Thus, those persons with code "A" imbedded in their cards can only enter portal A, code "B" will allow entry to portal B, and so on. Some such simple systems provide master key capability, so that the master code "M" will allow entry to all portals regardless of the individual code which opens that portal to the masses.

In systems which have more than the number of code combinations required to merely open a door, the extra digits can be used to store and control by employee number and shift. They can also be used to provide access by time of day and area of the facility. A log showing who passed through what portal and at what time on what day can be kept using these extra digits. This capability can be expanded into a personnel-locator function, and used to provide time-and-attendance (time clock) data for payroll purposes. These functions require that the access control system be controlled by a central computer, as opposed to free standing portal units which suffice for the simple door-control functions.

In a centrally controlled system which has an employee identification number encoded on each card, it is not necessary that the card contain an access code, since the central computer can contain a table that relates each employee to the portals through which he is allowed to pass, including the time of day during which access is permitted. In the event of failure of the central computer or communications between the portal equipment and the central computer, it is frequently prudent to provide some access code on the card by which the portal equipment alone can allow access under degraded-mode (fail-soft) conditions. Of course, goodies such as logging, time-period-control, and personnel-locator will be lost when the system operates in degraded-mode. When allowing for degraded-mode in a system design, one must consider that a sophisticated penetrator could take advantage of the reduced security by forcing the system into degraded-mode (by cutting the communications lines or the power lines to the central computer).

In a system without the central ability to correlate individuals using a central data base, the coding requirements might be compiled as follows:

- access codes (4,000 possibilities)   12 bits
- facility-plant-portal code (32 different doors)   5 bits

- time control code (16 shifts and combinations)   4 bits

  total coding capability required: 21 bits

In a centrally controlled system, the employee identification number is used against the internal data base to determine the portals, facilities, times, and so forth, at which that particular employee is to be admitted, and therefore there is no need for any of the codes listed above. One need only provide sufficient coding capability to accommodate the number of employees who are to be identified, for example, 12 bits for 4,000 employees. Any additional coding capability can then be used for other functions, some of which are described below.

Another feature inherent in the centrally controlled system is the ability to cancel the access privileges of a particular person or card. For example, when a person quits, is discharged, or loses his card, the appropriate employee identification number is simply removed from the data base. In a free standing system, lost cards can be used by whoever finds them unless the access code is changed at each portal, and on all of the cards in the system.

The ability to change the code that is contained on the access card varies with the kind of encoding used. Some cards have the coding embedded into the card during its manufacture, and there is no possibility of changing the code; should a code change be required, new cards must be issued. Other cards have the code recorded upon them magnetically, and the code may be altered at will. The various coding methods are described in detail in the next section.

Once a centrally controlled system has been put in place that controls access by use of the individual identification number on a card, the possibility exists for a "universal card" which can be used for many purposes in addition to access control. Since most cards have the capacity to contain more coded bits than are needed for personal identification, these bits can be used for other purposes. Cafeteria charging at companies and universities; purchasing at company outlet stores or university bookstores; recording of the student class schedule; these are all applications which have been added to centrally controlled systems.

An even more technologically advanced breed of plastic cards is beginning to emerge which has the capability of storing many times the number of bits used for any access control system. One of these cards is the "smart card," which contains a microprocessor integrated circuit and several thousand bits of memory. It is being pushed forward through the investment of many millions of dollars from the credit card industry, and some versions are beginning to be offered for access control purposes. A second is the "laser card," which can store 4 million characters—32 million bits—of data, more than the contents of this book; current applications include storage of a person's entire medical record, distribution of computer software, and storage of financial records. Access control and personal identification applications must be considered by-products of these technologies. The combination of laser storage and embedded microchips offers the possibility of a powerful multi-purpose computer system that can be carried in the wallet and plugged into computer terminals for access control, financial transactions, and other purposes as yet unconceived.

CODING TECHNIQUES FOR PORTABLE-KEY SYSTEMS*

There is a wide variety of techniques and technologies which have been and are being used to encode cards for use in access control systems. In the earliest days, the first card access systems were put together from components and techniques used in the fledgling computer industry: punched cards, embossed cards, and the reading equipment used with them. As card access grew to become a business in its own right, specialized card coding and readers were developed specifically for access control, although the mainstream of the technology continued—and continues still—to follow very closely the computer technology from which it sprang.

There are about a dozen techniques which have been used for embedding the access code into, or recording it onto, a card or token, and all (or nearly all, there was one which was widely deemed to be hazardous to the health, it being radioactive) are still in use today in one application or another. The mainstream, however, is comprised of half a dozen techniques which have been developed in the last decade or so, and the majority of them utilize one form or another of magnetic recording of the code. The non-magnetic coding methods in general are each peculiar to one vendor who has developed the method for his own reasons and for particular applications, and it is used in his product line alone.

We divide our examination of card-coding methodologies into groups consisting of the simple methods, which are also (not by coincidence) generally the oldest methods; embedded materials, which formed the second generation of coding technology, but which also include one of today's most popular methods; the magnetic techniques which have constituted the mainstream of card coding for the past dozen years; proximity-card coding, which represents an entirely new approach to the card access business; and the new technologies which may represent the future of card access control.

Simple Methods: The Hollerith Card

In the beginning was the Hollerith card, and the Hollerith card was with Thomas Watson, and without them was not anything made that was made. For five decades the 80-column card with the square holes** (universally known as the

---

*Some of the material in this section originally appeared in "Choosing The Right Card," by Dan M. Bowers, *Security World,* June, 1986.

**IBM's major competitor in the early days of the computing industry was Univac, which used a card having 90 columns and round holes (which are easier to make than square ones) for two decades; it finally succumbed to the marketing might of IBM, and in the late 1960s Univac systems were delivered with "IBM card" peripheral equipments.

"IBM card" but actually invented by Dr. Herman Hollerith to tabulate the 1890 census of the United States, 34 years before IBM was born; thus its official name of tabulation card, "tab-card" for short) served as the means for data recording, input, storage (there were no core memories and there were no solid state chips), and sorting for the computer industry. Data were entered into the card by punching physical holes into an array 80 columns wide and 12 rows high, and read by passing the card under a line of brush-type contacts. Current flowed through those brushes where the holes were located, but was blocked by the card where there were no holes (see Figure 6–2). In the 1960s, photoelectric reading replaced the brushes. A vast array of readers, sorters, punchers, verifiers, and duplicators were available for processing punched cards (an experienced manager of such an "electronic accounting machine" or EAM could frequently out-process the business computers of the day by using "tab card" machines entirely). The availability of this equipment facilitated the invention of the Hollerith card access control system. The manifestation adopted was the stubcard, which was a form of the standard tab card that was sent as an invoice to utility customers for example. The right hand portion of the card, containing 32 columns of data, was perforated so that it could be detached by the customer and enclosed with his payment. The 32-column stub was processed by the EAM machinery, thus eliminating the need for manual entry of the payment. This stub was a convenient size to use for an access control card, and all of the equipment needed to prepare and read it already existed.

Since the code on a Hollerith card is easily readable, and the equipment needed to prepare it was—and still is—readily available, it did not achieve much popularity as a security device. These cards are still in use in applications where there is no substantial motivation to duplicate them for illicit purposes, such as time cards and job-cost-accounting systems.

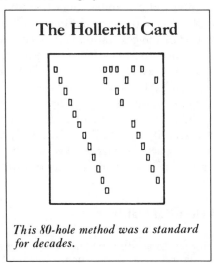

Figure 6–2 *The Hollerith card. (Courtesy of* Security *magazine, Des Plaines, Illionis)*

Simple Methods: The Embossed Card

In the 1960s the emerging science of optical character recognition, which now is used routinely in an ordinary office word processor, had reached the point where it was possible to reliably read numeric-only data written in a carefully controlled font; the reading of alphabetic data and of multiple fonts was still a decade away. This new capability was first put to useful work reading receipts from gasoline credit card purchases. These receipts were made by taking carbon impressions of the raised embossed printing of an account number on a plastic card, a procedure which for many oil companies has not changed to this day. As with the Hollerith card, the equipment for encoding the card and reading the code already existed, and the plastic card was a much more durable form of bearer identification than the cardboard stub (Hollerith cards could be made in plastic, but the normal punches, made for cardboard cards, quickly wore out when used to punch holes in them).

The embossed card, however, suffered from the same low degree of security as the Hollerith card, since the ID number was plainly visible, and card-making equipment was only slightly less available than punching equipment. A few access control systems were attempted but no widespread acceptance was ever achieved.

Simple Methods: Optical Bar Codes

Optical bar codes consist of a series of printed stripes spaced to represent coded data; they are now found on most grocery items and are automatically read by the new generation of supermarket checkout systems. The advantage of optical bar codes is that they can be read by passing a single photodetector over them, unlike optical character recognition which requires sophisticated optical and electronics systems, or even Hollerith which requires a multiplicity of reading heads in a line. Some early embossed cards of the gas station variety contained raised bar codes in order to make the reading process easier. The technology has been around since the 1960s; access control systems based upon it have been marketed for twenty years and are still available from several vendors.

Like the other early systems, optical bar coding suffers from the fact that it is visible to any observer, and is therefore not difficult to duplicate; it has therefore been relegated to the low security applications. Currently, however, versions for security applications are being actively marketed with the information encoded in non-visible form, and readable only by ultra-violet or infra-red light.

Simple Methods: The Electrical Matrix

As the technology developed for accounting and computing applications began to be adapted for access control systems in the 1960s, the search began for new techniques that would eliminate the easy-duplication and visible-coding defects, thus providing a higher level of security. One of the early attempts was the electrical matrix card, which was made of an electrically printed circuit containing a matrix of diodes connected to embody a unique code and was sandwiched between two layers of opaque plastic so the coding was not visible. The card was read by inserting it into a card-edge connector, which established an electrical connection with the decoding circuitry in the reader. Unfortunately, the card was somewhat bulky, it was not durable since the printed circuit could not withstand repeated flexing, and it was considerably more expensive than the alternatives then available. However, this card represented the state-of-the-art in electronic circuit fabrication and packaging for its day, and it should be considered a direct ancestor of one of the currently emerging card technologies, the *smart card*.

In the late 1960s, as the card-access business began the search for its own technologies, the majority of the early efforts concentrated on maintaining the basic coding concept—code bits arrayed in columns and rows—but replacing the visible bits at the reading positions with other kinds of material which would provide increased security without greatly increasing cost. This led to the embedded-materials group of cards. Although none of the early techniques is in widespread use today, they provided a necessary evolutionary link with modern technologies.

Embedded Materials: Magnetic Slugs

The first successful pure access control card employed bits of magnetic material that were arrayed in the conventional row-and-column form. The coding was established by the combination of present and absent slugs at the possible points in the matrix, just as it was in the Hollerith card or the electrical matrix (see Figure 6–3). The magnetic bits were arrayed on a sheet of material which was then laminated in opaque plastic so that they were not visible. The card was read by passing it along a row of magnetic-sensing heads. This product formed the backbone of the card access business for a decade. Its use has declined, not because of any inherent defects of its own, but because better ways to solve the problem became available as technology advanced. Improvements in the technology of magnetic materials and magnetic sensing, for example, have made it possible to store data on a film of magnetic material—also known as magnetic tape—which has a much smaller magnetic mass than the slugs that were required two decades ago. Magnetic slugs are the parent of the magnetic sandwich (also known as barium ferrite) card, which essentially uses different materials to solve the problem in the same way, and has been one of the most popular techniques of the past decade.

Embedded Materials: The Capacitor Card

Another row-and-column card coding method can be visualized as having bits of capacitive material at the appropriate points of the matrix. This type of card is

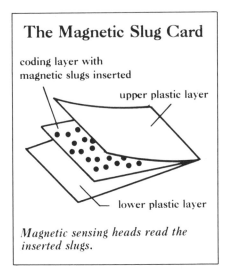

Figure 6–3 *The magnetic slug card. (Courtesy of* Security *magazine, Des Plaines, Illinois)*

read by passing it under a row of capacitance sensing heads; this is attractive because the sensing of a large difference in capacitance between those points that have slugs and those that do not is a relatively simple electronic proposition compared with other sensing problems, including magnetic sensing. In actuality, a center sheet of material laminated between two sheets of plastic was comprised of a high-dielectric material into which holes were punched, thus resulting in reduced capacitance at the hole locations. The technology was developed in the early 1960s as a read-only storage mechanism for the most advanced of computing equipment then available, IBM's 360 line; the holes were punched by standard Hollerith equipment, thus making this card a closet Hollerith. It never achieved much popularity, primarily because the access control system designers were directing their attention to the then new magnetic slug technology. It also did not achieve much popularity with its originator and in its original application, since it was replaced in the final version of the 360 by early solid state memory technology.

Embedded Materials: Other Slug-Type Methods

Other materials were used in a number of ill-fated attempts to create a row-and-column coded card. Non-magnetic metal slugs were introduced in attempts to overcome an inherent defect in magnetic slugs: the position of the slugs can be detected easily by scattering a handful of iron filings over the surface of the card. They were read by eddy-current sensors using the same principles as those now used in airport metal detectors, which proved somewhat more complex and expensive than magnetic sensing in the technology of that day. These techniques were offered from time to time by individual vendors, and never achieved any substantial acceptance. One memorable offering embedded the coding using bits of radioactive material, read by a Geiger counter kind of apparatus; it was not well received.

There is currently a token shaped like an ordinary ballpoint pen that contains non-magnetic slugs and is offered for access control.

Embedded Materials: The Wiegand Effect

In the group of access cards which are coded using embedded materials, the Wiegand-effect card stands alone: it is the only embedded-coding card to be introduced in the last decade; it is one of the few coding techniques that does not use principles of physics which have been known since Hans Christian Oersted; and it is one of the more widely used methods of card encoding today.

Although strictly speaking it is a magnetic method of coding, the Wiegand effect operates on a different principle and therefore has different characteristics from the other magnetic techniques. In this method, each bit of data is encoded in a wire which is twisted under tension and heat-tempered. Each wire has a magnetic snap-action which creates a large voltage under the influence of a given strength magnetic field, almost regardless of the speed with which it is moved past the read head; in conventional magnetic reading, the strength of the read signal is proportionate to the reading speed. Wiegand wires are embedded into positions in the access control card to create the codes, and dummy non-Wiegand wires can also be embedded so the position of the coded wires is less easily detected. Wiegand-coded cards and reading equipment are widely available, as is a key-shaped token with somewhat less coding capability, but which has become more popular than most non-card portable keys. The Wiegand-effect wires are also used in automotive ignition, sensing of key-depressions in electronic keyboards, and production line item-sensing applications.

The magnetic slug and the Wiegand effect utilize magnetic materials for the encoding, and magnetic-sensing read heads and electronics, but they are truly embedded materials, and once inserted into the card during its manufacture, the coding cannot be altered. True magnetic encoding as we are defining it herein utilizes a film of magnetic material which is similar (and in some cases identical) to that used for storage on magnetic tape and disk equipment for both computer and audio use. Each spot on the magnetic material can be magnetized or demagnetized using conventional equipment and circuitry, and the magnetized spots can be left in place permanently (defined as perhaps ten years) or can be changed at will. There are two magnetic card methods in use today, and both are among the prime contenders for the access control market.

Magnetic Techniques: The Magnetic Sandwich

In the magnetic sandwich card, a sheet of magnetic material is laminated between two layers of plastic. The magnetic material most commonly used is barium ferrite, and thus this kind of card is frequently called the barium ferrite card. A row-and-column array of spots on the magnetic sheet can each be magnetized or not (the spots are arbitrarily defined by the positioning of the recording and reading heads, since every spot on the magnetic sheet is equally capable of magnetization), thus creating the coding which is read by a row of magnetic-sensing heads. This seems to be an exact analog of the older magnetic-slug card, but there are important differences. First, the coding on the magnetic sandwich card can be altered by erasing the previous spots and recording new ones, whereas the magnetic-slugs and the coding that they represent are fixed into the magnetic-slug card when it is manufactured. Second, the magnetic sandwich card is easier to manufacture, since it requires only the lamination of three sheets of material, one of them magnetic; the slug card requires the precise placement of a number of small bits of material in the center layer of each card, and different cards will require different placement of the slugs so that they will have different coding. Third, the level of the magnetic field that is radiated from the card is lower in the sandwich than in the slug (although this is equally due to the age of the technology used in slug systems: modern materials and techniques could eliminate this defect, but development money is no longer being spent on magnetic-slug cards). The higher field of the slug card has been blamed for wiping out lesser magnetic fields, such as the one on your American Express card carried next to it in your wallet. Fourth, this lower level of magnetic field requires more sensitive reading equipment than is necessary for the magnetic slug card, but that is no particular problem with today's technology.

Magnetic Techniques: The Magnetic Stripe

A magnetic stripe is applied on the surface of the card, much as if a strip of ordinary magnetic tape had been affixed; the code is recorded on the stripe with equipment using conventional magnetic tape recording technology. Because this technology is well-known, and the stripe is visible and accessible, there is appropriate concern that the cards are easily duplicatable or that they can be erased or altered easily (see Figure 6-4), and a number of additional safeguards are provided in situations that require a high level of security. Many vendors encrypt the data on the card so that it is not useful to the perpetrator. In most high-security applications, such as using a magnetic-stripe card to withdraw money from an automatic teller machine, a keypad is used in conjunction with the card reader, so that the correct identification number must be entered in addition to an acceptable card. One manufacturer embeds a unique code into the stripe during the manufacture of the card, a code which cannot be altered or erased, and which can be read only by special equipment.

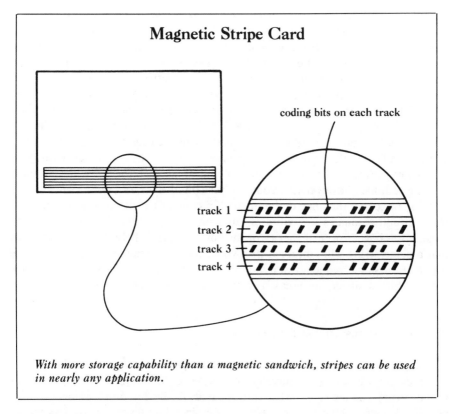

Magnetic Stripe Card

coding bits on each track

track 1

track 2

track 3

track 4

With more storage capability than a magnetic sandwich, stripes can be used in nearly any application.

Figure 6-4   *The magnetic stripe card. (Courtesy of* Security *magazine, Des Plaines, Illinois)*

There are also access cards and tokens that utilize surface magnetic recording for code storage, but this magnetic recording is not in the conventional stripe form. The magnetic area may be of some other shape, or in some cases (for example, some of the new hotel room access systems) covers the entire card surface—a kind of open-face magnetic sandwich with the magnetic layer on the outside.

Magnetic stripe recording is inherently capable of containing a much larger number of code bits than the magnetic sandwich, because the reading and writing heads can be brought closer to the surface stripe than to the internal sheet of magnetic material (the minimum size of a magnetically recorded bit is proportional to the distance between the head and the magnetic material). Both methods, however, have been proven to contain sufficient storage capacity for all access control purposes.

Proximity Systems: Passive Cards

Proximity-card access control systems require a different approach to encoding the bits into the card (or token), since the card will not be inserted into a reading mechanism and the code must therefore be sensed from some distance away. We devote an entire later chapter to proximity devices and technology, and will therefore dwell on the subject here only to the extent required for completeness of the understanding of card-encoding techniques. Passive proximity systems utilize access cards that contain no power source, and identify themselves by re-radiating radio waves at particular frequencies when they are interrogated by a radio-wave field at a particular, higher, frequency; the access code is embodied in the frequencies of the radio waves that are re-radiated, or in some instances in code bits modulated upon the radio waves. These cards are usually of the conventional credit card type with the usual three laminated layers, the coding layer being the center layer. Instead of the row-and-column array of bits with which we have become familiar, however, the coding layer contains a number of printed tuned circuits, or tuned antennae and a microchip containing the code. (An electronic tuned circuit resonates—or vibrates—at a particular frequency when it receives stimulation in the form of that frequency or a multiple thereof, in the same way that a piano string will vibrate at its own frequency when stimulated by a strong sound at the same frequency or a multiple of that frequency. It is the same principle by which a singer can break a crystal glass by singing at it.)

Proximity Systems: Active Tokens

Active proximity systems, the second type of proximity system, utilize tokens which do contain a power source (such as a battery), and identify themselves by broadcasting a coded signal when interrogated. Active proximity systems require portable keys which contain batteries, a fair-sized bundle of electronics, and an antenna, and they are therefore not yet available in a form that we could correctly call a card; most of them come about the size of a cigarette pack.

The new technologies are worth noting because of the impact that they may someday have on the field of access control: one (the laser card) promises to increase by a million times the amount of data that can be recorded onto a passive card, and the other (the smart card) promises to embed sufficient solid state electronic circuitry into a card to approximate the power of a small-size microcomputer along with its memory. We shall treat the future potential of these new cards at greater length in a later chapter, but it is part of our purpose here to describe their construction and coding.

New Technologies: The Laser Card

The laser card is credit-card-size and uses the same kind of technology developed for use in recording video and audio disks for entertainment purposes. One entire side is optically covered with bits that are read by a laser light beam (hence its name). Current cards can be written only once, since the information is recorded by burning a microscopic hole (using a writing laser) into a layer of photographic-like silver particles that cover the card; reading then consists of sensing the holes, which are the code bits. (It is worth noting that a re-writable laser card is not an ultimate impossibility: such a device was in the marketplace briefly more than twenty years ago. Honeywell introduced a high-density laser-magnetic memory that used laser recording and reading onto and from a magnetic surface. Writing was performed by placing the entire magnetic surface under a weak magnetic field; those bits to be written were then raised above their Curie point—the point of temperature at which the material loses its magnetic memory—using a laser for heat, and when the laser was removed and the temperature fell, the point aligned itself magnetically with the weak field. Reading was accomplished by shining a lower power laser onto the spots; the magnetized spots rotate the plane of polarization of the reflected laser light (the Faraday effect) thus allowing them to be differentiated from the non-magnetized spots. This memory system was pushing the leading edge of the late-1960s' technology from several directions, and a commercially successful product was never achieved.)

Laser cards are likely to be priced in the same range as most of the more conventional cards discussed above, once the technology is stabilized and some mass production usage is achieved. This could make them attractive for a number of applications.

New Technology: The Smart Card

The smart card is another of the laminated-layer variety, the size of a credit card but thicker. In the center layer, where we have seen slugs, sheets, and printed circuits, there is a complete microcomputer, its printed wiring, and a battery and radio communications circuit for communicating with the reader into which it is inserted. Considering the size of the pocket calculators that we all now carry, this is not too great an extension of the electronics packaging technology. Since the card represents a computer-in-your pocket, the capabilities for data storage and manipulation are well beyond those needed for pure access control. Card costs will be several times that of pure access control cards, even after significant production levels are achieved.

OTHER CONSIDERATIONS IN CARD SELECTION

We have described one of the important parameters of a card to be used for access control purposes; the amount of code bits it can carry, and the number of code combinations which it can therefore provide. We have also stated, however, that all the techniques that are in common use are capable of providing sufficient code combinations for access control purposes. The selection of a card technology will probably be based on considerations other than coding capacity; some of the other factors that should be considered are the following.

Age of the Technology

Many of the techniques described in the preceding section have been around for two decades or more, and in point of fact we have presented a few of them purely for historical interest, since they are no longer offered by any vendor (see Figure 6-5). The bad news with respect to these techniques is that the basic principles are well-known, and therefore anyone who intends to compromise the system will have no trouble getting access to the technology; and older systems will not have taken advantage of the advances in technology that have occurred during the past twenty years. The good news may be that the basic techniques of all card-coding systems are available to any person or organization with the training, motivation, and resources to pursue the subject; that ancient techniques can be updated and implemented with modern technology to create a system that is just as effective as any based on star wars kinds of discoveries; and finally, that there might be some additional security conferred by a system which is simply different from the

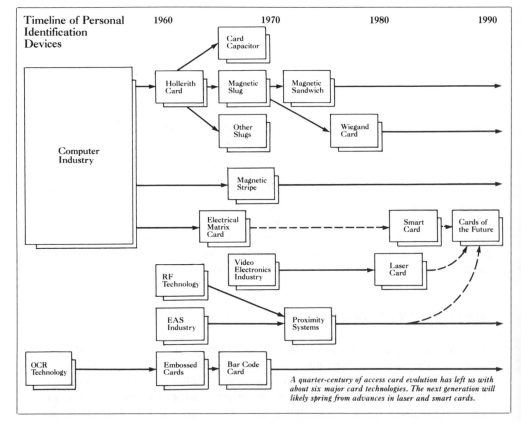

A quarter-century of access card evolution has left us with about six major card technologies. The next generation will likely spring from advances in laser and smart cards.

Figure 6-5 *Timeline of card access technology. (Courtesy of* Security *magazine, Des Plaines, Illinois)*

majority of those in place, that is, if the rest of the world is using magnetic-stripe cards, perhaps we can make life more difficult for the criminal-planners by having the only card-capacitor system in the world.

On the bottom line, neither the technique nor the technology of the access control system is of overwhelming importance; it is the operation of the access control system within the total security system that is the determining factor.

Changeability of the Coding

A consideration that *can* be of significant importance is the matter of whether or not the code contained by the card can be changed at will by the user. An effective aspect of a total security system can be the changing of access codes periodically or randomly, as we have discussed in Chapter 5 on keypad systems: it can also be very effective in a card-based system. The capability of changing the code, or the lack of that capability, is inherent in the kind of card and the means by which the code is embodied, as we have discussed in the preceding section. All cards coded by embedded materials have the code built-in during the manufacturing process, and the codes cannot be changed except by scrapping all of the cards (which can cost $6 each if they have pictures, pocket clips, and other goodies) and issuing new ones. All the simple methods—Hollerith, bar codes, and so on—are similarly encoded when manufactured and cannot be changed. The two magnetic methods of encoding—sandwich and stripe—are the only cards in the conventional access control spectrum on which the access code can be changed at will by the user. In the proximity systems, the passive versions are embedded circuits and cannot be changed, but the active versions can usually be re-coded using switches or jumpers that are provided in the internal circuitry.

Ease of Duplication

An important aspect affecting the security of a card access system is the difficulty which a prospective penetrator would encounter in duplicating a card, given that he knew how to properly code it. Since plastic card-making and laminating equipment is readily available from a number of vendors—it can even be obtained by mailorder—there is no particular challenge in creating any of the embedded materials cards, with two exceptions: the material which must be embedded into the Wiegand card is available from only one manufacturer, requiring some creative purchasing; and the circuitry contained within the passive proximity card requires sophisticated engineering and manufacturing. The surface-coded cards can be done by hand, even if this is tedious work: there have already been instances of magnetic stripe cards made with glued-on strips of magnetic tape, and bar codes can be done with a steady hand although the non-visible ones are more of a challenge. The powered proximity systems require the creation of some electronic circuitry, but not of a complexity beyond the capability of a journeyman laboratory.

Again, the bottom line is that there is no unduplicatable access card, provided that the adversary has sufficient motivation and resources; one can only raise the level of resource that must be expended to crack the system. And, again, there is not complete security in devices, but in the total security system.

Card Wear and Life

Cards are flexed, bent, abraded against other materials (such as in the wallet), compressed, and otherwise abused, and different kinds of cards can withstand these aspects of everyday use to different degrees. The old cardboard Hollerith cards didn't last long (on the other hand, they cost a dime) but the plastic Hollerith card is very durable (and costs a buck). Embedded slugs fare well, with solid bits of material doing better than more fragile structures such as wires. Printed circuits, such as are contained in the passive proximity cards (and will be present in even more fragile form in the smart card) must be protected from repeated flexing, which breaks the printed wiring and separates it from the card material. The surface-coded cards, such as magnetic stripe, are subject to considerable abrasion in addition to flexing; thus, the credit card versions are replaced every year or two avoiding any wear problems. The magnetic sandwich will probably last forever, having the recorded code protected by two sheets of plastic, and using magnetic material made for considerable flexing, similar to that used in a tape player.

External Effects

Some methods of coding can cause unwanted interaction between the card and other elements of the environment that have no relation to the access control system. Passive proximity cards have been known to trigger electronic article surveillance systems in retail stores, with resulting embarrassment to all involved. Active proximity systems, since they use radio wave communication, have the potential to be interfered with or to interfere. Some early magnetic stripe cards were wiped clean by magnetic fields emanated by everyday electrical devices (and some were reported to be affected by being carried in the same wallet with magnetic-slug cards), but better magnetic technology seems to have diminished this problem to an acceptable level.

Error Rates

There is very little probability that a Hollerith or bar code card will be improperly read, since the density of the code bits is low and the reading techniques can be relatively brute force. The accuracy of reading any of the magnetic techniques can be adversely affected by cracks, bends, and dirt on the card, misalignment of the card in the reader, dirt on the reader heads, and so forth. As a group, however, access control cards have a very-acceptably-low false-reject rate, and "for all practical purposes" a zero false-accept error.

A summary of the characteristics of the various access control cards is shown in Table 6-1.

READING AND READERS

Ignoring the proximity systems, which do not require that a card be inserted into any kind of reader, there are two basic methods of reading the code on an access control card. The fundamental operation which must be accomplished in reading a card is to move the coded portion of the card past a reading head—or an array of reading heads—in a carefully controlled manner such that the reading heads are positioned precisely over the locations of the code bits. In a row-and-column coded card, for example, there will be a reading head for each row, and the columns are read successively as the card passes under this line of heads.

Since the strength of a magnetic signal is proportionate to the speed with which the magnetic bit passes by the read head, the rate at which the card is inserted into or withdrawn from the reader (depending upon whether the card-reading takes place going-in or going-out) can be critical. In the early days of the technology this window of speed was sufficiently critical that motors were frequently provided to move the card into and out of the reader at a constant speed. Improvements in the circuits used for sensing the magnetic signal have greatly alleviated this requirement, to the extent that most readers can accommodate the range of speeds with which a human will manually move the card through the reader. There is still, however, a too-slow and a too-fast speed at which reading will not be reliably accomplished, and the card owner will be told to try again. Some technologies, such as Wiegand, Hollerith, and bar code, do not suffer at all from the reading-speed syndrome.

The traditional form of card reader presents to the cardholder a slot which is the size of the card when held on end; the card is inserted into the slot, passes the row of read heads, and is then ejected (using a motor drive, a spring arrangement, or pulled out manually), again passing by the heads (see Figure 6-6). Some card readers sense the code on the way in, some on the way out, and some sense at both times and compare the two readings: if they are different, a reading error has occurred and the card must be inserted again. This insertion type of card reader allows the use of the entire area of the card for code bits, since the entire card is swallowed by the reader and can be passed by the read heads. On the negative side, many users prefer to affix their cards with clips or neck chains so that they can be attached to the exterior of a person's clothing and be visible at all times, and the clip interferes with the process of inserting the card into the reader.

With the advent of the magnetic-stripe card, it was no longer necessary to use

Table 6.1   Comparative Characteristics of Portable-Key Devices in Common Use

Coding Means	Code Capacity	Code User Changeable	Ease of Duplication	Card Life	Typical Cost of Cards	Cost of Reading Equipment	Error Rate	External Effects
Hollerith	10^{32}	No	Easy	Poor	10¢	Low	Nil	None
Bar code	10^{10}	No	Easy	Excellent	$1	Low	Low	None
Wiegand	10^6	No	Very difficult	Good	$3	Medium	Very low	None
Magnetic sandwich	10^6	Yes	Moderate	Excellent	$2	Low	Low	Possible interference with other magnetic materials
Magnetic stripe	10^{12}	Yes	Moderate	Fair	$2	Low	Moderate	Possible interference from other magnetic materials
Proximity: user-activated	10^3	Yes	Moderate	Good	$25	Medium	Moderate	Possible interference with other wireless devices
Proximity: system-sensing, passive	10^4	No	Very difficult	Average	$5	Somewhat higher than mag cards	Somewhat higher than mag cards	Possible interference from other RF equipment and objects
Proximity: system-sensing, active but unpowered	10^3–10^{10}	No	Difficult	Average	$10	Relatively high	Relatively high	Possible interference from other RF equipment

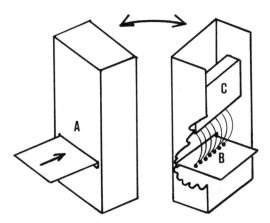

Figure 6-6 *Slot reader for a magnetic slug or magnetic sandwich card. Card is inserted into outside of reader (**A**). Cutaway view of inside of reader shows row of magnetic heads (**B**) positioned over the possible code-bit positions, reading each row of bits as the card passes by, and sending bit signals to the amplifier and decoder electronics (**C**).*

the entire area of the card to store a sufficient number of code bits for access control and other purposes: the stripe is entirely contained within one-half inch of the lower edge of the 2 1/8″ -high card, and contains more code bits than the other techniques that utilize the entire card. In the mid-1970s, the "swipe" card reader was developed, which allowed the user to grasp the card by its top edge and move it manually through a slot that encompassed the area of the magnetic stripe and enabled it to be read (see Figure 6-7). This development was—not entirely coincidentally—concurrent with the widening of the speed window for reading from magnetic material, which enables such human-powered operation. The first readers were used mainly for non-critical applications such as automatic telephone dialing (a person had a stack of magnetic-stripe cards on his desk and a card reader attached to his telephone; he selected the card having the appropriate number recorded upon it and passed it through the reader to dial the telephone), but as the technology matured the application area widened, and today the swipe reader is a reliable alternative to the slot reader, and is in fact preferred by most users of magnetic stripe access control systems.

The attractiveness of the swipe reader is due to several factors. First, the problem with the attached clip does not exist because the entire card does not need to be inserted into the reader. Second, it has fewer parts and is therefore cheaper than the slot reader, although this is as much due to the fewer reading heads required for magnetic-stripe recording as to the reader configuration. Third, there are no moving parts to break down, wear out, or jam. And fourth, there are no openings from the outside of the reader to the inner electronics, and it is therefore an inherently more weatherproof and jamproof reader.

Reading equipments for portable keys other than the standard credit card

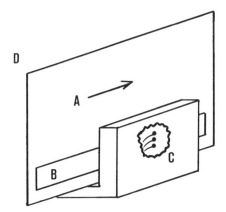

Figure 6–7   *Swipe reader for magnetic card. Card is moved through reader by grasping top edge (**A**). Magnetic stripe (**B**) is moved past internal magnetic heads (**C**) which are positioned to read and write on one or more tracks of the stripe. Electronics can be located within the portion of the reader that is behind the wall (**D**).*

form are generally of the insertion or slot type, with the slot being matched in size to the form of the portable key. For most of the key-shaped devices, the key is inserted into a keyhole-shaped slot and turned just as is a metal key, to activate the reading mechanism.

CARD-PLUS-KEYPAD SYSTEMS

Keypad access control systems are simple, reliable, and inexpensive, and the key to them cannot be lost or stolen. However, the key can be given away without penalty, and with most keypad systems there is no personal identification capability: everyone who possesses the code looks alike to the code recognition unit. Portable-key systems such as card access can have personal identification and can be virtually pickproof; however, cards can be used by non-authorized persons who came into possession of them through loss, collusion, or theft.

Key-plus-keypad systems combine the positive attributes of both of these simpler systems (see Figure 6–8). The person desiring admittance must possess the portable key, and he must know what code numbers to press on the keypad. The code numbers may be universal, that is, the same for every authorized entrant, or they may be different for each person. The number of mix-and-match combinations between the cards and the keypad codes, and the relationship—or the lack thereof—between them can be creatively used by the system designed to provide a high level of security along with personal identification, time-period control, and so on.

Two separate recognition devices are required in a key-plus-keypad system:

Figure 6–8 *A card-plus-keypad access control unit. (Courtesy of Continental Instruments Corporation, Westbury, New York)*

the portable-key reader and the keypad. The control electronics must be invested with sufficient intelligence to handle whatever creative coding combinations have been decided upon. For the simplest system, of course, the decoding circuitry of a simple keypad and a simple card reader can simply be ANDed together. The usual options of stand-alone portal units versus central-computer-control, the techniques of communications, the provision of fail-safe and fail-soft modes, sophisticated logging and control features, and the like, are as equally available with key-plus-keypad systems as they are with card-only systems.

Only a decade ago, the vendors of access control systems observed segregation into those vendors who sold keypad systems and those who sold card access systems; few vendors offered both kinds, and equally few offered card-plus-keypad systems. In today's marketplace, the "best buy" characteristics of the key-plus-keypad system have been recognized, and there is a broad range from which to choose. Since the equipment required for a key-plus-keypad system includes the equipment required for each of the two simpler systems alone, it stands to reason that vendors of the more complex system could also offer both of the simpler systems, and many do. On the other hand, a number of vendors of one kind of system (principally the card access folks) find it more efficient to purchase the other system from one of the established vendors thereof and integrate it into their final product.

In a particular security scenario, it would be unusual to find that all of the portals to be protected require the additional security provided by a card-plus-keypad system. Further, it might make good security sense in some instances to separate the elements of the card-plus-keypad system; for example, the card must be used to enter the front door, and all interior spaces are protected by keypad access. For this reason, a carefully designed access control system will usually be a mixture of card-only, keypad-only, and card-plus-keypad portal equipments. If the system is comprised of free-standing and independent portal units, this is not a problem since the individual units can be bought to suit, from different vendors if absolutely necessary. For a centrally controlled system, all equipment—the portal units, the local controllers, the communications equipment, and the central controller—must be compatible, and this is possible only if they are all procured from the same vendor. Many—but not all—of the centrally controlled systems offer the capability to mix card-only, keypad-only, and card-plus-keypad portals.

OPTIONS, FEATURES, AND FUNCTIONS

Portable key—principally card—systems in general are more sophisticated and provide more options, features, and functions than keypad systems. (Whether this additional capability and the concomitant additional cost provide greater security depends upon the total security system into which it is integrated: devices and gadgetry do not necessarily confer security.) As we have seen elsewhere in our study of access control systems, one of the basic decisions to be made is the distribution of the system intelligence at the portal, at a central controller, or somewhere in between. As we have also observed, if one requires or desires relatively sophisticated features such as logging and card-cancelling capability, one is almost certainly committed to a centrally controlled system. However, with card access and other portable-key systems, one is also committed to a certain amount of intelligence at the portal level, since there must be at least the code reading and interpreting circuitry located there: pure magnetic head pickup signals cannot practically be sent over the wire to a central location. Therefore, all card readers have the capability to read and recognize code; whether they decide on their own to unlock the portal, or send the code to a central location and await its command depends upon the system design philosophy.

A centrally controlled system has a multiplicity of portal readers (up to thousands in some systems) connected to and controlled by a computer or minicomputer, sometimes through intermediate-level controllers that pool the information from a few (four to eight or so) portals so as to make communications more efficient and less expensive. The coded information is transmitted from the reader to central, where it is recognized and processed, and a "door open" or "reject" signal is returned to the portal unit. The central unit provides all time and zone control, time clock, individual card lockout, logging, and so forth.

There is additional equipment required in a centrally controlled system, for example, the communications wire and circuits required to shuttle messages back and forth, and the computer power required to manage a central data base and prepare the separate portal logs. This is counterbalanced by the fact that the control functions are shared among many portals, and thus their cost per portal can be much less than if they were provided individually at each portal. Also, the relatively sophisticated functions such as time-clock and time-period control need only be added at central, thus having a low contributed cost per portal.

The selection between stand-alone and centrally controlled systems is based to a considerable extent, although not entirely, upon the number of portals to be controlled. In general, on a strictly cost basis, a centrally controlled system should not be considered for fewer than five portals. There are single-portal and several-portal systems which provide a reasonable selection of access control features. If, however, the more sophisticated features are required, then a centrally controlled system is the only economically feasible way to obtain them.

Other features and functions may be niceties and frills, or they may be the *sine qua non* of particular security situations. The following discussion represents a compendium of operational considerations that should be reviewed for their value to the design of any access control system.

Electrical Power

Most portal units require that standard 110 VAC electrical power be available at the portal; some will run on 24 VDC or 28 VDC, and there are a few that will operate on batteries (which one then has to remember to change). Unlike keypad units, there are no purely mechanical card access systems that can operate without electrical power.

Portal Unit Intelligence

Some portal units have sufficient intelligence to stand alone, others must be connected to a central system in order to perform the access control function.

Portal Unit Upgrade

Some single-portal units can operate in a stand-alone mode, and later be attached to a central controller if the user decides to upgrade or expand the system. Other single-portal units cannot be upgraded and must be replaced.

Portal Unit Degraded Mode

Most intelligent portal units, even when they are functioning under the jurisdiction of a central controller, can operate in a "degraded mode" so that if the central controller, or the communications between it and the portal unit, fails, the portal unit can still provide basic control of access. This usually consists of admitting all cards that contain the basic code for the portal without having the additional features of logging, individual card lockout, and so forth. Whether or not this is desirable for a particular facility must be decided by the security system designer.

Number of Portals

Manufacturers' offerings for centrally controlled systems will range from those that can handle a dozen or fewer portal units, to those that can accommodate up to 4,096. It does not make sense to install a vastly larger system than is needed, but one should provide for a reasonable amount of expansion capability. One usually will not go wrong by making certain that the central controller can handle twice the number of portals for which the system is initially purchased.

Form of the Portable Key

Plastic credit cards are the most popular form of portable key. There are also other sizes of cards (all smaller) and a variety of key- and pen-shaped tokens. The form of the key is not a major security consideration, but is more a matter of aesthetics and personal preference—this is the kind of decision that can be relegated to the upper management level so that they can feel closely involved with the process of designing the access control system. Some organizations opt for a universal identification card, which combines a picture badge with the access control card, and might also be used for other purposes, such as a charge card; the conventional credit card form is the best selection for such a multi-purpose card.

Coding Means

The defeatability of a pure portable-key system is largely determined by the encoding mechanism. Optical barcodes and Hollerith punches are clearly visible, recognizable, decodable, and duplicable by any person or organization with a little technical know-how. Magnetic stripes require more know-how and equipment, but should not pose a particular problem to the professional with some equipment and resources; the specifications are, after all, published by the American National Standards Institute. Embedded materials, both magnetic and non-magnetic, provide another step up in security, but readily available analytic equipment is capable of detecting and cracking the code. Organized criminals, competitive corporations, foreign governments, all these have sufficient financial resources to buy the technical capability to solve such problems. For every security device invented, a penetrating method can be devised, even as for every military weapon a counterweapon is made. Total security can be had not through the devices and their coding alone, but by incorporating the appropriate devices into a system that suits the organization's needs. Observe, for example, the magnetic-stripe card, the specifications for which can be bought through the mail: With the addition of other techniques and devices in the system (keypads, encryption, computer pattern analysis) it has become the single most accepted means for controlling access not only to physical facilities, but to all our money as well.

Coding Changes

As we have observed, there are some portable keys on which the user can change the access codes from time to time as his security plan dictates, and there are others which are born with the code and carry it, like DNA, to their graves. Probably the most important reason for choosing one coding method over another stems from whether or not the ability to change the code is important to the security system.

Number of Different Personal Identification Codes Available

We discussed in a previous section the theoretical maximum number of code combinations that could be made available with different encoding techniques. In commercially available access control systems these numbers may vary depending upon how the manufacturer has chosen to create his system, since he must allocate the codes among personal identification, time-period control, different space zones, facility codes, and so forth. In systems which are currently available from manufacturers, the number of different personal identification codes that can be assigned ranges from a few hundred to 65,000. The user is well-advised to provide for a 100% safety factor in the number of personal codes when procuring an access control system, i.e., make sure the system has the capacity to ultimately handle twice the number of persons that will be accommodated initially.

Time Period and Space Zone Control

Most centrally controlled card-access systems can restrict access of particular persons to particular areas during particular times and in a variety of combinations. Several hundred possible combinations are not unusual.

Individual Lockout

Individual lockout is the ability to cancel a card if it is lost, stolen, or the employee leaves the company, or to cancel the access privileges of a contractor at the end of a particular time period. This ability can be provided conveniently only in a centrally controlled system having a master personal data base; it is available with virtually all such systems.

Anti-Passback

Some card access systems have anti-passback protection, in which the card code (the personal identification number) is remembered when the card is used to enter a portal, and that card cannot be used again to enter until it has first been used to exit. This eliminates "passing-back" a card from one person to another as they enter in file, and allows only one-person entry per card. In order to accomplish this function, of course, there must be an exit reader in addition to the usual entry reader, which can substantially increase the cost of the card access system. A few systems accomplish anti-passback by recording magnetically on the card itself that entry was made, and erasing that entry upon exit. This illustrates one of the virtues of using a card upon which the codes can be changed, but alas, still requires the exit reader, or more appropriately, exit writer. Further, both the entry and exit card mechanisms are more expensive because they must have writing circuitry in addition to reading circuitry.

Dual-Card Control

In some very high-security situations, it is desirable that a portal (for example, the door to the vault) be opened only when two individuals present their cards at the same time at two readers, or one after the other at a single reader. A few systems offer this capability.

Duress Alarm

In the keypad system, this capability (also called a hostage alarm) is provided easily through the use of an extra or alternate digit in the code which the entrant enters. In a portable-key system, the code is embedded in the device, therefore changing the code or adding a digit on the spur of the moment is not possible. Several schemes have been devised, such as an over-travel switch on an insertion-type card reader: under normal conditions the user inserts the card to the first, or reading, position, and under duress he inserts it further to activate a duress alarm switch. In a card-plus-keypad system, of course, the keypad can perform the duress alarm function.

Computer Interface

Many systems provide a standard computer interface, such as RS-232, for general purpose use. This can enable a single-portal system to be connected to a centrally controlled system, a small system having few portals to be linked into a larger system, or access control equipment to be made a part of the user's general computer system.

Alarm Handling

Much access control portal equipment provides, in addition to the normal function of recognizing the code stored within or upon a card or token, the ability to recognize and report or act upon some number of electrical contact closures, that is, alarm points. These points may be door-open contacts associated with the access control function, or they may be unrelated points such as smoke detectors or intrusion alarms.

Time and Attendance

We have mentioned previously that the access control system, since it can monitor all comings and goings of employees, is well-suited to collect time-card data. In some systems this data is collected and organized to be turned over to a conventional payroll system on a general purpose computer; other access control systems offer payroll-processing software which can run on their own central-control computer.

Personnel Locator

Given full-scale card access at all locations within a facility, and the requirement that a person's card be read when he passes from one area to another, the information exists within the card access system to determine the location of any employee at any time; this is useful for locating managers and forwarding telephone calls, but the Big-Brother aspect tends to bother the human resource and civil liberties folks. A few vendors offer this capability with their access control systems.

Special Housings

Outside portals will require readers that can withstand extremes of temperature, rain, snow, and the like. Readers in the executive suite should be attractive and unobtrusive. Readers must be fitted to all types of doors, kinds of materials (wood, steel, cement, stone, brick, etc.), thicknesses of walls and doors. Many manufacturers provide a variety of housings and reader configurations for these various situations.

MANUFACTURERS AND THEIR OFFERINGS

More than 75 vendors offer portable-key access control systems as this is written, and the number rises continually as other companies enter the market with their own products or, just as commonly, add access control capability to their other security or building management systems by buying equipment from existing vendors and brand-labeling it with their own names. The forms of keys that are offered by vendors are distributed as follows. (N.B. the percentages in this and the following tables will add up to more or less than 100% because many vendors offer more than one form of portable-key product, and because in some cases the appropriate information or statistic was not divulged by a vendor, thus reducing the percentage tabulated.)

Plastic card	77%
Plastic token	16%
Metal card or token	6%
Cardboard card	1%

The means for embedding the code into or onto the portable key that are offered by manufacturers is distributed as follows.

Magnetic stripe	39%
Wiegand	22%
Magnetic sandwich	19%
Solid state chip and semi-"smart card"	6%
Bar codes, visible and infrared	6%
Hollerith and other punched holes	4%
Other one-of-a-kinds	4%

The capability of changing the access code in the portable key varies as follows among the available devices and systems:

User can change code	43%
New keys must be issued	57%

The number of individual identification codes that can be provided by the manufacturers' systems is distributed as follows.

No personal identification capability	11%
Up to 1,000 personal ID codes	15%
Up to 4,000 personal ID codes	11%
Up to 10,000 personal ID codes	26%
Up to 50,000 personal ID codes	19%
Up to 100,000 personal ID codes	17%
More than 100,000 personal ID codes	2%

The maximum number of portal units that can be connected to each of the systems is distributed as follows.

Single-portal equipments	33%
2-10 portals	8%
11-32 portals	8%
33-64 portals	13%
65-128 portals	8%
129-256 portals	17%
257-1,000 portals	8%
More than 1,000 portals	3%

The frequency with which the various options and features are offered demonstrates that card access systems are the current mainstream of access control, since the majority of manufacturers offer the additional features necessary to make these systems as secure as they can become, or as secure as the user is willing to pay for, at least. The duress alarm is infrequently offered, because it adds some otherwise unnecessary complexity to the card reader; if duress alarm is necessary in a system, it is most frequently provided by adding a keypad. Time-and-attendance data collection is another less frequent option, because it is out of the mainstream of the access control purpose for which these systems are mainly purchased, and the total integrated function systems are just beginning to emerge. The popularity of the various features and options, judged by the frequency with which they are offered by the manufacturers, is as follows.

Computer-standard interface provided	81%
Individual card lockout	73%
Multiple zoning, time and/or space	71%
Central controller for multiple portals	67%
Degraded mode of operation	67%
Keypad-plus-card available	59%

Antipassback	54%
Weatherproof model available	48%
Alarm points handled by controller	47%
Time-and-attendance data collection	22%
Duress alarm	10%

PRODUCT FEATURES AND COSTS

In surveying the offerings of the purveyors of portable-key access control systems and devices, there are a number of unique features, novel approaches, and singular contributions that come to one's attention. The following are topics of interest that follow from such an overview.

Special and Unique Features

The Wiegand Coding Technique

The Wiegand coding technique is based upon a process developed by John R. Wiegand, and is proprietary to Echlin Inc., a large manufacturer of parts for the automotive aftermarket. Wiegand-effect mechanisms have a number of applications within this aftermarket. Sensor Engineering Company was established by Echlin to pursue the applications of the Wiegand effect in the field of electronic access control. Sensor sells and licenses technology, cards, key-shaped plastic tokens, slot readers, and swipe readers to all and sundry; all of the vendors who offer Wiegand-type card-access systems purchase either the technology or the actual equipment from Sensor.

Watermark Magnetics

The Watermark magnetics is another technique that is proprietary to one company—Malco Systems—and is widely licensed for use by others. Watermark magnetics addresses a common concern with magnetic-stripe cards, which is that they are relatively easy to duplicate. During the card manufacturing process of watermark magnetic cards a unique code is permanently embedded into a portion of the magnetic stripe, and can be read only by a special reader.

The Laser Card

The laser card was also developed by and is proprietary to one company, Drexler Technology. Because of the vast amount of data storage which the card provides, Drexler's primary thrust is toward such customers as health insurers, banks, and software distribution; Drexler is also licensing its technology to other companies. Another optical storage card, by Optical Recording Corporation, has also been announced, and considerable competitive activity may be expected in this field.

(It is also worth noting that attempts to provide practical devices for the high-density optical recording of digital data have been coming out of research and development laboratories for more than thirty years, and none has yet succeeded in making inroads against the more traditional magnetic techniques. These devices, which are now as well remembered as Whistler's father, M. LeFarge, and Queen Kong, included some that came out of two of the most prestigious laboratories in the business, the IBM Research Laboratory and Bell Laboratories.)

Smart Cards

Smart cards are inherently proprietary to each company that develops such a card and the reading system to go along with it, but these companies view their development as representing a competitive edge in the marketplace, not as a technology to be licensed out to everyone, including their competitors. (This, of course, runs precisely counter to the kind of industry-wide standardization that was primarily responsible for the success of the magnetic-stripe card.) Several card access systems that contain integrated-circuit or microprocessor-level coding and intelligence are worthy of examination.

Codercard, Inc. offers a portable-key system for controlling access to personal computers and computer terminals. The access device is a one-half inch thick credit-card-size module that contains a microcomputer. It is plugged into a reader that connects to a standard RS-232 port on the computer, and must generate a code using its own internal algorithm to satisfy the computer before access is granted. A password or code number can also be required to be entered on the computer keyboard.

Cytrol, Inc. offers the CyLock system, which is designed to control access to the IBM Personal Computer. CyLock is connected intimately to the PC, and access is controlled through the use of a key-shaped token which contains a semiconductor memory chip, plus the usual entry of passwords on the computer keyboard.

Mastiff Systems U.S., Inc. was the first company to offer a proximity access control system, in the early 1970s. They also offer a portable-key access control system, using a plastic key-shaped token which contains a microchip within which the access codes are stored; the codes are read electronically when the token is inserted into a reader and turned.

Security Dynamics' system is based upon a plastic-card-type of device which contains a microcomputer, a liquid crystal display, and a battery to power it all. The microcomputer continuously generates a series of passcodes, which are displayed on the LCD; when access is desired, the code that appears on the LCD at that time is entered into a keypad or computer terminal. The central controller, meanwhile, has been generating the same sequence of passcodes in synchronization with—but independent of—the portable card, and can therefore determine whether or not the code is correct for that particular per-

son at that particular time of that particular day. The card can also be programmed to self-destruct at a particular day and time.

Much of the activity in smart cards is centered in the credit card industry,
with Visa and MasterCard in the forefront. Manufacturers in the United States,
France (where the smart card began), and, of course, Japan, are gearing up for
what they expect to be a massive market for these devices. If it indeed material-
izes, the resulting technology and mass production can be expected to stimulate
new kinds of access cards. This type of fallout has been used in this industry since
the days of the Hollerith card.

Encryption

Encryption of the code recorded on a card would seem to be a logical means of
providing some additional degree of security, but the use of this technique is not
widespread. Dorado Systems Corporation promotes such a feature; Dorado also
records the code redundantly for added reading reliability.

Elevator Controls

Elevator controls using the access card are frequently offered as an option to
security system planners. As in the keypad systems for elevator control, the card
system will permit the elevator to stop on a particular floor only after an
appropriately coded card has been inserted.

Loop Communications Systems

Loop communications systems are offered by Rusco Electronic Systems and
Federal APD. In such a system, instead of running individual wires to each portal
location, a single loop connects central with all of the portal equipments. This can
substantially reduce the wiring costs (which can be as much as 25% of the
installed cost of an access control system); however, if the loop is disrupted all of
the portals can be incommunicado. There is no free lunch.

Wireless Communications Systems

Wireless communications systems are beginning to make significant inroads in
the general security alarm field. In these systems there are no wires connecting the
alarm sensors with the central monitoring station, the alarm signals are sent by
radio-frequency transmission. The virtues and defects of wireless communications notwithstanding, there are applications where they are advantageous; no
vendor yet offers a wireless access control system, but this is only a matter of
time.

The Card Reader as a Computer Peripheral

Most access control systems—indeed, most security systems—are sold as a complete turnkey entity, including the card readers, central control computer cards,

programming, and so forth. Some vendors, however, are offering card readers that can be attached to the user's computer, thus making access card reading just another computer peripheral function: American Magnetics Corporation, Coastal Data Products, Magtek, Systematics and Xico offer readers that can be connected to virtually any general purpose computer. Other manufacturers have configured their readers to be attached to the IBM PC specifically: Alloy Computer Products, Elcom Industries, Intelligent Controls, and Northern Computers. National Control Systems offers readers and a complete software package for the DEC PDP-11 minicomputer to allow the user to assemble his own system using his own PDP-11. Many other manufacturers have interfaces which could be adapted easily if do-it-yourself access control catches on.

Access Control as Part of an Alarm System

Most of the companies that provide total security and alarm systems also offer access control as part of the system, integrated with other security functions such as perimeter protection, intrusion alarm, or CCTV. Large systems with the capability to handle thousands of alarm points and portals are offered by American District Telegraph, Diebold, and the Mosler Safe Company; these companies have been major factors in this business since before any of us were born. Total security systems including access control are also offered by GTE and Shorrock, and a smallish system is available from Vivitar Security Technology. Pasco International and Logiplex offer small total security systems that are intended to be monitored by a central alarm station, and include card access.

Access Control as Part of a Facility Automation System

Similarly, the vendors who provide total facility automation systems—security, fire and life safety, energy management, and so forth—frequently offer access control as part of the system; it should be noted, however, that the access control is not uncommonly purchased by them as an entity from one of the companies that specializes in the access control field, and integrated into the larger system. The big names in facility automation which also offer access control are Honeywell and Johnson Controls. Such systems are also available from Computer Applications Systems, Communication Manufacturing Company, Del Norte Security Systems, Kenilworth Systems, Kidde Automated Systems, and Security Control Systems.

Use of the Central Controller for Other Purposes

If the access control accoutrements can be affixed to the user's general-purpose computer, then it stands to reason that the central controller of an access control system, which is also nearly always a commercial general-purpose computer, could also be used for other purposes. Few access control vendors—Amtron Systems is a known exception—make a point of this capability, which could assist mightily in the cost justification of a system.

Special-Purpose Systems

Although they use the general-purpose techniques and technology common to all access control systems, and could be put to general access control use, a number of manufacturers have configured their systems for the specific requirements of particular applications, and direct their marketing efforts wholly toward one application and market. Anchor Pad International and Cytrol offer products which control access to the IBM PC. Card Lock markets to social clubs with a system in which the code can be changed easily to foil those who do not pay their dues. Federal APD, PPI Parking and Access Computer Systems, and Stanley Parking Systems all specialize in vehicle access control. The Safebox Company has a unique hotel-room safe. VingCard Systems and Winfield Locks have developed systems specifially for the lodging industry, which we discussed at length in Chapter 2.

Typical Cost Range of Portable-Key Systems

It is difficult to discuss the typical cost of a portable-key access control system, given all these variations, options, and features. There is probably no "typical" system and therefore no "typical" cost, so we are safer to speak in terms of cost ranges. There are vendors who offer basic readers and mechanisms for integration by OEMs, systems houses, and users into their own systems for sale or internal use. There are vendors who offer unsophisticated single-portal systems to the user. And there are vendors who offer thousand-portal systems with all of the access control goodies and facility management capabilities to boot. There are vendors who engineer and manufacture every ingredient of their system, and there are vendors who offer systems that are comprised largely or even entirely of components which they buy from other—sometimes competitive—vendors. The user has a broad choice of levels at which he can purchase his access control system or the components thereof, a choice of how much finished product he will purchase and how much value he will add to achieve the finished system to suit his requirements.

The cost of a single-portal card or token access control system begins in the $65 range and can go as high as $300. An intelligent single-portal system may provide some time-period control, individual lockout, and capability to be upgraded by being connected to a central computer. This will cost between $500 and $1,000; another $2,000 will add a logging capability.

Centrally controlled systems begin in the $2,000–$5,000 range for mainstream access control, go up to the $15,000 range for relatively sophisticated features and a large number of terminals, and can get into the hundreds of thousands of dollars when facility management capabilities are added; to this, of course, must be added the cost of the equipment at each portal. In most cases a completely satisfactory installation should be possible for $500–$1,000 per portal for a portable-key system, and $150–$200 more for key-plus-keypad. These cost ranges are, of course, for the purchased equipment, and do not include the wiring and installation costs, which will vary depending upon the physical facility.

The cost of the access control card or token must be considered when selecting a system. There are cardboard cards in the disposable range of a few cents each, but these are not suitable for permanent employee passes. Most of the conventional plastic cards can be obtained for one dollar to two dollars each in reasonable quantities, but the addition of logos, employee pictures, pocket clips, and the like, can easily drive costs into the four dollar to six dollar range.

Chapter 7

Proximity Access Control Systems

Proximity access control systems perform the usual functions, such as opening a portal or powering a computer terminal, based on a coded device that is in the possession of the person who desires admittance, but without the requirement that there be physical contact between the coded device and the reading and controlling mechanism or system. Some proximity systems operate like coded-card systems without the necessity of inserting the card into a reader; others are actually keypad systems without wiring between the keypad and the access control system; still others generate the appropriate access code on their own, like some forms of the smart card; they all can be considered to be a kind of portable key, since they are carried around by the authorized person.

In every access control system a code must be communicated from the user or from a device in his possession to a code recognition and comparison device in the system; in the conventional keypad or card systems this communication takes place electrically over physical wiring. In a proximity system the communication is accomplished through electromagnetic (including radio), or optical (including both visible light and the invisible forms such as infrared and ultraviolet), or acoustical (including ultrasonic) transmissions.

Proximity access control systems have been available for nearly twenty years, but they have only come into widespread use during the 1980s, primarily due to the technological advances and marketing prowess of the current prime mover of such systems, Schlage Electronics. The earlier systems were bulky, expensive, and contained batteries which needed to be recharged daily; Schlage broke open the market with a plastic credit-card device which needed no self-contained power, although it had to be placed much closer to the sending mechanism than did the previous devices.

During the same time period, kindred devices were developed for use in applications other than access control, primarily in the field which we shall call the **article identification** business. As these techniques and technologies have matured in the markets for which they were designed, primarily by small entrepreneurial companies, they are being viewed increasingly as possible bases for personal identification as well as article identification. One, somewhat unexpected, portion of the article identification business is concerned with animals (who, one presumes, will not be offended by being classed with inanimate articles). For many years we have been exposed to the means of tracking wild animals by Marlin Perkins and his cohorts, accomplished by placing a radio beeper on a collar around the neck of everything from wolves to polar bears to lions (which are all the while sufficiently sedated, the late Marlin's known bravery notwithstanding). Later, miniaturized versions were implanted or temporarily attached by dart guns (usually from the safety of a helicopter or Land Rover). These beepers emit a single radio frequency, from which the beast can be tracked; if there is more than one beast to be tracked, then there must be as many different frequencies as there are beasts, and the problem can swiftly become overly complex. The solution, of course, is to provide coded identification devices so that the tracking system can identify a large number of different beasts while using only a single radio frequency. Such coded animal identification devices and systems are achieving substantial usage in more mundane (and more profitable) applications than wildlife tracking. For example, coded tags are attached to each beast in a herd of milk cows: as each cow enters the feeding stall, its identity is recognized and it is issued the appropriate amount and kind of food for its size, weight, and age. The amount of milk given can also be individually measured and calculated as a return on the investment made in food, a kind of four-legged profit center. There are also coded animal tags which are sufficiently small and inexpensive that they are implanted into salmon so that the migration patterns of individual fish can be monitored as they pass by reading stations in a river.

Another form of article identification comprises a major industry, one which is in fact larger than the access control and personal identification business: the identification, locating, and tracking of products, parts, and the like through manufacturing processes, into and out of warehouses, and through shipping and delivery. The traditional means of accomplishing these functions is to attach a bar code label to each item (which in itself provides another link to access control technology and practices), and to scan and identify each item as it passes by a reading station on the manufacturing line, the shipping dock, or wherever. There are now devices and systems being introduced for this purpose which utilize identification tags using the same principles (and in some cases they are the same devices being offered for different applications) that form the bases of proximity devices used for access control. One major obstacle to displacement of the bar code in this application is that bar code labels cost only pennies, while proximity identification devices cost at least several dollars each; the proximity devices, however, are removable and re-usable in most instances.

The third form of article identification is the electronic article surveillance (EAS) business, which we described in Chapter 3. Current EAS tags are "screamers," that is, they emit a single-frequency signal when they are moved by a shoplifter through the exit of a retail store and thus past the EAS system interrogator. They, like the beast-tracking beepers, provide no individual identification, nor is such needed in the EAS business. The EAS manufacturers, however, are developing tags that will have the capability to communicate some level of coded information, for example they will be able to distinguish between shoplifting, tampering with the tag, authorized removal of the tag, and a tag which is not attached to merchandise.

The common characteristic of these article-identification devices and proximity devices for use in access control and personal identification, is that identification information is communicated from a person, an object, or an animal to a security system without need for physical contact between the coded device and its reading mechanism. Another common characteristic is that within both kinds of systems there are those devices that communicate individual identification of a person, article, or beast, and those that communicate only that the individual is one of a group for whom a door should be unlocked, or that communicate that an item should not be removed from the premises. We can safely predict that the trend that is now just beginning will continue until there is a single electronic identification industry replacing the now-separate industries of article identification and personal identification.

Probably the most widely-used form of proximity access control system is a common everyday object which one finds in many homes: the automatic garage door opener. For $150, one can carry a token into which one has set a code of his own choosing, and on command—by pushing one button—the code is transmitted by radio (or, in some cases, ultrasonically) to a controller into which he has set the same code. Upon recognizing the correct code, the controller activates a relay that turns on a motor which opens or closes the garage door. Home-oriented versions of the garage-door opener for ordinary doors are beginning to be offered, as are units for starting your car and turning on its lights from a block away. In fact, totally wireless alarm systems are becoming increasingly popular for both home and business use, systems in which the alarm sensors, arm/disarm keypads, and other elements all communicate using radio transmission rather than wires. The wireless keypad portions of these systems comprise a true proximity access control capability.

PRINCIPLES OF OPERATION

There are two basic classes of proximity access control systems: those in which the user initiates the transmission of the code to the system, such as in the garage-door opener, and those in which the system automatically senses the presence of a coded device without the user having to perform any action other than moving himself and his coded device within the prescribed range of the sensor. We call these two classes the user-activated and the system-sensing proximity access control systems.

User-Activated Systems

In a user-activated system, the system itself sits in a quiescent, listening mode until it is activated by a signal that is transmitted (usually by radio, but at least one manufacturer transmits by a light beam) by the access token carried by the user. Upon receiving such a signal, the system compares the received code with its stored access code (set, in the usual way, into jumpers, switches, or electronic memory). If the received code is correct, the system unlocks the portal; if the code is not correct, the system goes back to its listening mode. In order to transmit the signal, the token in a user-activated system must contain a power source, along with the electronics to generate the code and superimpose it upon a radio transmission. The power source is a battery in all currently offered tokens, but devices having other power sources are being developed. Since it must contain the battery plus the required electronics, the token in a user-activated system is usually rather bulky: observe your garage-door opener.

Within the class of user-activated systems there are two basic types, as follows.

Wireless Keypads

In a wireless keypad system, the user depresses a sequence of keys on an ordinary keypad, just as he does in the conventional keypad access control system. The coded representation of the keys is transmitted on a radio frequency as he depresses them, and the system detects the transmission and decodes it.

Preset Code

The code, in this system, is preset into the device (for example, the garage-door opener), and a single depression of a pushbutton causes the code to be sent all at once. This is the equivalent in concept to coded-card and other portable-key systems.

System Sensing Systems

The system sensing proximity systems utilize a variety of different concepts, operate at a wide variety of distances, and are dispersed over a wide range of costs. Some require that the token contain its own battery power and some derive their power from the system which interrogates them. Some of the battery-powered units will run for months between battery changes, and some must be recharged daily. The several types of system sensing systems are as follows.

Passive Devices

Passive devices contain no battery or other power, and communicate the code to the interrogator (the reader of the system) by re-radiating the interrogating RF signal back to the system at a frequency different from the original. This is the same principle upon which EAS systems operate, except that EAS tokens (tags) need have only one frequency at which they can re-radiate (scream), and they all scream at the same frequency. They therefore contain only one code bit, and can communicate only two items of information, screaming or not-screaming. In order to provide the degree of encoding capability which is required in an access control system, passive proximity cards are capable of re-radiating at several different frequencies simultaneously, and have dozens of frequencies from which the re-radiations can be selected. For example, the proximity access control system with which Schlage brought proximity into its current popularity uses a passive card that contains four printed tuned-circuits which enable it to re-radiate at any four frequencies selected from the 80 frequencies which the system can detect (except that adjacent frequencies may not be used in order to improve the accuracy with which the system can detect the codes) (shown in Figure 7-1). This provides a total system code capacity in excess of one million combinations. A second technique for passive proximity is known as surface acoustic wave technology, which provides the coding in the form of crystalline material on the surface of the card; the crystalline material is excited by the interrogating RF field, modulating the re-radiated signal with the code; this technique, developed in Australia, is just beginning to the be used in commercial access control systems.

Field-Powered Devices

These devices contain a relatively sophisticated complement of electronic circuitry, usually including solid-state storage for the code bits, microprocessor-level intelligence, a radio transmitter circuit with antenna, and a power supply circuit capable of extracting sufficient power from the interrogating field to operate the internal circuitry and to accomplish a brief, weak transmission of the code. Since the interrogating field that supplies the power for the device is maintained by the access control system, the code transmission will occur when and only when the device is brought within the appropriate distance of the interrogator. Despite the quantity of electronics which the device contains (about the same contained in a smart card), this proximity device, which is offered by several different vendors, can be obtained in credit-card form, in a disk the size of a dime, or in the form of a medicine-capsule-size cylinder which can be (and is) implanted in a salmon.

Transponders

Transponders are automatically operated two-way radio sets. The device contains a radio receiver, a radio transmitter, a receive-send antenna, and microprocessor logic with solid-state code storage, all powered by an internal battery. The access control system transmits an interrogation signal which is received and recognized by the device, which then transmits a return signal containing the access code. This operation is similar to the ordinary poll-response through which a computer communicates with its network of terminals, and to the IFF (identification, friend or foe) systems used on military radar systems (and, similarly, on air traffic control radars) to identify aircraft by interrogating an on-board transponder (enemy aircraft presumably do not have properly coded transponders on board). Transponder systems are more popular in the manufacturing segment of the article identification market, where the transponders are attached to automated

Figure 7–1 *A proximity-card system in operation. (Courtesy of Schlage Electronics, Santa Clara, California)*

vehicles, for example, that carry goods in warehouses and through production lines. Some of the vendors are beginning to approach the access control market using this technology.

Continuous Transmission

Continuous transmission tokens are used by one manufacturer; this would normally fall in the category of an aberration worthy of only passing mention, but in this case the manufacturer, Mastiff Systems, may be considered the Father of Proximity Systems, it having been (as Lewis Security Systems) the one lonely vendor in the mid-1970s. The device is battery-powered and contains electronic logic and a radio transmitter which continuously transmits the entry code. When the device is sufficiently proximate to the system and its receiver, the transmission is detected and the code is received and recognized. Mastiff ("Modular Automated System to Identify Friend from Foe") uses a cigarette-pack-size token that must be left on-premises every night so the battery can be recharged.

CODES AND CODING IN PROXIMITY SYSTEMS

Since there is a wide variety of proximity access control systems that operate on diverse principles and using markedly different technologies, there is a consequent wide variation in the methods that they use to store the access code, in the number of code bits that they can store, and the resulting number of possible code combinations that they can provide. Clearly, coding in these devices must be discussed separately with respect to each type.

Wireless keypads have the same coding capabilities as their wired brethren which were discussed in Chapter 5, since they are functionally the same devices. A three-digit code on a 10-key pad gives 1,000 combinations, four digits give 10,000 combinations, and so forth.

Preset code devices are limited in coding capacity only by the number of code switches which the manufacturer decides to incorporate into the equipment, and the electronic logic that is provided to organize and transmit all of the code bits. Most garage-door-opener level of devices have ten code bits, which provide 1,024 different combinations. To date, these devices have not been aimed at the high-security market with millions of combinations, personal identification, time and space zoning, and other sophisticated features.

Passive devices, using the current technologies, have theoretical coding capabilities in the millions of combinations. Commercially available systems offer personal identification capabilities in the range of 4,000 persons, along with time and space zoning and facility coding. This provides an adequate access control and personal identification system for most commercial and industrial situations.

Microprocessor-controlled devices comprise the remaining bases of proximity access control systems: the field-powered devices, the transponders, and the continuous-transmission system. Here also, as in the smart card, the amount of code storage which is made available is the designer's choice. Since solid-state memory requires very little space, tens of thousands of bits will fit onto an area the size of your little fingernail. Consequently, the designers have not been stingy with code capacity, which ranges from millions to billions (even the English billions) of combinations.

FEATURES AND FUNCTIONS

There are, as in other forms of access control systems, widely varying performance characteristics, features, functions, and options among the different kinds of proximity systems, and as always, there is no single choice as to which is best for every kind of application. The user's security system design must take into consideration the attributes of the various kinds of systems, and determine which, if any, of the proximity systems suits his needs. Following are some of the parameters which should be evaluated during the design process.

Activation Distance

The distance at which a proximity system can be activated by its token or card, or the distance within which the card or token can be sensed by the system, varies from two inches to nearly fifty feet with the various forms of proximity systems. The passive devices, which depend upon a low-level re-radiation of the interrogating signal, have the least range, from four to six inches for the tuned circuit (which requires that the prospective entrant hold the purse or wallet containing the access card up to the reader) up to a few feet for the surface wave. The field-powered devices are not much more powerful, since they must be relatively close to the source of the interrogating field to obtain enough power to operate: six inches to 12 inches distant is typical, with one vendor claiming operation up to six feet away. Devices that are powered by a self-contained battery are limited in range only by the power of the battery and the space provided to configure an efficient antenna within the device; some are intentionally held to an operational distance of a few feet (as a practical matter, effective security is not well served if portals can be opened while the authorized entrant is a considerable distance away), but others—including the garage door opener—can operate from distances of fifty feet or so.

Hands-Off Versus Triggered

User-activated systems, that is, the wireless keypads and preset-code devices, require the user to push buttons or depress keys to transmit the code to the system. All of the others require no user action, and thus need not be removed from pocket, wallet, or purse in order to perform their intended function.

Concealment of the System

Since there is no need for readily accessible and therefore very visible wall-mounted keypads, card readers, or reader slots, most proximity access control systems can be installed in an unobtrusive manner. Readers and interrogators consist of simple antennae, and these can be readily hidden or camouflaged to look like something else. This in itself can add to the security of an installation.

Physical Protection

Since electromagnetic and optical waves pass rather readily through sturdy materials (such as cement, wood, and brick for RF, and bulletproof and even tinted glass for optical), all parts of a proximity system, including the antenna, can be physically protected from assault and tampering, unlike conventional card and keypad systems which must have a card reader or keypad accessible in an unprotected area.

Form and Size of Device

Proximity tokens come in a range of sizes from one which could fit into an empty medicine capsule to another the size of a dime, to the conventional credit-card configuration, to cuboid packages ranging from the size of a matchbox to nearly the size of a pocket novel. Currently, the only credit-card versions are passive systems, but the activity in smart cards is certain to lead to field-powered and transponder proximity systems having tokens in the credit-card configuration. The capsule and dime-size tokens currently used for implanting into fishes and attaching to small manufactured parts are already beginning to be made into credit-card versions. The larger of the current versions is comprised of two groups: one consists of portable keypads, which need to be relatively large or else the keypad will be impossible to manually operate, and garage-door kinds of user-activated systems, in which size is of relatively little concern. The second group is comprised of devices that are currently marketed for manufacturing and inventory control applications, for which their size is not inconvenient. If and when the latter group begins to be adapted for access control use, one of the engineering tasks required will be repackaging. With today's proximity access control systems, the choice of token is between the credit card and a module which fits into the shirt pocket.

Cost of Token

The system portion of a proximity access control installation differs little in cost from a conventional card access system. The tokens, however, which must be issued to each authorized person, vary over a wide range of cost. The passive cards are on the high end of standard access cards, that is, four to seven dollars before imprinting, photographs, clips, and other accoutrements. Preset-code and other active tokens range from $15 to $75, with the wireless keypads on the high end of the range. Field-powered devices tend to run in the $10 vicinity. The devices that are currently used in the manufacturing area generally contain more sophisticated electronics than are required in devices for access control, and a $100 price tag is not uncommon. This identifies another area which must be re-engineered before these systems can compete effectively in the access control marketplace.

Code Changes

As in the other methods of access control, an important concern when selecting a proximity system is the ease with which code changes can be effected so as to provide additional security. With the passive cards, the code is constructed into the card when it is manufactured—the tuned circuits are contained in an internal sandwich, and the surface acoustic wave coding is contained in the surface coating—and changing the code would require issuing new cards, similar to the case with Wiegand or Hollerith cards. Most field-powered tokens have the code stored in solid-state memory, but this memory is not accessible and alterable like the memory in your personal computer, rather it is fixed when the circuitry is constructed and molded into the device; these are also unchangeable coded tokens. All the other tokens provide a convenient means for changing the code (and these are, not surprisingly, all of the more expensive tokens). The preset-code, garage-door types have internal code switches. The devices that contain microprocessors and solid-state memory, which include all of the manufacturing-oriented and transponder systems, and at least one field-powered device, can all be re-coded at the user's whim, usually using a separate programming unit supplied by the manufacturer with the system.

MANUFACTURERS AND THEIR OFFERINGS

At this writing there are sixteen companies (if we ignore the manufacturers of garage door openers) that offer products falling into the category of proximity access control systems. This includes several whose present primary markets are in the manufacturing and material control areas, but which are beginning to approach the access control market or are expexted to do so. It is of singular interest that six of the companies, 37 1/2 %, are non-U.S. companies that are making serious efforts towards gaining substantial shares of the United States access control market; three of these six have taken the route of alliances with American companies which already have good market positions, the others have established United States subsidiaries. Activity in proximity access control in Europe has been much more advanced than in the United States for at least a decade. (In fact, if we limit our statistic to the pure access control companies, eliminating alarm and material control systems, the non-U.S. vendors comprise over 50% of the contenders.)

The present offerers of proximity systems can be grouped into the following general categories.

Conventional Alarm Equipment Manufacturers

There are a host of companies that offer general purpose alarm systems for home and business use. Several of these now offer RF alarm systems, in conjunction with wireless keypads and panic alarms (a token of the preset-code type, which creates an alarm when its button is pressed) along with RF smoke detectors, lighting controls, intrusion alarms, and other sensors.

Mainstream Access Control Vendors

Seven of the companies offering proximity systems make their primary living in the access control business: they include Schlage, which pioneered proximity systems and now leads in its sales, and Rusco, Cardkey, and Continental, longstanding vendors of conventional access control systems which now offer proximity as well (in two cases with overseas technology). These vendors offer complete access control systems with all of the features—logging, central control, personal identification, time and space zone control, and so forth—which we have described in other chapters. Those vendors in this group who also offer card and keypad access in general will permit proximity-controlled portals to be mixed with the more conventional kinds of access in the same system. It is illustrative of the previously discussed trend towards the melding of personal and article identification systems to note that five of these seven companies, including Schlage, have either active enterprises in the article identification field or have made overtures toward gaining a market position therein.

Manufacturing and Material-Control Systems Manufacturers

Four of the companies involved in material-control systems manufacturing are marketing primarily proximity RF systems for use in materials-handling situations; two of these, however, are making overtures toward the access control and personal identification area. Typical applications of these manufacturers' systems are the following: "flexible manufacturing systems," using automatic guided vehicles or pallets, each of which has a transponder-type ID tag attached; warehousing of raw materials, work-in-process, and finished goods; transportation and shipping, with tags mounted on truck trailers; production-component tracking in computer-aided manufacturing systems; automated assembly operations; railroad car monitoring; package handling and sorting; machine tool identification for robotic tool changing in computer-controlled cutting machines; tracking of finished goods until sold, and asset management by the owner thereafter; vehicle identification, vehicle parking control, and automatic toll collection.

The leading company in this group is the Allen-Bradley Company, a subsidiary of Rockwell International, which is a major manufacturer of electrical and electronic equipment and components, and a principal player in the manufacturing-warehousing automation business using bar code identification, photocell detectors and counters, and the new breed of vision systems. Also members of this group are the companies that provide systems for animal monitoring, both wild and domestic.

A major obstacle to the crossover of the manufacturing system vendors into the access control business is the cost of the tokens that are used in the manufacturing systems: $100 per token is not unusual. A $100 tag added to each $20,000 robot or railroad car does not represent an important incremental cost, but a $100 access token issued to each of 2,000 employees will cost far more than the total access control system should cost. On the other hand, the tags used by those vendors that serve the animal identification application primarily are already in the right cost range, and can be adapted easily to access control. Both kinds of vendors, of course, lack the central control system and software, the door strikes and other mundane hardware, and the general knowledge of security system design. They must acquire these assets if they are to make a success of a cross-over attempt. No matter how effective the devices, the security objectives are achieved by proper design of the total security system.

Chapter 8

Access Control Systems Based on Physical Attributes

The ultimate access control system would uniquely identify a person and admit that person and only that person, independent of whether the person possessed a particular coded card or token, and/or knew a particular set of code numbers. This ultimate system would be based upon recognition of one or more physical or personal characteristics of the person desiring admittance. That such a system will eventually be a routine part of everyday security systems is indisputable, as any devotee of science fiction books and movies will attest. "Eventually," however, should be defined in this instance as occurring in the vicinity of the next turn of the century. Automated systems for accomplishing access control and personal identification based upon recognition of personal attributes do exist and have been in use since the early 1970s; they have variously been called physical attribute systems, personal characteristics systems, and—the current term in vogue—biometric systems.

The recognition of a "physical or personal" characteristic allows for a wide variety of characteristics which could be used as the basis for such a system, and not all of these characteristics are biometric* in nature. Physical characteristics such as the shape of the hand, the pattern of the fingerprint, and the appearance of the face are biometric. Other characteristics which are currently used in identification systems, such as individual's signature, are acquired mannerisms, and some, such as voice, are combinations of biometric structures (the vocal cords) and acquired mannerisms (voice training). Also, we must consider that certain inherent biometric characteristics are frequently and easily altered (changing the shape of one's face).

Which characteristics will form the basis of the ultimate personal recognition system is impossible to predict at this point; contenders range from the historical identifiers of face, fingerprint, and signature, to newcomers such as hand geometry, voiceprint, and eyeball retina, to possibilities as yet unexplored such as

---

*Biometrics: the statistical study of the laws and phenomena relating to a living organism or group of organisms.

brain waves, bone density, and the aura. Practically speaking, it may not matter which characteristics are used, since it is unlikely that a system can be devised which makes no false-accept errors, no false-reject errors, and provides no means by which a person can alter his characteristics to match those of another person. The probability of correct identification will always be maximized more easily by combining two access control systems than by trying to make either of them perfect (a concept which we observed in the efficacy of the card-plus-keypad system); it may be that almost any physical attribute will serve as the basis for identification in a combinational system.

Consider, for example, the following proposition. The average height of a person in the United States is 66 inches and the average weight is 155 pounds (men and women averaged). These are facts*; from this point, for the purpose of illustration, we indulge in a bit of fantasy. Presume that the population is evenly distributed in height from five feet to six feet, in weight from 110 pounds to 200 pounds, and that there is no correlation between a person's height and weight. Given these parameters, an identification system that could merely measure a person's height to the nearest inch and weight to the nearest pound would have an accuracy of 99.91%. Even a system which allowed for a five-pound variation in weight (due to differences in clothing, exercise, and food consumption) and a two-inch variation in height (for the days when some of us wear our Western boots) would be 99.1% accurate. The point of this exercise is that, as we have said before and will say many times again, high security does not require high technology and exotic concepts, and, conversely, high technology and exotic concepts do not by and of themselves confer high security. Security is achieved when and only when a properly conceived total security system is put in place.

HISTORICAL USE OF PHYSICAL ATTRIBUTE SYSTEMS

Access control systems based upon physical attributes have been in use for centuries in the non-automated form. **Face recognition** dates back to aboriginal man who recognized all of his friends by sight, and in the security business it dates back to the guard at the plant gate who knew by sight everyone who worked at the plant. When the number of persons, and also the number of guards, became too large for everyone to know everyone else, picture-badge systems were introduced, allowing the guard to compare the face on the badge with the face of the person presenting the badge. Such systems which use a person's face as the unique physical attribute, are considered sufficiently secure and reliable, to the point that they are still a mainstay of security provisions used by the Government at Washington, in maximum security installations and, for example, on your passport. Many states also use the picture-badge for the drivers' licenses, and this document has become the most commonly accepted form of identification for banking and credit transactions.

---

*From the *Statistical Abstract of the United States*, U.S. Department of Commerce, 1966.

Two other forms of physical attribute identification systems also have long histories of non-automated usage, although neither goes back as far as Og in his cave: they are the signature and the fingerprint. The **signature** is required as the means of identification and authentication on all of the checks we write, the credit card purchases we make, and the legal contracts—including loans, home purchases, and business agreements—into which we enter. The fact that these signatures are almost never verified except by ourselves when we receive the cancelled checks and credit card bills (which is discussed at some length later in this chapter), does not detract from the fact that it is the identifier for these transactions, and is subject to satisfactory scrutiny in the event of a dispute between us and the bank or the credit card company.

The fingerprint has stood alone for half a century as a unique and legally accepted means of personal identification, and the Federal Bureau of Investigation maintains a file of fingerprints for the 23 million people who have criminal records (contrary to popular belief, they do not maintain a file of everyone who has ever been fingerprinted, only the bad guys). This file is organized by the type of pattern that the fingerprint forms; in this way, a relatively small group of potentially matching fingerprint records can be quickly located when an unknown person's fingerprint is submitted for identification. The final match with a single fingerprint record is then done one by one by comparing the unknown person's fingerprint with each of its potential matches in the group. Until the 1960s, this entire process was performed effectively and efficiently by hand. During the 1960s, systems were developed (principally by McDonnell-Douglas and Cornell Aeronautical Laboratories) under FBI contracts that could optically scan the fingerprint records (which were, and still are, on the 6 inch by 9 inch cards with which all of us who have ever been fingerprinted are familiar), digitize the fingerprints, and identify both their patterns and their individual characteristics using digital computers and pattern-processing software algorithms. The descendents of these early systems form the backbone of the FBI's fingerprint-matching process today, and the technology developed also provided the fundamental principles which led to today's fingerprint-based access control and personal identification systems.

Automated and semi-automated access control systems using these three basic, and universally accepted physical attributes have been developed by the score; many are still offered and in common use, others have been relegated to the Boot Hill of new inventions. Three other physical attributes have also been the basis of access control systems: the voiceprint, hand geometry, and the retinal pattern of the eye. Systems based upon all of these attributes are currently being marketed.

EARLY DEVELOPMENTS

Access control systems based on physical attributes were first offered for sale during the early 1970s, during a period when massive amounts of money were being expended on research and development by private companies, by the FBI, by the United States Air Force under its BISS (Base Identification Security System) program, and by LEAA (Law Enforcement Assistance Administration). By 1974, there were six systems on the market. Two were semi-automatic, or if you prefer, machine-assisted, systems for face recognition; there are a number of systems available today, although the original two vendors no longer offer them. One was a voiceprint system which, along with its manufacturer, has vanished from the scene; after a ten-year hiatus, voiceprint systems from new manufacturers are being offered again. Two systems were fingerprint-based and used two entirely different methods: one compared the overall pattern of the fingerprint, and the other utilized the minutae approach which is the basis of the FBI's matching method; neither of these products or companies is among us any longer, but the minutae-based system technology had several inheritors who have subsequently offered kindred systems.

The sixth system was based upon the notion, greeted with some skepticism, that the geometry of a person's hand is unique to that person. This system alone survives, prospers, and is imitated by new competition today, under the Stellar Systems subsidiary of the Wackenhut Corporation, who acquired the originator, Identimation Corporation. It remains to be seen whether the current crop of physical attribute systems will prove any more durable than those of a decade ago and whether these systems will prove to be the Cadillacs of access control, or the Edsels, or perhaps even the Tuckers.

THE PROGNOSIS

Industry experts, ourselves included, have been predicting for a decade that physical attribute systems are the future of access control, but that future has persistently been much further away than the experts and hopefuls in industry have expected. Despite the massive amount of money expended during the 1970s, no durable, pervasive systems resulted. The vaunted technology of the microchip, which has foisted upon us the wonders of the personal computer, has yet to bring us into the age of the physical attribute access control system.

A substantial part of the problem has been and continues to be cost: the per-portal cost of a physical attribute system is four to ten times that of a sophisticated card access system (in fact, during the 1970s heyday, costs of up to $15,000 per portal were not uncommon for physical attribute systems). The second problem was and is the unavoidability of false-accept and false-reject errors, which we discussed in Chapter 4: even though the physical attribute may be unique, the measurement of it may be imprecise. The designer of a security system must resolve a number of questions when he considers a physical attribute system as a possible solution to his access control needs: is it really more secure than the alternatives, for example, a card-plus-keypad system? If it really is more secure, is it worth the added cost? Is there penetration potential by those who successfully fake the particular physical attribute, just as a card can be stolen and a number learned? As always, there is no standard, universal answer, each security situation must be analyzed and the choices made which are appropriate for that system.

One last comment is appropriate regarding the prognosis for automated physical attribute systems, which is to note the possible parallel with the development of automated equipment for reading printed or written material. For two decades, beginning in the fifties, inventors, entrepreneurs, large companies and government agencies poured research and development money into what began to look like a black hole, with spotty results and flash-in-the-pan products akin to what we have experienced with physical attribute access control systems. One of the early successes was the ability to read the numbers on gasoline credit card slips, made by the embossed plastic cards which we discussed earlier. By 1960, this application and the ability of the Post Office Department to recognize a few city and state names was the sum of the accomplishments in this business. The problems were similar: measurement of an analog entity which could vary from case to case, be smudged, light, dark, marred, and scarred; false-identity and non-identity problems; and costly technology. But in the 1970s, with most of the pioneers having passed on to that happy hunting ground in Chapter 11 (of the bankruptcy law), the technology finally came of age; and today reading of the printed page is commonplace in the most mundane of word processing environments. (Reading of handwriting, also a goal of the industry since the 1950s, has, however, some obstacles yet to be conquered.) Soon the physical attribute access control systems may also have served their time wandering in the wilderness.

FACE RECOGNITION SYSTEMS

Access control based on recognition of the human face is, as we discussed earlier, the most venerable form of physical attribute system. There is not now, nor has there ever been, a fully automatic system based upon this attribute, although there have been efforts in a number of laboratories to use modern pattern recognition techniques to provide such a capability. There are, and there have been for more than a dozen years, semi-automatic systems of several kinds.

Side-by-Side CCTV Systems

The first such system was introduced by Ampex Corporation in 1974. It was a guard-plus-machine system which stored an image of the face of each authorized person on a video disk (which had just been invented, primarily for use in television "stop-action"). The filed face was called up by the guard onto a TV screen, and compared with the actual face of the person at the portal, either directly or via a CCTV camera, thus allowing the guard to cover a multiplicity of portals. A system capable of storing 4,000 faces cost $97,000. This was an improvement on the concept of a picture badge; instead of the picture being carried on a card outside the system's control, and therefore subject to counterfeiting, the reference picture was stored internally where it could be protected. An employee number was used to retrieve the reference picture from the system file, thus making this a sort of face-plus-keypad system. A similar system had been introduced by 1973 by Mardix Security Systems. It utilized two side-by-side display screens, one a microfilm viewer and the other a CCTV monitor. The person desiring entrance was photographed by a CCTV camera at the portal, and his face appeared on one monitor. He then keyed his employee number into a keypad at the portal, and this was used to automatically locate his picture in a microfilm file; the file picture appeared on the other screen, and the guard then decided whether or not the two faces represented the same person. The system could handle multiple portals, and was priced at a very reasonable—for the time—$3,000 or so.

The Ampex system died somewhere along the long, long trail, but there are a number of conceptually similar systems being offered today, including a descendant of the Mardix product. Panasonic Industrial Company offers a close cousin, with a photograph stored on an optical disk and accessed by a magnetic-stripe card carried by the prospective entrant. Chorus Data Systems has a video camera and a digitizer which stores the image in digital form, and allows it to be presented on the screen along with text related to the person, all operating on a personal computer. Visual Methods offers a remotely related system in which the person inserts his picture badge into a CCTV reader, and the guard is presented with side-by-side images of the picture on the picture badge and of the real person. (Visual Methods also offers an instant visitor-picture-badge machine which prepares temporary badges that fade after 24 hours.)

Video Intercom

Probably the most popular form of machine-assisted access control system using the face as the physical attribute is the CCTV intercom (see Figure 8–1). Developed primarily for use in apartment houses, this system consists of the usual call-up intercom in the apartment lobby, but with the addition of an integral CCTV camera. The intercom in each apartment contains a small TV monitor, so the resident can identify a visitor by face as well as voice before admitting him beyond the lobby. The systems are reasonably priced at a few hundred dollars per apartment, but the entire building must be wired with coaxial cable in order to carry the CCTV signals. This is no different from the cable TV connections which are supplied to most apartments anyway. Siedle Intercom/USA, Lee Dan Communications, and Panasonic offer apartment-building systems, and a number of residential security firms offer more limited systems for home use. One of these, from Panasonic, will record in its video memory the faces of all persons who approached the entrance door during the owner's absence.

Technology will no doubt ultimately provide us with a fully automatic face-based access control and personal identification system, although "ultimately" may well be in the next century. This ultimate system may be based on pattern recognition techniques such as are used in today's fingerprint recognition sys-

Figure 8-1   *Apartment building CCTV-intercom. (Courtesy of Seidle-Intercom/USA, Wynnewood, Pennsylvania)*

tems. It may be based upon physical measurements such as are used in the hand geometry system, or it may be based upon the composite process used with such positive effect by police forces, for example, Sirchie Fingerprint Laboratories' Photo-Fit System, or Smith & Wesson's Identikit, which assemble faces by the piece and can create more than twelve billion different faces.

SIGNATURE VERIFICATION SYSTEMS

The signature has traditionally been the means of identifying the owner of a bank account, and today it remains the final means of verification, despite the increasing importance of electronic fund transfer, the ATM, the bankcard, and the PIN. Further, it has become even more pervasive as we endorse billions of credit card transactions each year. Despite the major advances in technology in other areas, including fully automatic recognition of fingerprints, handwritten numerals, and typed or printed material, there has never been a machine that can compare two written signatures and determine whether they were or were not written by the same person. For three decades, there have been machine-assisted means (similar to those that we have described for face comparison) for assisting in signature verification, and more advanced, reliable, and speedy methods are now coming into use, but the final determination is always made by a human (with, incidentally, little or no training in the subject).

Signature-based access control systems have existed for over ten years, but these systems are based on the dynamics of the signature as it is written, not upon comparison of the written signature itself. We shall review these systems later in this section; first, we believe it instructive to review the current technology in signature comparison since it is in such widespread use for control of access to our money, and also because it might provide clues as to the nature of an ultimate fully automatic signature-comparison system.

Banking Systems

The signature storage and verification process in banks, where most of the activity occurs, has evolved as follows, with the single constant being the 3×5 signature card which we all fill out and sign when we open an account. In the beginning, when banks were self-contained stone monoliths on prominent downtown corners, a file of signature cards was kept in the teller area on the main floor of the bank. When signature verification was required, a teller found the actual card and visually compared the two signatures. When banks began to establish networks of branches, two copies of the signature card were made: one was kept at the branch where the account was opened and the other was sent to the main office, on the theory that these were the two most likely locations for the customer to be doing his banking business. If the customer did appear at another location, the teller placed a telephone call and another teller retrieved the card and verbally described the signature.

There are clearly risks and potential imprecisions in this verbal correlation of signature characteristics between tellers, and a variety of equipment and techniques have been developed to assist in the signature verification process. They can be grouped into the following general categories.

Customer-carried verification. In this category the customer has in his possesion a means by which his signature can be verified which he presents to the teller and the teller makes the verification. Usually the customer-carried signature is in such a form that it can be read only by special equipment, such as the venerable "black-light" and ultraviolet light source. There is also a scrambled-image signature in which the signature is optically distorted for recording and can be read only through equipment having the proper reverse-optics. There is considerable reliance upon the modern driver's license which contains both the signature and the person's picture, and the bank card and PIN are also frequently used.

Full signature file at all branches. There are a number of manufacturers offering microfilm and microfiche systems that can be used to provide a complete duplicate set of signature cards at each branch.

Telecommunication of signature as needed. There are both facsimile and CCTV systems that provide a modern version of the old teller-to-teller verbal description, by transmitting the image of the signature on the card to the branch where the signature is needed for comparison.

Computer-stored signatures. The most modern technology is used to store a digital image of the signature within the memory of the bank's central computer, and to transmit that image automatically to the teller's display terminal, upon which the other account information—balances, and so forth—has always been presented.

The products which are offered to provide these capabilities range from very inexpensive and simple devices to rather exotic and expensive systems, and are offered by vendors ranging from small, one-product companies to the largest names in the computer and graphics fields. The categories of equipment, and the levels of security that they provide, are the following.

Black-Light Imprinting and Reading Equipment

This method has been in use since World War II, and has obviously provided a satisfactory, if rudimentary, first level of security. It is also the least expensive signature-coding that can be provided, since the bank need only purchase the imprinting equipment and some $20 reading lamps. The bad news is that any teenager with a hobby catalog can also read the imprinting, and modifying the signature is no great technological challenge. Any means of identification in the possession of persons outside the bank must be considered to be susceptible to forgery, regardless of the technology that is used to encode the signature or other means of identification, since the technology is available to any who have the resources and the motivation to forge.

Scrambled-Image Equipment

This technique raises the level of customer-carried verification both in security and in cost, because it requires more sophisticated technology to forge. Early versions used optical elements—lenses, prisms, mirrors—to print the elements of the signature in a scrambled form, and identical-but-reversed optics in the readers. More modern versions use digital scanning of the signature and print a scrambled image of the resulting dots. This class of equipment has not achieved widespread popularity.

Facsimile Equipment

Using ordinary telephone lines, the teller requesting a signature calls the teller or a clerk where the signature card is located; that person obtains the signature card and places it onto a facsimile scanner, and the image is reproduced at the teller's location within approximately ten seconds. This automates the old teller-calls-teller method, and provides a greatly superior ability to compare and validate the signature. There are also facsimile systems which transmit the signature from the branch as it is written to the central office, for verification at central where the signature file is located. This requires either that each teller window have writing-and-transmitting equipment, which is expensive, or that the customer be required to walk to a central location in the branch, which is awkward and aggravates the already-vexing service delay at most bank branches. It is also, of course, of no use when third-party checks (the person cashing the check is not the person who wrote the check) are presented at the branch.

Closed-Circuit Television Systems

CCTV has been used to assist in signature verification since the early 1960s, when Stone Laboratories installed a system in the main office of the Provident Institution for Savings in Boston. Tellers entered the account number on an electronic keypad, the number was displayed in the central room where the signature-card files were located, a clerk retrieved the appropriate card and placed it under a CCTV camera, and the signature image was transmitted over coaxial cable and displayed on a TV monitor at the teller's window; the entire process took less than ten seconds. The process has changed little since then, except that remote branches are now served by the systems, and ordinary telephone lines are used instead of expensive coaxial cables. (This is possible because the transmitted signature image can be a single-frame snapshot, unlike a moving TV picture which requires that 30 images be sent every second; using the low bandwidth of a telephone line, the signature image requires about 8 seconds to transmit.) The total time elapsed from placing the request to receiving the image is about 30 seconds.

Microfilm and Microfiche Equipment

Microfilm (images are recorded sequentially on a roll similar to movie film) and microfiche (images are recorded in row-and-column format on a flat sheet of film) are alternative photographic processes for making the entire signature file available at each branch location. New account signatures, deletions due to closed accounts, name changes, and so forth, are added to the file on a periodic basis, usually every two weeks, and a complete new set of files is distributed. There are mini-computer-based systems for storing directories of account numbers so that the files need not be completely redone. These systems are in numerical order just to accommodate the frequent additions and deletions, but are not widely used in banks, by far the most substantial user of micrographic signature storage systems. These systems provide an effective means of enabling signature comparison to be done at all branch locations; the downside is that there is a significant capital expense for cameras, film-preparation equipment and film readers, and a significant recurring expense for the periodic updates. Also, of course, any additions, deletions, or changes made since the last update will not appear in the files.

Computer-Stored Signatures

Systems were developed in the mid-1970s by IBM, Signature Technology Inc., and Bowers Engineering Company that scanned the written signature (using digital tablets, flying-spot scanners, or video cameras), stored the resulting signature image in digital form within conventional computer-disk memory, and presented it automatically to the teller on a TV monitor or upon the screen of his teller terminal, upon entry of the account number into a keypad or onto his teller terminal. In that time frame, few banks believed the systems—in the $150,000 to $250,000 range—to be cost-justifiable, but advances in the technologies of computer graphics and computer memory have resulted in greatly improved performance of these systems at substantially reduced cost, and there are now a greater number of vendors offering products to a more receptive group of customers.

Vendors of Signature Presentation Systems

There is a separate set of vendors for each of the products offered for signature verification (used almost entirely in banks). Black light equipment is produced by a small set of small companies who are well-entrenched in the business and are well-known to the customers, and the scrambled-signature vendors are also a small set with specialty products. The facsimile-product vendors, also a small set of small companies, offer their products to a wider base than only financial institutions, but are not among those companies who have made a success of the commercial facsimile and remote-copying business involving transmission of printed pages, drawings, and documents.

CCTV signature systems are provided by two classes of vendors. The largest companies are those which are in the general purpose CCTV business, and will design and install a custom CCTV system for any purpose, using standard off-the-shelf subunits. The largest domestic CCTV companies—General Electric (GE) and RCA—sell only the subunits (cameras, monitors, transmission and switching equipment, and so forth; custom systems are provided by local dealers and systems houses. These are the same vendors who design and install all of the CCTV systems for all of the security applications, which we discussed in Chapter 1; they also do industrial CCTV systems, and would be the sources from which we would expect a signature-based access control system if one were to be marketed. The second class of vendor, for example, Antronics, offers a system that is custom-designed for the bank signature application and is sold directly through local representatives who call on the banking industry.

Microfilm and microfiche systems can be more general purpose, since the signature-storage application does not differ materially from the other uses to which these systems are put. 3M, Bell & Howell, and Eastman Kodak have always been the big names in this business, and there are nearly a hundred other companies offering micrographics (the name by which this business is generally known) products that are appropriate for this application.

Computer-stored signature equipment, shown in Figure 8-2, is offered in two versions, and by two classes of vendor. At the top of the heap, as usual, is IBM, who along with most of the other suppliers of banking computer systems and their attached teller terminals can provide signature capture, storage, and presentation as an optional capability on their standard systems. The other class of vendors includes all of those who do not also supply on-line banking systems. Their products are either free-standing, which means that separate computers, communications equipment, digitizers and signature-presentation monitors must be separately installed; or they provide equipment and software that can be added onto the (usually IBM) mainframe computer already in place at the bank.

SRI Signature Dynamics

All the systems and techniques for signature comparison that we have discussed thus far are semi-automatic, or machine-assisted, systems, the purpose of which is to facilitate the presentation of the unknown signature alongside a reference signature, so that an individual can compare them and decide whether or not they are the same. None of these machine-assisted signature comparison systems is in common use as an access control technique; and, contrarily enough, the fully automatic systems existing for comparison of signatures are used exclusively in the access control application.

The fully automatic signature verification systems, however, do not use as the physical attribute the appearance of the finished signature, but rather the manner in which the signature is written. The speed, acceleration, and pressure with which the person produces the signature are measured and stored, and these parameters are measured and compared when the unknown person writes his signature. The technology was developed by Stanford Research Institute during the late 1970s, and was licensed to a number of companies (including, for a time, IBM itself) which developed, introduced, and abandoned products in rather swift sequence. These systems still come and go seemingly every year (as this is written, the latest and only current offerings are by companies called Signify and Ion Track Instruments).

The Future of the Signature

The future of the signature as an important means of personal identification, and, consequently, of access control, seems questionable; but, because it is one of the three most venerable and historically trusted forms of identification using physical attributes, it should not yet be lightly dismissed. In the banking business, historically the mainstay of the signature as the ultimate authority on personal

Figure 8–2 *Computer-based signature comparison system. (Courtesy of Autosig Systems, Inc., Irving, Texas)*

identification, passbooks are being phased out in favor of the various forms of electronic banking. When signature verification is needed, the driver's license is increasingly accepted. In the one place where our signature still always appears, on the checks we write, the signatures are not (and never have been) verified as the check is cleared through the bank; there simply isn't time, and the risk of loss due to signature fraud is much less than the expense of verifying the signatures. There is about one forgery per 2.5 million checks written, and about 80% of the forgeries are so good that an ordinary examination of the signature would be unlikely to detect them.* The bottom line is that it is not worth a great deal of expense to a bank to implement a system that provides comprehensive automation of the signature storage and retrieval process. (This is not the only industry where this phenomenon can be observed; many industries find it more profitable to accept losses which are covered by insurance, the premiums for which are added to their costs and then their prices, rather than to invest in preventing the losses in the first place: cargo transportation is a very visible example.)

For the banking industry, given the low and diminishing importance of the signature, and the low importance that is placed (probably very properly) upon signature fraud, and the technology and products that are available or are likely to be available within a reasonable period of time, we are led to the conclusion that signature verification will continue to be utilized at the lowest (that is, the cheapest) level that provides some intimidation and keeps most people honest. This argues for continued reliance on technology at the level of the black light and the driver's license. At the same time, we believe that the cost of computer-stored signature systems will continue to be reduced, until they reach a level where they represent an insignificant incremental cost to the bank's on-line computer system network. The sum of our predictions then, is that in the 1990s most large banks will have inexpensive computer-stored signature systems, and that nobody will care.

A fully automatic system that automated the process from file-signature capture to storage to automatic comparison with the signature in question, at reasonable cost, and with reliability and accuracy comparable to today's print-reading systems (or even to today's physical attribute systems using fingerprints or eye retinas) could make the signature once again a viable contender as the means of identification, if it were available soon enough. The pattern-recognition technology and all of the corresponding equipment exist, but there is a lack of development activity directed towards this purpose. We are therefore forced to conclude that no such system is likely before the turn of the century, and we believe that the importance of the signature in financial transactions will by then have diminished to insignificance in comparison with identification methods which are more compatible with the electronic forms of banking.

The signature-dynamics system, as the Stanford Research technique is

---

*For a very instructive analysis of this subject, see "Signature Verification: an Exercise in Futility", by Dr. Allen H. Lipis, in the February 1987, issue of *Bank Systems and Equipment,* from which these statistics are taken.

known, has achieved no penetration of banking operations, even though it could solve the part of their problem having to do with a live person at the teller window (it is of no help in validating third-party checks), for the reasons discussed above. It is certainly as viable a personal identification system for access control purposes as any of the other physical attribute systems from a security point of view, but it does suffer from being considerably slower than the other methods: writing your signature takes more time than presenting your face to a CCTV camera, your finger to a scanning aperture, or your eye to an eyepiece. It might be found most useful in low traffic situations such as access to computer terminals, with the computer itself storing the signature dynamics characteristics and the comparison algorithms.

Access control using the already written signature as the attribute could be done on a machine-assisted basis, using side-by-side presentation of the written and the reference signatures, similar to what is done in the face-comparison systems described earlier. Any of several techniques used in banks—CCTV, microfiche, computer-stored signatures—could be readily adapted; the equipment and techniques already exist, and a marketable system could be made ready within six months. To our knowledge, such a system has never been offered.

FINGERPRINT RECOGNITION SYSTEMS

Fully automatic systems for the recognition and comparison of fingerprints have been marketed since the early 1970s by a continuously changing series of vendors, driven originally by large expenditures of the DOD, FBI, and LEAA during the 1970s. Despite the presence of the substantial and productive automated fingerprint search operation at the FBI, and despite massive research and development efforts by very substantial companies, including what looks like a list of the top aerospace and DOD contractors, there has not been a profusion of successful products for the access control application.

Pattern vs Minutae

There have been two fundamentally different approaches taken to solving the problem of comparing two fingerprints. The first, and the earliest to be represented in automated access control equipment, is a pure pattern comparison; the whorls, loops, and tilts of the reference fingerprint are stored, either in image form or in a digitized representation of the image, and compared with the fingerprint of the prospective entrant. Comparison electronics then measure whether or not the two images are the same to within a pre-established percentage of what a perfect match would be. (It is interesting that this same approach was one of the more successful during the early years of optical character recognition: each character on the printed page was compared in succession with a series of masks which included all the letters, numerals, and other characters to be recognized, and the decision as to the identity of the character was made on a best-match basis.)

The second approach to matching is the minutae method which, because it is the basis of the FBI technique, has had conferred upon it a certain amount of credibility over the pattern method. Minutae are the endings and branching points of the ridges and valleys which comprise a fingerprint; in the center of the fingerprint, where the pattern is most dense, there can be several dozen minutae. Minutae-based systems locate these minutae on the image of the fingerprint, and identify each according to its location and orientation (similar to identifying each ship on the ocean according to its longitude, latitude, and heading). False-minutae (for example, a break in a ridge due to dirt or a cut, resulting in two false ridge endings which face each other) are mathematically located and eliminated, and the final identifying numbers for the minutae are stored as the reference print. Each unknown print is also identified by its location and orientation of minutae, and comparison of the two sets of minutae numbers determines the degree of correlation between the two prints; those which correlate to within the percentage which is decreed as acceptable by the system are declared to be successful matches.

A word is appropriate concerning the number of possible combinations available with fingerprint recognition systems. There are about one billion (American billion: 10^9) possible minutae combinations on a fingerprint; since there are about 5 billion people inhabiting the Earth, and each has ten fingers, this means that statistically it is likely that fifty people on Earth share a fingerprint. Lest we panic, however, remember that the FBI uses all ten fingers to establish an identification, not just one.

Commercial Systems

KMS Security Systems

The earliest automatic fingerprint system for access control was a pattern-matching system marketed in the early 1970s by KMS Security Systems. The reference fingerprints were stored in holographic form on a film chip which was affixed to an access card; the prospective entrant inserted both his card and his finger into appropriate openings in the machine, which made the correlation measurement between the images. A second model stored the reference cards internally and retrieved them for comparison based upon an ID number entered into a keypad by the prospective entrant. The system was free-standing, one was required for each portal, and each cost about $7,200. A number of successful installations were made, primarily at Federal Reserve Banks.

Calspan Corporation

The second commercial system was introduced in 1974 by Calspan Corporation, which was the commercial reincarnation of Cornell Aeronautical Laboratories, one of the principal contractors who developed the fingerprint technology and systems for the FBI. Having sprung from FBI work, the Calspan system was naturally minutae-based. It was a centrally controlled system which could oversee up to 16 portals from a minicomputer wherein was stored the minutae characteristics of all the authorized entrants. The prospective entrant placed his finger onto a reader at the portal, the minutae were extracted and sent to central, and central compared the minutae against the entire file of authorized persons to determine whether or not that particular person should be admitted. Time-and-attendance data collection, payroll generation, logging, and control of other security systems such as alarms were also offered for use on the system. A few systems, in the $15,000 per-portal range, were placed in military installations.

Fingermatrix, Identix, and Metron

The KMS and Calspan systems, and the companies as well, faded away like old soldiers during the mid-to-late '70s. There was sporadic activity in the field, primarily by a number of inheritors and licensees of the Calspan Technology, until the mid-1980s, when a new crop of companies entered the field with products that had a much more reasonable cost per-portal than had been the case in the earlier generation. Two of the approaches represented by the current group (Fingermatrix and Identix, shown in Figure 8-3) are fully automatic. The third (Metron Optics) is a machine-assisted system for presenting the reference print and the unknown print side-by-side on a projection viewer for comparison by a human, just as we have observed being done with signatures and faces. The two fully automatic systems are based upon minutae-comparison, with some pattern-matching features added for additional reliability. Both Identix and Fingermatrix offer single-portal, stand-alone systems and centrally controlled multi-portal systems, and both incorporate a keypad so that an individual user ID can be used to select one individual fingerprint from the file for comparison, rather than comparing the unknown print with the entire file of the fingerprints of authorized persons. As we have noted before, this keypad-plus-fingerprint system is greatly superior in security and has a substantially lower error rate than a fingerprint-alone system. Both offer a smart-card version in which the fingerprint parameters are stored within a card carried by the user and read by free-standing portal equipment, rather than being stored centrally.

Fingermatrix also offers equipment for reading and verifying from FBI fingerprint cards, and for preparing FBI cards without the inking process. Both companies offer a two-finger access control system wherewith two fingers of the prospective entrant are compared rather than the single fingerprint which has been the basis of all other systems. Fingermatrix specifies a false-accept rate of 0.001% and a false-reject rate of 0.5% for its systems. Identix offers a false-accept rate of less than 0.0001% and a false-reject rate of 2%.

THE HAND GEOMETRY SYSTEM

One of the only three personal attribute access control systems available in 1973 (the other two being the KMS fingerprint system and Mardix' side-by-side face

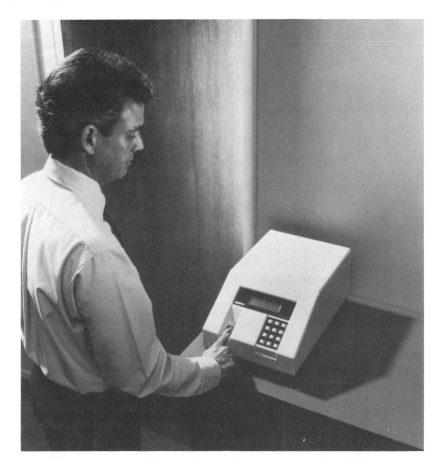

Figure 8–3 *Fingerprint-based access control system. (Courtesy of Identix, Inc., Palo Alto, California)*

system) was based upon the premise that the geometry of a person's hand was unique biometric identifier. This premise sprang from a study performed in 1971 by Stanford Research Institute to analyze glove measurements for pilots in the U.S. Air Force, with the object being to reduce manufacturing variability and increase inventory efficiency. SRI concluded that hand geometry is a distinct, measurable characteristic which can be related to individuals, and that tolerances can be established so that the probability of a particular individual cross-identifying can be reduced to one out of thousands.

Based upon this premise, and adding additional parameters such as the light transmissivity of an individual's skin, Identimation Corporation introduced an access control system in 1972, during a time when interest in physical attribute identification systems was reaching a peak. Most of the efforts were concentrated in the more accepted attributes of face, fingerprint, and voiceprint; the professional pattern recognition community looked upon hand geometry recognition in much the same manner as the American Medical Society views a faith healer. Yet Identimation's Identimat system alone survives, in substantially the same form (and with the same name) as it had fifteen years ago, from among the many systems which were introduced and sort-of introduced during the 1970s (see Figure 8-4). Identimation is now owned by Stellar Systems (the big name in fence alarm systems) which is in turn owned by Wackenhut (one of the big names in overall security services and systems).

The Identimat system is offered in both a card-verifying mode and as a com-

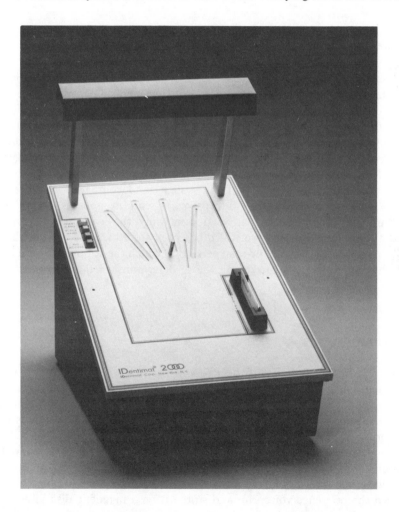

Figure 8-4 *The Identimat hand-geometry system. (Courtesy of Stellar Systems, Santa Clara, California)*

puter-based system. In the card-based system, the reference measurements of the subject's hand (length of the fingers, curvature data, handwidth, webbing between the fingers, and so on) are magnetically encoded on an access card, which is presented along with the hand. The computer-based version stores all the measurements for all the authorized entrants within the disk memory of the computer, which serves as central controller of a multiportal system. Keypads or magnetic-stripe cards can be used with the system. Stellar quotes a false-accept rate of 1% and a false-reject rate of 1.5% for the Identimat system. There are both single and multiple-portal versions, and a model adapted for control of access to computer terminals.

RETINAL PATTERN OF THE EYE

Another one-of-a-kind biometric access control system was introduced in 1983, and is based upon the premise, presented in a 1935 medical paper, that the pattern of the blood vessels on the retina of the human eye is a unique individual identifier. The system, from EyeDentify, requires that one place one's eye 1/2 inch from a lens and focus on a visual target, while one's retinal pattern is scanned by a low-intensity infrared light beam, detected by a photosensor, and digitized (see Figure 8–5). As in all biometric systems, this digitized reference pattern is stored within the computer-controller of the system, and compared with the actual reading that takes place when a prospective entrant appears at the portal. EyeDentify offers both a keypad version in which the scanned pattern is compared against the single pattern which has been stored for the person whose ID number was entered, and a file-scan version in which the scanned pattern is compared against all of the patterns on file to determine whether or not there is a match.

VOICEPRINTS

During the frenetic activity of the 1970s in the field of access control systems based upon physical attributes, there was a considerable amount of research and development work devoted to the development of a system based upon voiceprints. Although they did not—and still do not—have the legal status of the fingerprint, the signature, or the face, there were a number of court cases in which voiceprint evidence was admitted, and there were those who believed that the individuality of the voiceprint would soon achieve legal status on a par with the fingerprint. Datawest introduced a short-lived commercial product in 1974; it digitized the reference voiceprint and stored it on a magnetic disk in a PDP-11 computer, then compared this reference with the digitized voiceprint of the prospective entrant using a "convolver/correlator"; a basic system could handle

Figure 8-5   *Retinal pattern access control system. (Courtesy of EyeDentify, Inc., Beaverton, Ohio)*

eight portals for $150,000. Texas Instruments was reputed for a decade to be on the verge of introducing a commercial voiceprint system, and indeed conducted research and development for a decade and made a few test system installations, but never seriously pursued the market; one of the systems on the market today is a descendent of that work.

For fifteen years the access control industry anticipated the advent of the voiceprint system in vain, and then in 1986, within months of each other, two products arrived on the market. VoxTron Systems acquired the Texas Instruments technology, and was formed as a subsidiary of Detex (which was one of the few companies offering card access systems in the early 1970s and also vends security hardware such as door controls, alarms, and indicators). Voxtron was sold in 1987 to Camarilla Corporation. The second entrant was a new venture in Massachusetts called Ecco Industries. Both systems use a telephone handset as the voice-entry device and a keypad as the personal identifier. Reference voice patterns for selected words are digitized and stored in a central computer-controller, which is capable of controlling a multiplicity of portal units. Error rates for false-reject and false-accept, respectively, are quoted as 0.1% and 0.01% by VoxTron and 1% and 0.1% by Ecco. Costs range in the $2,000 per portal area.

ERRORS IN PERSONAL IDENTIFICATION SYSTEMS
BASED ON PHYSICAL ATTRIBUTES

In Chapter 4 we discussed the fact that, unlike keypad systems and card systems, there are unavoidable errors (both false-accept and false-reject), in physical attribute systems, and further, that there is an unavoidable dependence between the two. Let us examine why this is so, using our simple weight-and-height system as an example.

False-Accept and False-Reject Errors and the
Balance between Them

Assume that the measured weight and height of a person can vary up or down by as much as a tenth of a pound and a tenth of an inch; that is, the combination of the variation in the person's height and weight, and the accuracy of the measurement device can result in that difference from day to day. Further, a person whose reference measurements are 140 pounds and 5'6", was actually measured anywhere between 139.5 and 140.5 pounds and 5'5 1/2"–5' 6 1/2", since we are using weight to the nearest pound and height to the nearest inch. Assuming that height and weight are uniformly distributed, 10% of the population will fall between 139.4 and 139.5 pounds, and another 10% will fall between 139.5 and 139.6 pounds. An upward variation in measured weight by a tenth of a pound for those persons in the 139.4–139.5 category, whose reference measurements put them in the 139-pound category, will place them into the 140-pound category, and their identity will not be verified. Similar logic applies to a downward variation in the 139.5–139.6 category, and to the height measurements as well.

Probability calculations (approximate, rather than rigorous, since we are only interested in illustrating a point) tell us that 5% of the variations in measured weight will cause a person to be tipped into the wrong category, and thus cause his identity to not be verified—a false-reject error. But since the identification is based upon both weight and height, and there will be another 5% of errors due to the same phenomenon with respect to the height measurement, the total false-reject error rate will be 10%.

On the false-reject side, an error in either height **OR** weight will cause rejection. For a false-accept error, both height **AND** weight must be in error in the appropriate direction, and for our example the probabilities are multiplied, resulting in a false-accept rate of 0.25% due to the measurement variations. To this must be added the normal probability of cross-identification due to the nature of the physical attribute and the fineness to which it is measured (to the nearest inch and pound), which we calculated earlier in this chapter as 0.0009, giving a total false-accept rate of 0.34%.*

To illustrate the dependence between the two kinds of errors, let us assume that the false-reject error rate of 10% is unacceptable, since it means that one of every ten authorized persons will be inappropriately rejected each time they present themselves to the system. We can adjust this parameter by loosening the size of the measurement categories; as we described earlier in this chapter, we could measure weight to the nearest five pounds (instead of the nearest pound), and height to the nearest two inches (instead of one inch). By doing this, the number of categories is reduced and their size is increased, and the variations of a tenth of a pound and a tenth of an inch have an effect only at the boundary points between categories; since there are one-fifth the number of categories in weight, there are one-fifth the number of boundaries, and the weight false-reject rate is reduced to 1%. The height categories are reduced by half, and the false-reject rate therefore also by half to 2 1/2%. The combined false-reject rate will be 3 1/2%.

On the false-accept side, the combined rate due to measurement variations is now improved by a factor of ten, to 0.025%; but the coarser nature of the measurements has resulted in fewer total combinations being available, resulting in a cross-identification probability of 0.009, for a combined false-accept rate of 0.925%. We have therefore succeeded in reducing the false-reject rate by two-thirds (3.5% from 10%), at the expense of raising the false-accept rate by three times (0.925% from 0.34%). There is no free lunch.

These principles apply to all physical attribute systems, whether the characteristic being measured is the fingerprint, hand, voice, or any other. There is an inherent imprecision in the measurement and an unavoidable variation in the characteristic, both of which will combine to create false-reject errors. The rate of false-reject errors can be reduced by loosening the requirements for identification, and this will also increase the false-accept rate.

A common method of decreasing the false-reject errors while creating only a minor concomitant increase in false-accept errors is the try-again; the rejected person submits his physical attribute for a second and even a third time. If the original reject was due to measurement error, poor placement of the finger in the window, background noise during a voice verification, or the like, the try-again frequently will be successful. Of course, if the rejected person has gained ten pounds because of last night's black forest cake topped with chocolate ice cream and Hershey's syrup, he will need to run around the block a few times before the system will accept him on a weight basis. Try-agains are usually limited to about three, on the theory that any temporary aberrations will be overcome within three tries, and extended ability to try-again increases the chances of success of prospective penetrators who are looking for a false-accept error.

---

*Note that probabilities are expressed as quantities between 0 (the event will never occur) and 1 (the event is certain to occur), and error rates are expressed as percentages. Therefore an error rate of 0.34% has a probability of occurrence of 0.0034, and will occur an average of 34 times out of each 10,000 trials.

The balancing of false-accept and false-reject errors is an important part of the design of any system that will include an access control capability based upon physical attributes, and neither of these error rates can ever be brought completely to zero. The system, therefore, must incorporate means to deal with both kinds of errors: there must be an alternative means to admit those authorized persons who are for whatever reason unable to pass the scrutiny of the system on a given day; and there must be a means to deal with attempted penetrators who are detected by the system, a deterrent to that small percentage who will be falsely-accepted, or a second level of defense to apprehend them using different identification criteria. The total security system, not exotic technological mechanisms, is the only certain means of protection.

COMBINATION SYSTEMS USING PHYSICAL ATTRIBUTES

As in all security systems, and as we have observed several times before in access control systems, the use of combinations of devices can result in greatly increased security, in many cases at modest additional cost. Nowhere is the efficacy of this phenomenon more apparent than in physical attribute access control systems. In many of the early physical attribute systems, the characteristics of all authorized persons were stored in the system's file, and the characteristics of a prospective entrant were compared against the entire file to determine whether or not there was anyone in the file who matched those characteristics. Most of the modern-day systems, on the other hand, require that the person identify himself using an access card or keypad, and then his characteristics are compared with those on file for that particular person only.

Let us examine the significant difference in error rates between these two approaches of the physical attribute alone, and the card/keypad-plus-physical-attribute system, using again our simple weight-and-height system with one-pound and one-inch resolution. In such a system there are 1,080 possible combinations of weight and height (and remember that we presumed for the purposes of illustration that the population was uniformly distributed over weight and height and that there was no correlation between the two). Using the old, pure physical-attribute approach, the chance of a successful penetration depends upon the penetrator matching one—any one—of the descriptions stored in the file. If there is only one authorized entrant, the penetration chances are 1 in 1,080, or 0.0009; with 100 persons stored in the file, the odds rise to 0.086, with 500 they are 0.363, and with 1,000 authorized persons, the odds are on the side of the penetrator at 0.594: 59.5% of attempted penetrations will be successful! If, however, a combination system is used that requires the person to identify himself through card or keypad, the odds of penetration will remain at 1 in 1,080 forever.

These illustrative numbers, of course, should not be taken at face value, since the available combinations of physical attribute access control systems on the market can be much greater: a billion, for example, in a minutae-based fingerprint system (but some, we suspect, are closer to our height-and-weight system than to the fingerprint system). These examples illustrate the increased security that can be achieved through simple combinations of systems rather than through high technology.

The major decision with respect to physical attribute systems, of course, is whether they provide additional security commensurate with their greater cost. If a keypad or card system must be added in order to provide an appropriate level of security and reliability, is the physical attribute system any more than a verifier for the ID entered by other means? Can equivalent security be provided using a well-conceived card-plus-keypad system within the envelope of a well-designed total security system? At current cost levels, is there really a great deal of difference between the installed cost of a personal attribute system and the installed cost of a sophisticated card-plus-keypad system? These kinds of questions must be faced individually by each security system designer, and the answers provided that are appropriate for the particular requirements of his operation.

Chapter 9

Command and Control Systems

From the simple lock-and-key to a fingerprint recognition system, an access control system or device contains a means for command and control of the functions which it is designed to perform. For the lock-and-key, control is exercised by a mechanical means of recognizing that the shape of the key is correct, and the prospective entrant is permitted to turn the knob, releasing the bolt that holds the door closed. In the mechanical keypad, a mechanism recognizes that the correct sequence of buttons has been depressed, and the prospective entrant may turn the knob and enter. Electronic keypads recognize the correct sequence of pushbutton depressions through electronic circuits and withdraw the bolt automatically so that the prospective entrant need only push open the door. Card and token systems recognize electronically that the proper code is contained on the card or token, frequently also ascertain that the person to whom the code is assigned is permitted entrance to that space at that time, and also automatically withdraw the bolt. Physical attribute systems verify that the person submitting the card or token, or depressing the keypad, is (within reasonable lack of doubt) the person to whom the code is assigned, before withdrawing the bolt.

There is a wide range of choice regarding the location and distribution of the intelligence—whether limited or sophisticated—required in access control systems and devices. There is, however, not a complete choice among all the combinations of access control methods and ways in which the intelligence can be distributed, since some methods of access control afford only one means of command-control (for example, mechanical keypads cannot be controlled from a central computer) and some access control features can be achieved only through certain command-control means (for example, logging and selective-person control can only be practically achieved using central computer-control).

169

ALTERNATIVES FOR COMMAND AND CONTROL IN
ACCESS CONTROL SYSTEMS

There are really only two alternatives for locating the command-control functions—at each portal or at a central shared location—but there are half a dozen variations on these two basic themes, and they each deserve explanation.

Self-contained portal units: all the required intelligent functions are located within the unit mounted at the portal, and no control is exercised from elsewhere. Examples are all mechanical keypads, many electronic keypads, and some card-reader systems. Sophisticated functions, such as logging, individual card lockout, and time and space zoning are usually not provided with these single-portal units because the entire cost of including these features must be borne by each portal; this can make the per-portal cost twice that of other methods. There are, however, single-portal units available that provide all of these features.

Portal-group controllers: a single controller system controls several (typically four) nearby portal keypads or card readers. There are two principal varieties: the first is simply a means of sharing the already simple electronics of a self-contained portal access control unit among several doors. The second is a means of concentrating control and communications between a group of several portals and a central-control computer, both in order to share the cost of the electronics and to reduce wiring costs by eliminating the need for direct wires from each portal to central. As before, there are portal-group controllers which stand alone and still provide most of the relatively sophisticated functions normally associated with central control.

Central control: a computer system is provided that is connected with and controls all of the portal equipment. This is the only really economical method of providing the full range of sophisticated access control and other security functions in a security system which encompasses a large number of portals. It also provides a means for general data communications, so that the access control system can be integrated into a total information management system which may include building automation functions, personnel control, planning and forecasting, and so forth.

Distributed system: the command and control functions are distributed throughout a network comprised of a central-control computer, and some number of regional (building or floor or area) and/or portal-group controllers. If such a system is properly designed, and the intelligence properly distributed, the distributed system can combine good cost-effectiveness with the capability of the system to continue to perform a major portion of its security functions even if some portion of the system has failed.

Combination and multiple systems: a central-control computer serves as the means for a multiplicity of different systems, such as access control, time-and-attendance, energy management, and factory data collection. As we observed in Chapter 1, this appears on the surface to be efficient use of computing equipment, but opens the user to the dangers associated with massive software systems and the collapse of all functions pursuant to a single computer failure. There is also risk from a security point of view in allowing other users to meddle with the innards of the fundamental control mechanism of the security system; even if the security software is an independent module, there are common areas of the computer system hardware and operating software through which the security system can be subverted. It is instructive in this context that virtually all fire safety codes forbid the mixing of fire alarm systems with any other functions.

Central alarm station control: really a form of central control within the facility, since the wiring from various portals must be brought to a central location and consolidated for communication to and from the commercial central station. In practice, this configuration usually is an unmanned centrally-controlled system that reports alarms and trouble conditions to the central alarm station where there are people who can initiate the appropriate actions.

The command and control functions for the self-contained portal units and the simpler portal-group controllers are easily defined, and pretty much come with the territory when the products of particular vendors are evaluated for a particular application. There is much greater variance among the systems offered with central control of the various sorts described above, and we shall devote the remainder of this chapter to consideration of the centrally-controlled system; its functions, features, capabilities, and shortcomings.

THE CENTRAL-COMPUTER CONTROLLER

There are seven elements that make up the central-computer controller; the seven elements are the same for any computer system, regardless of whether it is used for accounting functions, manufacturing process control, battlefield strategy assessment, or spaceship launch. The seven elements are described in the following sections.

Processor

Comprised of solid-state integrated-circuit chips which process information at rates of millions of operations per second and store data in amounts of millions of characters in a volume which will fit in the palm of your hand, the processor is the brains of any computer system. Processor power, which only a decade ago cost tens of thousands of dollars, is now available (thanks to the continuous advances in semiconductor technology that each year make possible putting more circuitry into a smaller space, performing more functions faster and at lower prices) for a few thousand dollars, and resides on the desks of half of America's professional workforce in the form of the ubiquitous personal computer. The processors which are used in central controllers for access control systems are almost universally standard, off-the-shelf commercial computers, and an increasing number of them utilize the popular IBM Personal Computer as the central controller.

Peripheral Equipment

Peripheral equipment is generally the electromechanical devices that connect to the processor in order to perform functions that need not, cannot, or should not for economic reasons be performed by the millions-of-operations-per-second circuitry of the processor. Examples of peripheral equipment are printers, magnetic disk storage units, magnetic tape storage equipments, keyboards, CRT displays, and graphic plotters. Peripheral equipment is usually procured from the processor manufacturer along with the processor, and in many cases as a non-separable package including processor, keyboard, display, and disk. The combination of the processor, the peripherals, and the operating software, described below, constitutes a **computer system.** Peripherals for the more popular processors can also be bought from indepedent vendors and plugged in directly.

Operating Software

Comprised of computer programs, the operating software causes the processor to interact appropriately with the various peripherals, and to perform the internal functions that enable the computer system to do useful work with the direction of humans. When the computer is instructed to "multiply," the operating software organizes the two numbers to be multiplied, feeds the digits in the correct order to the solid-state multiplier chip, takes care of the carries and adjusts the decimal point, and places the result into the register where the human expects to find it. When the computer is instructed to "store" or "fetch," the operating software locates the affected data and writes it onto the disk such that it can be easily located later, or finds the appropriate information on the disk, reads it, and places it in the register or memory location where the human expects to find it. When the computer is instructed to "print," the operating software organizes the data in the proper format and sends it slowly to the printer until it has all been printed. In summary, all the wondrous pieces of physical hardware which technology has presented to us would be useless lumps of silicon, plastic, and metals without the operating software to organize and coordinate them.

Applications Software

The assemblage of computer programs that cause the computer system to perform a specific function is known as the applications software. The operating software is concerned only with the mechanics of multiplying, storing, fetching, and printing; the applications software utilizes these mechanics to multiply an employee's pay rate by the number of hours he has worked, store the result as a daily wage, fetch seven days' entries every Friday, and print the employee's paycheck. In a security system, the applications software contains the specific instructions which enable the computer system to allow access to particular persons through particular portals at specific times of day, sound the alarm when a door is propped open or the cover is pried off the control box, and print the daily log of all activity in the system. Whereas the operating software is a part of the computer system and is purchased from the computer system vendor along with the processor and the peripherals, the applications software is added to the system by the company that designs the security system and also adds the card readers and keypads.

Communications Capability

Communications capability assumes two forms in a security system. The first kind of communications capability that is required is that which enables the computer system to exchange information and control with the card readers, keypads, and alarm devices attached to it (and which could be considered in a security system to be peripheral equipment). This is usually accomplished using the intimate and custom kind of interconnections that also characterize the computer's relations with its own directly-connected peripheral equipments, such as printers and disk storage. The second kind of communications capability is required to exchange information with other computers, remote terminal equipments, central stations, and so forth. This is accomplished using generic industry-standard protocols that have been developed to facilitate communication among computers and other systems regardless of their make, model, or manufacturer.

Interface With Humans

Interface with humans and other elements of the real world (such as the mixture of chemicals that results from a chemical processing system or the pointing of a missile in a gun-fire control system) is required in order for the computer system to complete the purpose for which it was designed, since a processor endlessly performing calculations internally for its own amusement has no purpose except in the more abtruse science fiction novels. In a security system these interfaces take the following forms.

Interface with general users: the readers and keypads at the portals into which the coded cards or the codes are entered; the red and green lights at the portals that indicate "access granted" or "access denied"; the withdrawal of the bolt in the door; the bell that sounds when an emergency exit is opened; and the picture that is automatically taken when a forced entry is perpetrated.

Interface with system operators and managers: the keyboard through which the opener enters lists of authorized persons, opens doors manually, acknowledges alarm conditions, and orders the computer system to print certain reports; the CRT display which presents status and alarm messages to the operator; and the printer which prints the activity log, the lists of authorized persons by portal and time, and the usage statistics on the system.

Systems and Procedures

Systems and procedures connect and coordinate all the equipment, software, and human elements of the central-computer controller into an integrated, computer-controlled security system. There must be well-planned procedures for every contingency, and a system of people and equipment prepared to deal routinely with every situation. The following is illustrative of the kinds of systems and procedures that must be instituted in a computer-controlled access control system.

- Authorization and data base entry of changes to the lists of authorized persons for all portals and during all time periods.
- Procedure for dealing with lost cards, both temporary and permanent.
- Procedure for changing access codes and informing the authorized persons of the new code.
- Schedule for printing and distribution of reports.
- Emergency procedures for forced entry and other alarm conditions.
- Security procedures during periods of non-functioning equipment, power failure, or interrupted communications.
- Authorization and procedure for changes to the applications software.
- System of data base backup, safe storage, and data base restoration after emergency or equipment failure.

EQUIPMENT FOR THE CENTRAL-COMPUTER CONTROLLER

The equipment complement for the central-computer controller of an access control or general security system will vary greatly depending upon the number of portals and alarm points in the system, and the overall level of security which must be provided in order to counter the threats and risks associated with the facility. The following ingredients must generally be considered for inclusion in the system.

Processing Equipment

Processing Unit

A processing unit having sufficient power to perform all system functions without untoward delay is the heart of the system. Access at the portals should be granted or denied within two seconds of entry of the code or card, even under maximum traffic conditions. Alarms should be presented at the console within a few seconds. The access control functions of the system should not bog down when reports are being run.

Selection of a processing unit with sufficient power is the responsibility of the vendor of the access control system, but it is the responsibility of the buyer to insure that this has been properly done, since it is he who may be stuck with an ineffective system. The most effective method of insuring that the system is based upon an adequate processor is to visit previous customers who have installed the identical system in a facility of approximately the same size and of the same security level, and determine how effectively it has performed. Performance guarantees can be written into a purchase contract, but they are difficult to construct and time-consuming to litigate; meanwhile, the system is in place and frustrating one and all.

Input-Output Processor

An input-output processor capable of controlling all the peripheral equipment that will be attached to the system, and of controlling the card readers and other portal equipment must be provided. The capability of the input-output processor is equally as important as the processing unit in determining the performance of the system, and it should be evaluated with the same care described above for the processing unit.

Disk Memory

Disk memory must be provided which is sufficient to store all necessary operating software, applications programs, the cardholder data base, and the transaction log for as long a period as deemed necessary. (At least one week's worth of logging data is usually kept in the system, although some users prefer a month or more of data. Logging data can be kept permanently and more cheaply by periodically dumping it from the disk storage to a magnetic tape, by accumulating it on a removable magnetic disk, or by printing and microfilming it.)

Printers

Logging Printer

A logging printer is used for on-line logging of access accomplished and denied, alarms, and operator functions; it is usually a slow-speed, typewriter-type printer. We usually recommend that it also be capable of acting as a backup printer for the high-speed system printer in case of failure of the system printer.

System Printer

The system printer is a high-speed page printer used for the production of voluminous material such as reports. It is also useful for it to be capable of backing up the logging printer.

Displays and Consoles

Operator Console

The operator console contains a CRT display and keyboard, and is the means through which the operator interacts with the computer system for receiving alarm displays and responding to them, for updating the data base, for ordering the system to print particular reports, and for system and programming functions. The operator console frequently comes integrally packaged with the computer system.

Additional CRT Display Terminals

Additional CRT display terminals may be provided, with or without keyboards, for remote or alternative alarm display and processing and a possible alternative operator's console. Also, graphic displays are frequently provided in large and sophisticated systems, which can display maps and floor plans to identify the location of an alarm, describe the nearby presence of hazardous or valuable materials, and so on. Color display terminals rather than monochrome display terminals are useful in security systems because priorities and emergencies can be more easily and quickly identified through the use of distinctive colors for those portions of the graphic display.

Communications Equipment

Multiplexers and Concentrators

Multiplexers and concentrators are units of communications equipment that combine messages for and from several or many remote terminals or devices, so that each portal need not be directly wired to the central computer, thus reducing wiring costs. One must take care that too many portals are not combined on a line; this creates the potential for a traffic jam and consequent delays in the communication path. Care must also be taken that the combination of signals does not allow subverting of security at all portals by manipulation or tampering at one of them.

Computer-Industry-Compatible Communications Port

A computer-industry-compatible communications port allows the computer system to communicate with other computers for the variety of purposes already discussed. Even if there is no need for this capability when the system is procured and installed, the system designer should provide for it to be painlessly added in the future.

Power Protection

Power protection can provide any of several levels of continuation of operation of the system after and during a failure of the primary electrical power provided by the power utility. Many computer systems routinely provide sufficient battery backup for the system to maintain the continuity of its real-time clock and the contents of its high-speed memory. From there it is only a question of money: How much should be spent to insure against power failure? The answer to this question is three-fold:

1. What is the probability of power failure as to frequency and duration?
2. What is the security impact of the probable power failure upon the facility?
3. What other means of security might be employed to cover during a power failure?

Alternatives

There are four alternatives to implementing power protection and they are summarized briefly below.*

Relax and Enjoy It. If the security system is not critical, or if there are other means of providing adequate security, such as guards, there may be no need to provide any means to continue operation during a power interruption, nor justification for the cost of doing so.

Orderly Shutdown. If the system need not continue operation, but the data being processed at the moment of power failure—such as the activity log—is critical, then power must be maintained long enough to complete current processing, save data, and place all equipment into a safe condition. A few seconds of power-continuation are usually sufficient for orderly shutdown.

---

*For a complete discussion of power problems, their causes, effects, and solutions, see "The Importance of Power," by Dan M. Bowers, *Datamation,* January 15, 1985.

Graceful Degradation.   In this form of power protection, the high power consumption portions of the system—printers and disk drives—are shut down in an orderly fashion, but sufficient power is provided that basic functions can continue. In a security system this might result in a loss of time-and-space zone control, logging being limited to critical functions and only stored, not printed and so forth. Since the degraded mode might continue indefinitely, a substantial power-support system will be required.

Damn the Torpedoes, Full Speed Ahead.   The ultimate, and most expensive, power protection system is one which continues to provide full power without interruption, regardless of any hiatus on the power company's line: it is appropriately known as an Uninterruptable Power System (UPS to its close friends). The designer's challenge in UPS is to provide adequate protection without squandering money. For example, for how long a period will power be needed—a day? a week? an aeon? Should a second UPS be installed to provide power if the first one fails?

Redundancy

Redundancy of equipment can be provided, if the security requirements indicate the need, so that the system can continue to operate even if a portion or portions of it have ceased to function. Power protection by means of the UPS is one form of redundancy that protects against failure of outside agency, the power company. In a distributed system, portal-group controllers or intelligent portal readers may continue to function at a degraded level after the central computer or communications with it have failed. In the highest security situations, such as nuclear power plant security systems, every element, including the central computer, has a redundant twin that continuously operates in parallel, so that no failure will degrade the operation to any degree or for any period of time.

Expansion Capability

Expansion capability should be allowed for in any computer system that is procured, and security systems are no exception. As a rule of thumb, we recommend that expansion of 100%, in both the number of portals to be controlled and the number of people to be accommodated, is possible by routine additions of additional circuitry or subunits to the computer system.

CONTROL OF ACCESS AND ALARMS

The rules and regulations for access control and the definition of alarms and other unusual conditions are embodied in the applications software which is contained in the central-computer controller. Like the complement of equipment which will be provided, these rules, regulations, and procedures will vary depending on the level of security required for the facility. Following are representative procedures and variations that might be appropriate.

Access Control

Access control to particular spaces might be continuous, as in a laboratory or valuable-storage area, or it might be in force only outside of normal working hours, for example in an office area which needs free flow of people during normal working hours, but restricted access outside those hours.

Failure of Access-Controlled Portals

Failure should be to the locked condition, else the access-controlled portals provide no security at all. This means that an alternative entry must be provided, lest a particular kind of equipment failure be allowed to permanently close a space. This alternative means, usually mechanical since one of the most common failures is that of electrical power, must be carefully controlled if it is not to become a weak point in the security system. If there are always people within the space, of course, there is no need for alternative means since the door must always be capable of being opened from the inside, for safety reasons.

Control of All Portals from the System Console

It should be possible for all portals to be controlled from the system console. The system operator, under proper control, should be able to unlock or lock a portal either temporarily or permanently.

Alarm Handling

Alarms should be presented on the operator display using plain-English messages, so that the operator can take appropriate action without reference to code books, charts, or lists.

Alarms should continue to be displayed until they are acknowledged by the operator and the appropriate action has been taken.

Alarms should be prioritized so that the most important are brought to the operator's attention first. A common method of penetrating an alarm system is to set off all the alarms so that the security force cannot tell from whence the real penetration is coming; the security system program must be able to instantly resolve this confusion.

Alarms may include certain valid accesses, for example, if a personal-locator function is included.

An alarm summary line should appear on the operator's display, presenting data on all outstanding alarms: number of alarms by priority level, number unacknowledged.

All alarms should be printed on the logging printer, or at least stored in the log, including time and date, portal number, type of alarm, operator acknowledgement, and how they were resolved.

An Unattended Mode

An unattended mode may be included in the system repertoire; in this mode, alarms are presented on the operator display as usual, but acknowledgement and operator clearing are not required. All activity is recorded in the log and printed on the logging printer as usual.

SYSTEM FUNCTIONS AND OPERATIONS

The functions and operations that are controlled by the system but performed at the portals, such as time and space zone control, anti-passback, and the like, are well-defined as basic functions of access control systems. There is another class of operations performed by the central control system, having to do with the features of the central system itself. The following describes a number of these operations.

Password Control

Password control is commonly used to allow access to the operator console, and several levels of password are usually provided. The first level is the operator, for ordinary monitoring and control functions. The system operator, for system functions such as printing of reports, and resolving problems and ambiguities in the normal alarm monitoring operation, is the second level of password. Data base alterations, for making changes to the authorization list, persons authorized, time and space zones, and the like, form another level. The applications programmer, for making alterations to the fundamental rules of the game embodied in the applications software is the final level of password.

Access to the ability to make data base alterations and changes to the applications software represents carte blanche to compromise, circumvent, and penetrate the security system, and this access must be more protected than any other point in the system. As we discussed in Chapter 3, the password alone is not sufficient protection against unwanted access to any computer system, and additional measures should be provided, such as card-plus-password, dual-passwords (that is, two people must be present in order for access to be granted), detailed documentation of the programs and strict control over alterations to them, and a comprehensive audit trail that is frequently scrutinized. But, no matter what additional measures have been taken, the security manager must realize that *an expert programmer who has unlimited access to the computer can circumvent any protection that is built-in,* while leaving no trace of his activities in the log. Protection against this threat requires that programmers' access to the system be carefully controlled, and under the supervision of a trusted person (the programmer might, of course, be that trusted person); ultimately, someone must be trusted.

Logging

All activity should be logged and preserved on magnetic storage so that it can be called back as needed; alarm activity should be presented on a terminal and printed on the alarm printer as well. Logged activity should include: all log-on and log-off activity of operators and other persons; entry into and exit from the unattended mode; enabling/disabling/locking/unlocking of portals; all card or keypad accesses; all data base alterations; and all system functions such as initiating of report printing, file backup, or interchange of data with another computer over the general communications capability.

Database

The database will contain all the information describing the authorized individuals the spaces to which they are permitted access, the time periods during which access is permitted, and so on. Alterations to the data base must be conveniently accomplished while at the same time being carefully controlled; these alterations should be capable of being accomplished while the system remains on-line performing its normal access control and alarm monitoring functions.

Degraded Mode

A degraded mode of operation will be possible in a variety of forms, depending upon the design of the overall access control system and the characteristics of the equipment and software provided by the particular vendor. The user must consider how the various functions of the system will perform (or be absent) during the degraded mode, such as allowing or denying access, treatment of alarms, logging capabilities.

Reports

The complement of reports which are provided will vary with the manufacturer, but at the least, the following should be available.

Daily Alarm/Access Listing: by portal; by building; by total site or facility; by person; by department.

Daily Operator Log.

Data Base Maintenance Audit Trail.

Cardholder Listing Dump: by priority level (time/space); by portal or building; by department.

Definition of Access Levels.

Table of Alarms: location, priority, response.

Password and Permittee List.

OPERATIONS AND FACILITIES

The proper operation of any computer system depends as much upon factors that fall in the systems and procedures area as it does upon the hardware and software that is installed. In addition to the control of access to the system, the logging of all activity, and the procedures necessary to insure the integrity of the data base, the following processes and procedures must be carefully considered in light of the specific requirements of the particular system and its environment.

Archiving Capability

The logging of access activity, alarms, data base alterations, and the like, requires that space be made available on magnetic media for its storage. The amount of logged information that can be retained depends on the amount of magnetic media which is allocated to it. Due to cost, it is clearly impractical to provide enough space to store this information *ad infinitum;* even one year's worth could be burdensome. The most practical solution is to contain a limited amount of logged information—one week to one month—within the on-line disk memory of the system, and to transfer all older information periodically to a cheaper form of archival storage. Commonly used methods of storage are the following.

- Print the information and microfilm it for permanent storage. There are microfilming services that will do the microfilming at modest cost, but the user must purchase microfilm readers in order to read the information when it becomes necessary.

- Utilize removable-disk magnetic storage so that the disk-pack containing the archived material can sit on the shelf and not on the expensive disk drive until it is needed to read information from it or to add additional archived material to it.
- Use a magnetic-tape storage unit for the archived material. This can be a cheaper unit than a magnetic disk drive, and also provides the removable-medium.

Operating Statistics

Operating statistics on the system have a number of uses, and are easily accumulated by the computer. Statistics collected should include such things as accesses by portal by time period, percentages of access denied, and so forth. Site and building managers can utilize this information to optimize the efficiency of their operations. Some systems will provide the capability for the user to collect and analyze statistical information on an ad-hoc, homegrown basis.

File and Program Duplication

This is necessary for backup of the system; for example, if fire or other catastrophe occurs in the computer room and ruins the disk-packs that contain the data base, it is prudent that a copy of the data base was previously made and stored in another location; it this was done, operations may continue with little perturbation; if not, the system could be inoperative for weeks or months. The computer system must provide a convenient means for accomplishing this duplication of magnetically stored files, since it will be done relatively frequently—daily or weekly, depending upon the frequency and volume of alterations to the data base information. Also, since the computer system may be shut down for access control purposes (or, perhaps, be put into degraded mode) while the duplication process is being performed, it must be accomplished as swiftly as possible.

Changes and Enhancements

Changes and enhancements to the equipment, operating software, and applications software represent exposure to the integrity of the security system, and must be carefully controlled. A strict policy must be instituted which governs the process of authorization, design, installation, and documentation of any changes, enhancements, or alterations.

Facility Plan

A facility plan and policy should be created which covers the following important areas.

- Housekeeping: organization of the computer room, standards of cleanliness, access by janitorial personnel.
- Data Flow: into and out of the facility, logging of incoming and outgoing documents, distribution of reports.
- Control of Programs: when they are to be run and who may run them.
- Control of Files: programs with which they are to be used, when to be mounted on the system, storage places and procedures, and updating procedures.
- Control of System Documentation: descriptions and source listings of programs, updating requirements and restrictions.
- Fire Protection: evacuation procedures, notification and admission of emergency services personnel.
- Power Control and Conditioning: noise filtering, backup power, and UPS.
- Climate Control: air conditioning, dust filters, and anti-static.
- Surrounding Hazards: for example, a dynamite storage locker in the room immediately below, or a powerful source of electromagnetic radiation in the next room.
- Operating Procedures: duty roster and log, startup procedure after degraded mode, priority-level alarm handling, what to do when the system fails, and so forth.

Security Plan

A security plan must be created that addresses the following subjects.

- Physical Access Control of persons to the computer room.
- Electronic Access Control to the computer system over communications lines.
- Operational Security of printed reports, documentation of programs, validation of authorization for alterations, and so on.
- Audit Trails, computer-recorded logs and manual logs, periodic examination and analysis.
- File and Data Backup Procedures, secure offsite storage for the backup copies, backup for the backup, procedure for utilizing the backup copies under emergency conditions.
- Periodic Security Review of all plans and procedures: surprise attempts at penetration of the system are frequently a good means of testing the efficacy of the security plan.

Contingency Plan

A contingency plan provides a means of coping with any disruptions or failures in the security system, and should provide a step-by-step procedure for the operations personnel to follow under any set of emergency conditions that can be foreseen. It should include the following kind of considerations.

- Fail-Soft Operation (degraded-mode): what kind of failures may occur, what fail-soft operation should be instituted using the equipment which remains operational?
- Back-Up Site or Equipment: in the event of the ultimate catastrophe—for example, the entire computer room is destroyed by fire—can the operations be transferred to an alternative site, using the backup files?
- Emergency Processing Procedures: when operating under emergency conditions, what are the alternative procedures that must be followed in place of the normal procedures for archiving, operations, backups, flow and control of data, computer-room security, and so on.

Chapter 10

Selecting and Implementing an Access Control System

Every management decision requires the balancing of risk and expenditure, and in choosing an access control system for his facility, the manager must decide what expenditure is warranted for the solution to the facility's security risks and threats. A total security system will encompass fire detection, perimeter control, internal surveillance, access control, and non-physical security items such as employee screening and audit trails. In all cases there will be existing measures in place for most or all of these aspects of security, and the manager must weigh the cost of new or additional security measures against the cost of those which are already in place.

The simple keypad-only access control system is merely a combination lock that is quicker to operate, can be more difficult to defeat, and that has more features and options than the version which is sold at the corner hardware store. Features such as remote indication, error alarm, and hostage alarm can be deciding factors in some situations. Pushbutton systems cannot be employed where there is a large risk of collusion, since the combination can be told without penalty if there is no individual identification feature, and few keypad-alone systems incorporate such a feature. Keypad systems can cost ten to twenty times the cost of a common lock, but the increased security and extra features will justify the cost in many cases.

On the subject of locking mechanisms, it should not go without mention that an access control device such as a keypad, card reader or physical attribute system must be associated with a mechanical means of unlocking the door; this is usually called a door strike, and is comprised of an electrically-operated solenoid which moves a bolt similar to the one in the ordinary lock-and-key mechanism. (There are also fully electrical locking mechanisms which lock the door using the force of a powerful electromagnet, and unlock the door by removing power from the magnet.) Just as there are mechanical locks that can be purchased for five dollars,

$20 or $50, there are door strikes available over a wide range of cost and providing a commensurately wide range of protection. It does not make much sense to purchase a card access system that costs $300 per portal, and attach it to a $10 door strike that can be subverted easily. It also follows that an important part of calculating the cost of an access control system is to include the cost of the door strikes and jimmy-proof plates and barriers.

The card-only system is equivalent to a conventional lock-and-key, in which it is more difficult to duplicate the key without authorization, and which can have a large number of useful additional features. When equipped with personal identification, the ability to cancel the access privileges of individual persons, and logging of accesses and attempts, these systems provide sufficient control, history, and identification, and are virtually undefeatable by an amateur outsider. They can in many cases be completely cost-justified through side benefits such as time-clock information. The risk of lost or stolen cards is still present, since entry may be effected before the card's loss is known and the card's access privileges cancelled. Card-only systems can cost ten to one hundred times the cost of the lock-and-key, and with the logging and cancel features they can provide sufficient additional security to justify that cost when the security need requires it.

A few observations should be made about the method of encoding a card. Since no amount of ultra-high technology can create an un-lose-able or un-steal-able card, it does not make much sense to pay much more money for exotic coding techniques. Even though sophisticated coding requires the would-be penetrator to expend more effort and resources to crack and duplicate the code, if the stakes are worth it he will proceed to do so; further, in most cities he can hire a burglar, pickpocket or mugger to obtain a real card cheaply. The security provided by card systems does not depend a great deal on the code or its embodiment.

Card-plus-keypad systems plug the loss and theft loopholes in card-only systems, and the collusion loophole in keypad-only systems. Card-plus-keypad systems do not cost much more than card-only systems, and they provide considerable increased security: on a cost/performance basis we consider them to be a "best-buy." The increased security provided by adding a keypad to a card system may be sufficient enough that a simple, stand-alone system will satisfy the user's security needs, and he can dispense with the expensive central processor and its options—along with its expensive wiring. If this is deemed so, card-plus-keypad could be a cheaper system than a sophisticated card-only system.

Physical attribute systems are, or will be, the ultimate in access control systems, but they have yet to stand the test of time in the mainstream of access control applications. Standing alone, they still suffer from the false-accept and false-reject error problems, but in combination with a keypad or card they are even today a reliable top-of-the-line means of access control. At present costs, however, there is a rather limited portion of the spectrum of security situations in which they can be justified.

SUPPLIERS OF ACCESS CONTROL EQUIPMENT AND SYSTEMS

There are several categories of vendors who offer access control and personal identification systems and products for user applications; the following material describes the general characteristics of these vendors, from amongst which the user must choose.

Large Security and Facility Automation Vendors

This vendor category is comprised of substantial companies which can supply a complete turnkey system including all of the user's needs for security electronics and also, in most cases, the added capability for life safety (fire detection and alarm, smoke exhaust, and the like), facility management (heating, ventilation and air conditioning control, energy management), and personnel management (time and attendance, personnel locator). Two of these companies, Honeywell and Johnson Controls, are the major forces in total facility automation. Two are primary among suppliers of equipment and systems of all kinds to the banking industry: Diebold and Mosler. And two are leaders in supplying security equipment and services: American District Telegraph and Wells Fargo Alarm. These vendors do not in all cases install systems that are comprised wholly of products of their own manufacture, but may purchase, for example, card access and keypad access subsystems from vendors of those products, and integrate these subsystems into the total security or facility automation system.

General Security and Alarm Equipment Distributors

These companies are retail and wholesale resellers of products ranging over the spectrum of security devices and equipments, from door contacts and strikes to sirens to CCTV equipment to keypad and card access control equipment. They do not design systems or install equipment, and their offerings in the access control area are generally limited to the simpler, one-portal devices.

Local Alarm Companies

These companies service a limited geographical area with the design of security systems for particular users, and the installation and maintenance of the equipment. They install systems made up of subunits and equipment which they buy from the distributors described above; some may also be factory-franchised dealers for systems such as CCTV and access control. They are generally low-overhead, and therefore economical, sources of routine alarm systems, but few are well-equipped to handle large or multi-capability security or facility management systems.

Security System Houses

This category of vendor is similar in capability to the large security system vendors described above, but is populated by much smaller companies than ADT, Diebold, Johnson, Honeywell, et al. The system house is expert in security system design and in designing a special purpose or customized system to fulfill the user's needs. In general, they purchase all of the equipment needed to create the system—CCTV, alarm components, central computer, access control equipment—from the manufacturers thereof, and their contributed value is in assembling the correct subunits in the correct manner to create the desired system. They frequently also offer the capability to customize the applications computer programs that run on the central computer, even though the principal bulk of the software may be brought from another company.

Access Control Product and System Vendors

These are the approximately 150 companies that are the original manufacturers of the access control equipment included in the products and services purveyed by the other categories of vendors. In a few cases the large system vendors also manufacture their own access control equipment, in a few cases the access control vendors also offer complete security systems, and in a few cases the access control vendors also offer other security products, but in general the access control vendors have always represented a rather pure breed. They, in turn, can be subdivided fairly neatly into the following sub-categories.

Vendors of Keypad Systems

These vendors are generally small companies offering single-door mechanical or electronic keypads, some intended for special applications such as vehicle or boat entry.

Vendors of Card and Token Systems

This sub-category is comprised of two kinds of vendors: one of systems houses that have developed control software for access control and that buy magnetic card readers from other vendors to furnish a complete card access system; the other of vendors that offer other than the conventional magnetic-card system (ultraviolet, various token systems, and so forth) for a specialized purpose such as hotel room security, computer terminal access, social clubs.

Vendors of Card-plus-Keypad Systems

This is the mainstream of access control vendors, offering card (usually the mainstream magnetic coding), keypad, and card-plus-keypad systems, with the access means usually mixable on the same system. The systems can range in size from one or a few portals to many hundreds of portals, and the number of identifiable entrants can range to the tens of thousands. Although they are capable of supplying very large and sophisticated access control systems, these vendors do not in general offer total security systems or facility automation systems. Leading vendors in this category have for many years been Cardkey Systems and Rusco Electronic Systems, but their historical dominance is being challenged by two dozen smaller, aggressive companies with attractive products. Within only the past year, these companies have nearly all rushed to add proximity-card (and in some cases physical attribute) access to their product line, making them complete suppliers of access control systems.

Vendors of Proximity Systems

A small but growing community of vendors that competes with ever-increasing effectiveness with the conventional card access industry, these vendors each offer their own proximity technology within their own access control system; no two are alike, and there is no standardization. Schlage Electronics pioneered, developed, and is the leader in this market segment; Sielox Systems and Mastiff are also long-time suppliers, there are a number of companies with recently developed technology, including old-line access control companies Continental Instruments (using a smart token developed by N.V. Nederlandsche Apparatenfabriek of Holland), Cardkey (using a surface-wave card developed in Australia), and Rusco (with an adaptation of the fish-ID system, from Identification Devices, Inc., of Colorado).

Vendors of Physical Attribute Systems

These vendors each have built their business on a particular kind of physical attribute recognition, and each offers only that one system; keypads or cards are commonly used in conjunction with the system, but that is incidental to the main thrust. The long-time survivor in this business is Stellar Systems' handprint system, but Identix and Fingermatrix are strongly pursuing their fingerprint systems, and Eye Dentify, recently joined to Cardkey, is aggressively marketing the eye-retina system. There are a number of machine-assisted face and signature comparison systems; new announcements are made every year in this area, such as the two voiceprint systems which appeared almost together in 1986.

Vendors of Components

There are also vendors who do not deal with the user of the security system, but offer component parts—card readers, keypads, plastic cards, computer software—to the vendors in the other categories. One noteworthy among these is Sensor Electronics, the owner of the Wiegand-card technology, which either manufactures or licenses every Wiegand card and reader in use anywhere.

Central Station Operators

Central station operators were, until a decade or so ago, strictly in the burglar alarm business, but many are now capable of installing and monitoring access control systems as well.

THE PROCUREMENT PROCESS

Procurement of an access control system or, for that matter, procurement of a total electronic security system, a facility automation system, or a business computer system must be viewed as a project in itself, one which must be approached with thorough management planning and conducted according to a firm list of tasks and a sensible schedule. There are several well-defined phases in the procurement process, and it is important that they all are performed, and that they are performed in the proper order. These phases can be described in terms of the goals that must be reached in order to accomplish a successful procurement.

Understand the Problem that needs to be solved, and decide upon the appropriate solution.

Describe the Solution desired in a form that is definitive and unambiguous, so that the prospective vendors will understand what is required, and people within the organization understand what will be installed and what functions it will perform.

Select a Vendor who can be relied upon to install a system that provides the desired solution, at an appropriate price.

Monitor the Project continuously until the system is installed and working satisfactorily.

We suggest that the following sequence of tasks be carefully followed as the user wends his way through the procurement process.

Initial Education

Before deciding upon the means of access control or electronic security to be used to protect one's facility, one must first have a general understanding of what equipment and systems are available and satisfactory for the purpose intended. These are the tools that will be used to create the system; if one does not have a general understanding of the tools which are available, and the costs of the various kinds of tools, one runs the dual risk of designing a system that requires tools that do not exist, or designing a system that does not take advantage of all the tools which do exist.

There are a number of means through which the prospective user can gain a sufficient education to enable him to make intelligent decisions during the procurement process.

Books

Books such as this one are created to perform the task of educating the user so he can make intelligent system design and buying decisions. One must remember, however, that technology marches on after the book has been published, and any book that has been in print more than five years without revision is likely to be missing some important recent developments.

Trade Magazines

Trade magazines are a source of up-to-date information. There are tens of thousands of trade magazines that are dedicated to every imaginable industry and interest, and among them are several (*Security, Security Management, Security Dealer, Security Systems Administration*) which serve both vendors and users of security equipment and services. A public library having a decent business periodical section will have at least some of these magazines, which present product information and advertisements, how-to articles, and case studies describing how certain kinds of equipment have been used to solve particular problems. One must, of course, be careful to separate objective editorial material from the blatant product promotion present in any trade magazine. There are also trade magazines dedicated to the user's business, whatever it may be, and these will frequently publish articles on security applications in that industry.

Contact with Peers

Contact with peers in the same industry is also useful, but must be approached with some caution. It is useful to know how others in the user's business have approached their security problems, what solutions they have elected, and how satisfactory the results have been. In accepting this information as the basis for his own actions, however, the user must identify and take into account any biases that the informant may have (for example, your informant's brother-in-law works for the company that installed his system), or differences between his security requirements and yours, or flaws in his analysis and procurement procedure (for example, his system does not work satisfactorily because he did not convey all of the appropriate information to his vendor).

Conventions and Trade Shows

Conventions and trade shows can be a convenient and condensed means of conversing with a large number of peers (if it is a convention of the user's own business) or of gaining extensive exposure to security electronics (if it is a security industry trade show, the major of which are the annual convention of the American Society for Industrial Security, and the quarterly International Security Conference Expositions).

One must also approach the security industry trade shows with some caution. In order to gain an understanding of what equipment exists, what functions they perform, and at what price, it is necessary to talk with the salespeople who staff the booths, and to gather descriptive literature; the necessary *quid pro quo* is that the inquirer's name and company are left with the salesperson, and this frequently results—if the sales force is as aggressive as they should be—in intensive exposure to too few vendors before the users has properly defined the system that he plans to purchase. Vendor input is appropriate, desired, and valuable, but it must not be allowed to pollute the initial phases of the procurement process. (As an example, we were called into a situation some years ago where the user's first step had been to invite several vendors whom he encountered at trade shows to analyze his requirement and submit proposals: three sales engineers from three different companies submitted proposals with costs of $135,000, $275,000, and $425,000—all for solving presumably the same problem. The requirement cannot be left to the eye of the beholder.)

Consultants

Consultants are another alternative, one which provides instant education if the consultant is one whose continuous practice is in the security electronics area. The consultant acts as counsel to the user for this purpose just as his attorney and accountant do in their areas of expertise. There are a number of reliable and reputable independent consultants in security electronics (check the trade journals, ask peers for references, call the editor of one of the security trade magazines or of a publishing house specializing in security books—this one, for instance), and several of the larger architect-and-engineering firms provide this service.

System Analysis

Before any operation can be automated, it must first be understood. The various spaces to be protected must be surveyed and described, the population which must be permitted to move about the facility must be known and categorized, and the potential threats from outside must be anticipated. Then, the degree of security which is required must be decided upon: There are various degrees ranging from the relatively loose (for example, a college dormitory or a public lodging facility) to the "moat-and-drawbridge" philosophy (for example, the nuclear power plant or the prison). There are also those situations where the security philosophy must be different at different times (for example, the security required at a bank during business hours is different from the security required at night).

This analysis should be done without specific consideration of security equipment, products, and services, although it will be aided by the knowledge gained during the initial education task. The result should be a description of the facility and its various spaces in terms of the access to be granted to them for various categories of persons, and at various times of day and week. In nearly all cases, of course, there are existing—even if manual and even if minimal—security provisions and procedures that will serve as the starting point for this total analysis of security needs. The improvements in security should be considered as to whether they are essential, desirable, or merely wishes, so that when cost analyses are later done, those items that are not essential can be included or not depending upon whether or not they are deemed worth the price. The anticipated growth and other changes in the business over the next five years should also be described in the system analysis, along with their impact upon the security requirements, so that sufficient expansion capability is provided for in the final system.

The Functional Specification

The functional specification is the most important document in the procurement process; it describes the security requirements of the user, the equipment which he requires to satisfy those security requirements and the performance required from the equipment, and the systems and procedures that will cause all of the equipment and people which are parts of the system to meld smoothly together into the total security system.

The functional specification combines the system analysis task with the initial education task, resulting in a document that describes the security requirements of the facility in terms of the equipment that will be procured and installed. It will contain diagrams of the facility, all of its spaces, and all of its portals. It will specify which portals are to be controlled and by what means. It will itemize those persons who are to be allowed access through each portal, at what hours and on what days. It will describe the reports that are required from the system, and what special features—for example, logging, duress alarm, anti-passback, and so forth—are to be included in the system.

There are also a number of items which the functional specification should not include; most of these are overly specific, or overly restrictive: the user should remember that he is not the only person in the world capable of coming up with a good idea, and should leave room in the specification for the vendor to suggest ways and means that may be superior. Some common areas where specifications are overly restrictive are described in the following sections.

The Tailored System Pitfall

There is a frequently overwhelming temptation to require that the system be totally tailored to the user's needs and that it be capable of performing all operations automatically, down to the last detail. The cost of any automated system can be reduced dramatically by taking advantage of the standard capabilities already developed and offered by vendors, and by not automating operations for which the cost exceeds the value received.

Level of Detail

The user is not equipped by education, experience, or expertise to specify the kind of computer to be used, the amount of high-speed or disk memory, the kind of solid-state chips to be used, the rates of transfer of data, and so forth. The user should specify the performance to be achieved in terms of response time at the portals, printing time of the reports, how many days or months of logging records must be kept on-line, etc.; it is the vendor's responsibility to select the appropriate hardware and software to do the job. Minicomputer equipment, on which most centrally controlled access control systems are based, can pretty much be chosen at random from any of the top dozen computer vendors, and they will all do the job with comparable speed and reliability, and at a comparable cost. The computer itself contributes a minor portion of the cost of a system, the major cost elements being the peripherals, software, portal readers, wiring, and installation.*

Similarly, the user should not describe in detail how the software should be written; it is a legitimate action, however, to require that the software be written in a language which is in common industry use and not a singular invention of the vendor. This will enable the user to make modifications to the software himself, if he chooses, or through a software contractor. This will also ensure that the user is not left stranded if the vendor goes out of business. The user might also require the ability to locally and quickly create ad hoc reports on the system, other than those that were originally specified and written into the software.

The Perfect System Temptation

Life is a series of compromises. There is no perfect job, there is no perfect legislation passed by the Congress of the Government at Washington, there are no perfect children (notwithstanding the syrupy mimeographed letters we get from old friends every Christmas), and there is no perfect access control system. One must strive to make the functional specification an effective combination of the available technology, the personnel who will use the system, the stated security requirements, and the vendor who will install the system, while recognizing that compromises will have to be made among all these ingredients if a working system is ever to be installed.

The reverse of being overly restrictive when writing a specification is to be overly vague so that virtually any system proposed can be considered to be responsive to the specification. A proper balance must be achieved, one which

---

*Twenty years ago we calculated that if the cost of the processing electronics in a large computer installation were reduced to zero, the total EDP costs would be reduced by less than 5%; the calculation would be even more dramatic today.

presents clearly the details of the security requirements and the equipment complement that the user estimates will satisfy the security requirements, but just as clearly encourages alternative solutions which are advantageous as to cost, performance, reliability, and so forth, and still satisfies the security requirements.

Compare with the Real World

Notwithstanding that the functional specification has been prepared after having conducted the task of initial education, the equipment requirements of the specification should now be compared against the offerings of the many dozens of vendors who compete in the real world to supply such systems. The user should find that the system that he has described matches the offerings of a substantial number of vendors; if not, he has probably specified a system that is impractical or impossible, or, at best, is a customized system (see "The Tailored System Pitfall") which does not take advantage of the technology already developed and being offered by vendors. There are, of course, occasional security requirements that are far outside of the norm, but these rarely occur in ordinary business and commerce; they are most commonly found in James Bond movies.

Selection of Vendors

One must now select the vendors that will be invited to submit proposals for the system as described by the specification, and the task of comparing the specification with the real world will have identified a number of possibly suitable vendors. For most access control systems there will be from a few dozen to about one hundred vendors that are apparently suitable (and if one spent some time searching, even these numbers could be raised).

The methods of identifying potentially suitable vendors include those methods which were described in the task of initial education, augmented by the use of security industry directories such as those published by *Security Magazine* (Cahners Publishing Co., Newtonville, Mass.), *Security Letter* (New York), and the *Buyers' Guide,* and *State-of-the-Art Report* (published by the author Dan M. Bowers, and described in the Introduction). The *Buyers' Guide* presents sufficient information on all known companies and their products to identify potentially suitable vendors; the various directories give only name and address information for each of the product categories, and one must then go through the tedious process of obtaining literature from all the companies, and the even more tedious process of reviewing the literature and evaluating the products against the user's requirements. Fortunately, there are a sufficient number of vendors who are very visible and the techniques of initial education will usually identify more than enough potentially suitable vendors.

The larger problem, usually, is finding a rational basis for reducing the number of vendors to a manageable quantity, so that the proposals received can be properly evaluated—and interactions with vendor salespersons coped with—without unduly taxing the user's manpower, or requiring an inordinate length of time to complete. As a general guideline, it is most prudent to receive between six and ten proposals, to make certain of being exposed to a reasonable sample of the vendors' capabilities, and to have a reasonable data base across which to compare prices. In order to achieve this, between ten and twenty vendors should be invited to bid, since some will submit nonresponsive proposals, some will combine with others and submit jointly, and some will lose the invitation in their internal paperwork and you will never hear from them again.

Reducing the number of vendors from the fifty or so which are likely to be unearthed during the average search, to ten or even twenty, based solely upon literature and other commonly obtainable information, requires that criteria be adopted that are arbitrary, frequently unfair, and occasionally capricious. It is usually prudent to include some or all of the large companies on the invitation list, since they have demonstrated and established capabilities which should not be ignored. One can include or exclude the smaller companies based upon their geographical proximity and capability. Companies which have installed similar systems in similar industries might be preferred over those whose experience has been in totally different applications. And companies which have been mentioned by your Chairman of the Board—regardless of where he got his information—should probably be included.

The Bidding Process

The bidding process is initiated by sending the invitation to bid (IFB) to the selected vendors. The IFB is comprised of the following three principal ingredients.

The Functional Specification.

Contractual Terms and Conditions under which the user desires to procure the system: these are discussed in detail in the following section.

Description of the Bidding Process. The format in which proposals are desired; procedures for getting additional information, asking questions, getting answers; schedule for bidders' conference and site surveys; procedure, if any, for amendments and addenda to proposals; cost breakdown desired.

About six weeks should be allowed for the preparation of bids. This time period should be divided roughly as follows:

Weeks 1–3: vendors study the IFB, generate questions, decide whether or not they are interested;

Midway: a Bidders' Conference is held (see below);

Weeks 4–6: vendors prepare their detailed proposals.

The *Bidders' Conference* is held for the purpose of efficiently and equitably answering all of the detailed questions which the vendors will generate as they review the detail of the IFB, and should include a site survey so that the vendors can study the actual locations into which they will be required to install equipment, run wiring, and so forth. If a consolidated Bidders' Conference is not held, the user must answer questions and conduct site tours for each of the vendors individually, and this process has the dual drawbacks of a much greater consumption of time of the user's personnel, and the likelihood that different information will be imparted to different vendors, resulting in less uniformity of vendor responses.

Even though the IFB is specific and detailed, and even though there is a Bidders' Conference, there will still be questions and requests for clarification and various other kinds of communications from the vendors during the proposal period; a person within the user's organization should be identified in the IFB as the contact point for these random communications.

The First Cut

Even though the number of potential bidders was intentionally limited, it is efficient business practice to further limit the number of vendors which will have to be examined in detail, by executing a first-cut process using the received proposals alone. Usually about 25% of the proposals received can be immediately rejected because they were unresponsive to or did not understand the specification, did not choose to respond to the user's desires, or are so much higher in price than the other bidders that it is clear they did not perceive an economical solution to the problem. The remainder should be reviewed thoroughly and each vendor should be given the opportunity to explain his proposal and to present his case in person. Vendors, after all, contribute a substantial amount of resources, time and money to analyzing and attempting to solve the user's problem.

Detailed Proposal Evaluation

The user should prepare a checklist of the items that are important to his system, for use in conducting a detailed analysis of the proposals which survive the first cut. This list will vary from one situation to another because of the different security requirements for different facilities, but the following items are generic and should be part of every list.

Security Hardware

Does the equipment proposed satisfy the requirements as to number of portals, number of different persons to be identified, number of time and space zones, logging capability and other options, alarm handling capability, reports to be provided, and so forth?

Is the level of security of the card or keypad units (number of available codes, method of card encoding, and so forth) sufficient for the stated security requirements?

Is the technology used consistent with the state-of-the-art, and not likely to be obsolete within a few years?

Computer Hardware

While the user is not sufficiently expert to evaluate a system in terms of bit densities, semiconductor technology, transfer rates, and so forth, there are some parameters which are both understandable and important to the user.

Is the equipment configuration calculated by the vendor to do the job (amount of high-speed memory, disk storage capacity, printing speed, number of terminals and printers, number and speed of communications ports, and so forth) reasonable? Is it consistent with what the other vendors have estimated? If something sounds too good to be true, it probably isn't.

Is there sufficient expansion capability of memory, disk, portals and alarm handling capability, terminals, printers, etc., to keep pace with the user's growth? Can he migrate upwards to a larger processor without having to replace major elements of his system, most notably the software?

What is the cost of the equipment?

What are the continuing maintenance costs, who will maintain and from where, where are the spare parts stored?

Who will install the equipment, what is the cost of installation, what space is required, what are the environmental requirements?

Is the technology used consistent with the prevailing state-of-the-art?

Computer Software

The user's view of the computer system is perhaps more directly concerned with the software than the hardware, and there are several key points according to which he should evaluate the vendor.

Terminals: base of operation of the terminals, prompting methods, display of alarms, initiation of disk backup, report printing, and so forth.

Standard and operating software (operating system, file management, terminal handling, etc.): features of operation, who makes them, where is the source of support, are they standard or have they been modified?

Applications software: are they standard and proven packages, are they being created especially for this system, or are they combination packages?

Programming language: in what language is the applications software written, is it an industry standard, does it allow transfer to another computer if that becomes necessary?

Ease of modification of the software: can the user change a report or a screen or create a new one?

Continuing support: by whom, from whence?

Training: what is provided, for whom, at what cost?

Additional applications: can they be added easily to the system?

Continuing Costs

The purchase price is paid but once, but there are other costs that will continue for as long as the system is in operation, and these can sometimes exceed, in the aggregate, the purchase price. It is useful to consider the system costs on a five-year basis when comparing different vendors and different purchase options: the purchase or time-payment cost, plus the yearly operating costs for five years, plus the earning value of the cash money paid out computed from the time it was paid out. The following continuing, or recurring, costs should be examined.

Maintenance and repair costs on all the equipment.

Software license fees (some are one-time up-front, others are yearly) and continuing maintenance and upgrade fees.

Supplies and expendables for the computer: paper, ribbons, disks, and so forth.

Other expendables, such as replacement access cards.

Operations and management labor.

Cost to upgrade as increased level of user's business requires additional hardware and/or software.

Expandability

When planning a system, we consider it wise to provide for easy expandability to accommodate the user's projected five-year growth, and then to make certain that the system that is procured can ultimately be expanded to twice that capability. Items which determine the expandability of a system are the ability to add additional terminals, additional high-speed memory, additional disk memory; ability to add additional portal equipments, alarms, and so forth; sufficient number of available codes in the access control means; ability to transfer software to another larger processor in case the current one becomes completely inadequate; and possibly the addition of other programming packages to perform new functions or expanded versions of current functions.

Security and Contingency Capability

Integral to any system is protection against loss and unauthorized use of the system or the data within it, the ability to recover and continue operations after a system failure, and the ability to operate (perhaps for a period of several days) if the equipment ceases to function. In determining whether or not a proposed system provides these capabilities, the user must explore the following kinds of questions.

What facilities are provided to limit access to terminals, data bases and files, programs, and so forth, to authorized persons only? (Access control capabilities for the access control system, as it were.)

What procedures are standard for copying of files so that a backup file is available in the event of destruction of the main file? What are the recovery procedures under these circumstances?

Does the capability exist to carry on limited and less efficient operation in the presence of failure of some portion of the system (degraded mode)?

Can an alternative site or loaner equipment be made the basis of a contingency plan, enabling operations to continue after a disaster?

What is the availability of spare parts and replacement equipments: where are they and how fast can they be put in place when needed?

Vendor Credibility

This is the most important consideration of all. The best written specification, the most thorough proposal evaluation, and the most tightly written contract cannot insure a satisfactory system if the contractor is inept or a charlatan, or if he goes broke. The user must carefully examine the vendor's integrity, capability, and responsibility through analysis of the following areas.

What is the vendor's financial strength? The transient nature of the computer and electronics business, where any two engineers or programmers gathered together in a garage can become a company, has left many a user with an incomplete or unsatisfactory system because the vendor was underfinanced, or had poor business judgment, or was a charlatan.

How many contractors are there, how much of the system is supplied by the vendor and how much is supplied by other companies? The user is equally at risk if one of the suppliers of a critical subunit fails, and they, therefore, must be evaluated as thoroughly as is the prime contractor.

Who does the maintenance, and from whence? If there are units supplied by other companies, who services them? Where are the maintenance persons located, how long does it take them to arrive, is coverage available other than prime shift, where is the backup support in case the local person cannot solve the problem?

What is the history of the vendor's company, how long has it been in business, how stable is it, what is its financial position, who are the key personnel and how commited are they to the company?

Visit the vendor! No quantity of slick proposals, well-written literature, and expensive dinners with the salesman can substitute for the on-the-spot impression of the vendor's office, engineering laboratories, and factory.

Talk with his customers! Visit them! See an installation similar to yours that the vendor has installed, and review with the customer—uninhibited by the presence of any vendor personnel—his degree of satisfaction with the performance of both the vendor and the system, and the quality of his working relationship with the vendor personnel from the president to the salesman to the engineers to the installers.

Contractual Terms

The following sections of this chapter are devoted to the details of contractual terms and conditions, which will be specified in the IFB. Part of the proposal evaluation process is to assess the vendor's compliance with the user's desires as specified in the IFB, to evaluate any deviations in terms of their seriousness, and to identify any terms that represent unacceptable risk. Following are some of the areas to be examined.

How many vendor contracts are there? Is there one prime contractor, or are separate contracts to be written with separate vendors for the computer hardware, software, access control equipment, electrical and mechanical installation, and so forth?

How many maintenance contracts are there? Does one vendor service all of the hardware?

What are the financial alternatives? Purchase, lease, rent, license, and so forth.

What are the acceptance criteria and procedures?

What are the payment terms, what is the schedule of payments, is the schedule tied to milestones in the completion of the work?

What are the warranty terms and guarantees? Are there performance bonds and penalty clauses? What are the means of recourse and settlement of disputes?

Selection and Contract Negotiation

After having done a thorough job of conducting the procurement process as described in the foregoing material, the user will usually find himself in the pleasant circumstance of having two or three vendors with which he is completely satisfied; a choice must then be made and the contract negotiated and signed with the successful bidder. We deem it prudent to complete the contractual process before advising the losing companies that they will not be granted the work since there might be surprises when the lawyers get into the act, and these surprises may be of sufficient import to warrant a change in the decision as to the identity of the successful bidder.

CONTRACT TERMS AND CONDITIONS:
SUPPORT REQUIREMENTS

In addition to the performance requirements that will be thoroughly covered in the functional specification, there are a number of items related to the access control system which must also be adequately described. If a card access system is to be implemented, there are a number of considerations and logistics with respect to the cards themselves that must be noted. Installation, documentation, training, acceptance criteria, maintenance: all must be discussed between the user and the vendor, and the final contract should describe how all of these requirements have been agreed to be performed. The following material describes the kinds of details that must be included in this portion of the IFB, and later included in the contract in such modified form as the user and vendor have agreen upon. Clearly, an important part of the proposal evaluation process is judging how closely each bidder conforms to the user's stated desires, and how serious are any proposed departures.

Access Control Cards

Access control cards are an integral part of most access control systems, and they must be durable and readily available.

Availability: does the vendor supply the cards? are there alternative sources as well?

Coding of cards with the company code, employee identification, and other information required by the system, must be carefully controlled and secured so as to prevent both duplicating and counterfeiting of cards.

Pocket clips, employee pictures, company logotypes, and the like, are frequently affixed to the cards. How is this done, and by whom?

Cost of cards, and the delivery time for the cards, must be quoted by the vendor, both for the initial quantities required to begin using the system, and for smaller quantities for later additions and replacement.

In-house preparation of cards can be done by the user if he so desires; in this event, the vendor should be required to quote on the cost and delivery of the necessary card preparation equipment and materials.

Installation

Installation requires skills that range from sophisticated computer equipment and software, to tradesman-level electrical wiring, to the bang-holes-in-the-walls class of carpentry and masonry work. Sometimes the user has maintenance people who perform the contracting work, sometimes the vendor does the work, more frequently neither of them does and a local electrical contractor will be engaged. These details, including who is responsible for identifying and handling union requirements and problems, and applicable building code and safety requirements, must all be addressed.

Communications wiring from portal equipment to multiplexers to central computer site. Wiring distances must be determined, gauge and number of wires must be specified, responsibility must be assigned.

Electrical power will be required at the central controller site, at the multiplexer sites, and at the portal for the card readers and keypads, and also for the door strikes and any alarm points.

Installation of portal equipment will require electrical work and also the mechanical work of making holes in walls, installing door hardware, and so forth.

Central computer and control equipment is normally installed by the vendor, including all peripheral and communications equipment. The vendor must specify the site requirements for wiring, climate conditioning, electrical power, and floor space layout, for the equipment that he proposes.

Testing and Commissioning

Testing and commissioning of all equipment and software is performed by the vendor. Any faults due to installation and construction performed by the customer should be repaired by the customer, unless they were due to faulty specifications received from the vendor. All other faults discovered during the testing and commissioning phase should be repaired by the vendor.

Complete Documentation

Complete documentation should be submitted by the vendor at the completion of the contract, and before final payment is made. The documentation package should include at least the following materials.

As-Installed Wiring Diagrams of site and subunit interconnections.

Specifications and Description of Operation for all units of electronic equipment.

Maintenance Manual for all units of electronic equipment, including instructions for initial installation, setup and calibration, test, diagnosis, repair, and preventive maintenance.

List of Parts for all units of equipment, along with prices and sources for each.

Recommended Spare Parts List for all units of equipment.

Software System Description, including flow charts, parameter tables, narrative description of operation, and so forth.

Software Applications Source Code and Listing is required to be in the user's possession so that the user is protected against the untimely demise of the vendor, or the vendor's abandonment of the access control business. Since this source code is frequently regarded as a proprietary and confidential business asset by the vendor, the vendor is frequently unwilling to provide it to the user; another means of providing adequate protection to the user is for the source code to be placed into escrow in such a manner that the user will have immediate access to it if the vendor becomes incapable of or unwilling to support the user's system.

Operator's Manual with detailed instructions for performing all operator functions, such as alarm handling, portal control, and data base alteration.

System Manager's Manual with detailed instructions for performing all management level functions such as password control, priority level assignments and alterations, file backup and reloads, and so forth.

Training

Training of the user personnel should be performed by the vendor to the appropriate level of effectiveness. The following kinds of training programs are typically required as part of an access control system contract.

Management Indoctrination Seminar for site managers, senior company management, and other personnel not directly involved with the system but who need to be conversant with its functions and operations.

Operator's Training Course should be exhaustive, and should include testing for proficiency as a requirement for successful completion.

System Manager's Training Course should also be exhaustive and include a final exam.

Site Maintenance Personnel Training Course will be required if the user's personnel are going to perform some of the maintenance of the system, for example maintenance of the portal hardware, subunit-level replacement of card readers, alarm sensors, and so forth; this training should be exhaustive within the boundaries of the maintenance to be performed, and should also include proficiency testing.

Videotaping of the training sessions should be considered by the user, so that they can be repeated later for training new personnel, and as refresher courses for all personnel. The user may also want to require that the vendor be willing to repeat the training sessions—for additional money—at future times for refresher and new training purposes.

CONTRACT TERMS AND CONDITIONS:
PRICE, DELIVERY, GENERAL

There are a number of contractual items that have to do with the purchase of any equipment or system, whether it be an access control system or a crusher-sorter for strip mining of coal. The following material presents a suggestion list; the user's contracts department and legal counsel will doubtless have contributions to make in this area as the purchasing policies of the user's company are melded with the specific requirements for the access control system.

Warranties

Warranties on all the equipment included in the system must be specified. Warranties may be different (and may be from different sources) for the computer equipment, the software, the access control equipment, and the portal hardware.

Beginning of Warranty

The beginning of warranty must be specified. Does it begin when the equipment is delivered to the user or when it is accepted by the user? In cases where the vendor buys subunits from a third party, the original manufacturer's warranty might begin when the equipment was delivered to the user's vendor.

F.O.B. Point

The F.O.B. point must be known. That is, does the vendor's quotation include freight?

Transfer of Title

Does the user own the equipment when it is delivered on his premises, when he pays for it, or when he accepts it?

Liability for Loss

When does the user assume liability for loss of or damage to the equipment?

Price Quotations

Price quotations should be broken down into the system constituents, in order to make it possible for the user to evaluate specific capabilities in terms of their cost to him; price breakdowns also make vendor-to-vendor comparisons more easy to do on a rational basis during the proposal evaluation phase. A typical level of price breakdown is as follows.

Cost of Central Computing Equipment, including peripheral equipments and software.

Per-Unit Cost to Expand the complement of computing equipment, for example, additional memory, disk, terminals, printers.

Portal Equipment cost per unit, expanded to total site costs.

Multiplexers or Concentrators required for the portal equipment: unit costs and total site costs.

Cost of any Proposed Alternative or optional feature.

Labor Cost breakdown: site survey; engineering and design; electrical contracting work; mechanical contracting work; installation; testing and commissioning; training; documentation; support during warranty period.

Cost of the Access Control Cards whether they are supplied by the vendor or produced in-house.

Cost of Maintenance Contracts for computer equipment after the warranty period, for computer software and for access control equipment.

Price Quotations

Price quotations should be required to be firm on the vendor's part for a sufficient period of time to allow the user to evaluate all proposals and make a selection. A reasonable period is 90 days.

Acceptance Test

Acceptance test criteria and procedures must be described in detail in the contract.

Remedies

Remedies should be agreed upon, in the event that all does not go as wonderfully as planned during the performance of the contract. Will there be penalties paid by the vendor if the vendor fails to complete the project on time or does not achieve

100% of the performance specified? Will there be costs paid by the customer if the vendor is delayed due to actions of the customer, if, for example, the computer room is not made ready on time? In the event of irreconcilable differences between the parties, will there be provisions for arbitration or shall we all go to court?

Payment Terms and Schedule

Payment terms and a payment schedule must also be agreed upon. Typical terms are of the following sort:

- 15% of the contract price upon delivery and acceptance of all design and installation drawings and detailed equipment specifications;
- 50% of the contract price upon delivery of all materials to the jobsite;
- 25% of the contract price upon completion of installation and commencement of commissioning;
- 10% of the contract price after acceptance of the system including completion of all training, documentation, and the like.

PROJECT MANAGEMENT AND MONITORING

The most certain method of insuring that any system project will be a disaster is for the user to assume that after the contract has been signed, all responsibility rests with the vendor, and the user can ignore the project until the vendor returns some months later with the completed system. The customer cannot assume that he has perfectly described his needs and desires in the performance specification, and the vendor cannot presume that he can accurately divine the nature of any pieces that are missing from the specification, or resolve by himself any conflicts within the specification. There must be continuous interaction and interplay between customer and contractor as the project proceeds.

Phases of the Project

Each project proceeds through a well-defined series of phases from the signing of the contract to the signing of the final acceptance papers, as follows.

Site Survey, Investigation, Data Gathering. First, all the detailed information required for design and construction must be obtained and analyzed.

Design, Engineering, Programming.

Site Preparation. Running the wiring, installing the portal access control equipment and hardware, making the central control room ready.

Delivery of Equipment. Equipment is delivered to the site.

Installation of Equipment.

Unit Testing. The individual units of equipment are tested in place.

System Testing and Commissioning. The entire system is tested, one function at a time, one portal at a time, one alarm at a time, then in combinations until the total system has been fully tested as an entity.

Training. Customer personnel are trained.

Delivery of Documentation. Materials.

Acceptance Testing. The customer—who is now the owner—may accept the system subject to the correction of some remaining defects which were identified during the acceptance testing; the list of defects is commonly known as the "punch list."

Correction of Punch List Items.

Submittals

One means of maintaining effective and accurate communication between the vendor and the customer during the project is known as the submittals process. Submittals are various documents which the vendor must create and submit to the customer for approval before certain phases of the work may begin, or before the work may progress from one phase to another. Typical submittals during an access control system project are as follows.

Site Construction Drawings including wiring and installation drawings and instructions.

Equipment Specifications including installation requirements, electrical requirements, climatic requirements, size and weight.

Central Site physical layout including power and wiring.

Training Schedules and Curricula.

Unit Test Procedure and Schedule.

Commissioning Procedure and Schedule.

Final Test Procedure.

Supervision

Supervision of the project will usually be the responsibility of the vendor, except for any work items which have been defined as the responsibility of the customer. Electrical and mechanical contractors, if they are under contract to the vendor, will be managed by the vendor, and must be held subject to all conditions of the contract which have been agreed upon between the vendor and the customer.

Progress Reports

Progress reports, in writing, should be required from the vendor at intervals which can range from weekly to monthly, depending on the length of the project and the buyer's desires. They are a means of enforcing the discipline of organization upon the project team. To the report prepared by the vendor should be added a similar monthly report prepared by the customer personnel who are responsible for monitoring the project; this packet should be circulated among the appropriate management persons of the customer organization, so that those not directly involved with the project will be kept continuously appraised of its progress and problems. In addition to these written progress reports, there should be regular and formal meetings between the project personnel of the vendor and of the customer, at which meetings progress, plans, and problems are discussed in a constructive manner. Such meetings should generally not be held more frequently than monthly, since they can consume appreciable manpower to prepare for, travel to, and attend; and they should not be construed as sufficient to replace a close day-to-day working relationship between the vendor and customer personnel working on the project.

Changeover and Parallel Run

Special attention needs to be given to the changeover period, where the old security procedures and mechanisms are changed over to the new system which the vendor is installing. Until the new system is accepted, the old—presumably manual or semi-automated—methods must remain in place. These will need to be adjusted, sometimes on a daily basis, during the construction phase, due to such events as the need for outside contractors to be allowed inside normally secured spaces, changing of wiring to old alarm systems, temporary disconnection of power while new equipments are installed, and so forth. The customer must be certain that adequate security continues to be provided during this period of continual disruption and unique exposure.

When the new system is complete, but before it has been fully tested and accepted, both the old system and the new system will be in place. The old security system should not be dismantled until the customer is fully convinced that the new system is completely working and that his operations personnel are completely capable of coping with any eventuality using the new system. Until that time, we recommend that both the old and the new system be kept in place and working in parallel, and that changeover to the new system be made gradually on a piecemeal basis, perhaps over a period of several weeks.

Chapter 11

The Future of Access Control and Electronic Security Systems

Predicting the future can be a chancy business, notwithstanding the claimed successes of Nostradamus, the Oracle of Delphi, and King Arthur's Merlin (all of whose successes probably ensued from the fact that their predictions were sufficiently vague and ambiguous that nearly any eventuality could be deemed as having been predicted). It is far safer to identify trends and to analyze how specific areas of security practices and technology might sensibly progress in concert with those trends, and we shall offer our prognostications on that basis.

Since security electronics, of which access control is a part, is fundamentally based upon electronic and computer technology, it is therefore appropriate to begin with a review of the important trends in that technology.

The solid-state revolution will continue unabated for the foreseeable future; even though it is certainly a misnomer to call something a "revolution" that continues for half a century, the results continue to be dramatic from one decade to the next. In the first decade of the revolution, the transistor freed us from systems that occupied large amounts of space, consumed enormous amounts of power, and generated tremendous amounts of heat that had to be carried away. In the second decade, the integrated circuit gave us tenfold improvements in space required and power consumed, and a more than tenfold increase in the speed and reduction of the cost of the electronic componentry within a system. In the third decade, large-scale integration has given us hundred-fold improvements in these important parameters, with the net result that we can now carry in our hand computing equipment power that would have filled up a room before the revolution. There will unlikely be a lessening in the pace of these improvements within our working lifetimes.

Increasing computerization of all the mechanisms we encounter in both our working and personal lives has resulted from the improvements made during the solid-state revolution, and this will also continue apace. Microcomputers are now incorporated within our telephone, copying machines, and desk calculators, as well as our television sets, washing machines, and automobiles (thereby making obsolete the single automotive skill of those of us who finally learned to tune the ignition: the points, vacuum advance, and rotor are now buried in an electronic chip). In general, these electronic controllers are both cheaper and more reliable than their mechanical or electromechanical predecessors, although there is still progress to be made, as anyone who has just paid to replace the electronic ignition system in his automobile can attest.

Decreased power consumption of the new solid-state mechanisms has been and will continue to be important to the increased computerization. Decreased power consumption permits tremendous computer power to be implemented without requiring special electrical service and wiring, and special air conditioning to remove the heat generated. It permits modest, but very useful, amounts of computing power to be run from ordinary batteries. And it enables simple functions to be performed for a period of years using small batteries the size of a dime.

Greater reliability will continue to be one of the most important benefits of the solid state revolution, and it is also very visible in the non-electronic mechanisms of the computer—printers, disk drives, and keyboards. Those who were not part of the industry thirty, and even twenty, years ago may have difficulty appreciating how much the improved reliability over that period has contributed to the ability of the computer industry to permeate and improve all facets of our working and personal lives. A computer with the power of today's PC would have experienced at least one breakdown per month, with consequent disruption of vital operations (since it was likely to be the only computer within the company) and cost of the service personnel; today few of us even carry a maintenance contract on our PC. (Of course, rare is the PC which is assigned to any operation which might be termed "vital.")

Throw-away components, the basic building blocks of an electronic equipment (transistors, integrated circuits, CRTs, and so forth), are inherently unrepairable, just as were their predecessors the vacuum tubes. But the dramatic cost reductions engendered by the solid state revolution have now brought us into an era where many items are economically unrepairable, even though they are physically capable of being repaired: thus the term "throw-away components." If you bought an electronic watch or calculator for $20, and the repairman's charge is $40/hour, you cannot afford to have it repaired if it will take more than a few minutes of his time. If you bought a home computer on sale at Kiddie Korner for $69, can you afford to even have a serviceman look at it? (Actually, for most home computers, you are better off looking in the local "bargain news" for the many advertisements from those who discovered that even at $69 there was no useful function for the machine in their home, and are willing to part with it for $20.) As the cost of skilled labor continues to rise, and the cost of the electronic equipment continues to decrease, the amount of electronics in our junkyards will burgeon.

Regarding human comfortability with computers, in the early days of computerization, we included as part of the project the careful indoctrination, education, and coddling of the users of the new systems, and we were not unfamiliar with reluctance, resistance, fear, and occasional sabotage and violence from those who believed that their way of worklife, or even their jobs, were threatened. Twenty years of the permeation of computer equipment has convinced the users that progress is inexorable, and that so is the change in work methods and the threats to jobs. The microwave oven controls, the TV games, the digital watch, along with all the computerized systems in the workplace, have made for a familiarity with these formerly fearsome mechanisms. The children are learning computers in school and with Speak-and-Spell, and the toddlers have digital talking teddy bears. And every third program on television features robots, a talking computer named HAL, or James Bond-type gadgetry for use in quickly dispatching one's enemies (the other two-thirds feature old fashioned means for dispatching one's enemies, like a .357 magnum, and soap opera *menages-a-trois* which are definitely nontechnical). This hard-won familiarity with high technology will be a considerable boon as the applications of electronic and computer equipment continue their geometric progression.

These trends in the advance of technology, coupled with an increase in the number and level of security threats, real or perceived, as opportunities and temptations increase and morality and respect for property and authority decrease, lead us to anticipate a dramatic growth in the use of electronic security equipment and systems. In the following sections we shall preview the likely progression in each of the constituents of electronic security which we have discussed.

THE FUTURE OF ACCESS CONTROL

The following trends in access control technology, equipment, and practices in coming years should be considered by vendors as they plan their new product offerings, and users as they design their new security systems, in both cases for the purpose of creating systems which will not be obsoleted by new developments too rapidly.

The Active Card

The active card, also known as the smart card or token, is a developing area which cannot be ignored: complete microcomputers, along with their power source, can now be self-contained on a credit-card-size card. The major credit card companies are already testing these cards, and this will result in cards being produced in sufficient quantity that prices will begin to approach those of the simpler present-day access control cards. If one adds the storage capability of the laser card concept to the computational capability of the smart card, the result could be a powerful multi-purpose computer system which can be carried in the wallet and plugged in to computer terminals for access control, financial transactions, medical history, and other purposes as yet unconceived.

Notwithstanding the vast potential of this personal-computer-on-a-card, there are several arguments against a swift penetration of it into the access control application. First, security is generally better served when the ingredients—access codes, time zones, and so forth, are kept within the system; that is, the less intelligence that is outside of the system's control (in the wallet of the user) the more security is provided. Second, the more mundane current cards have completely adequate coding capability for all access control purposes. Third, even at only a few dollars difference in cost—and the current difference is much larger than that—several thousand cards and their continuing replacements and additions will result in a substantial cost difference.

The Universal Card

Although competition among all the services that are based upon plastic cards, and among the companies that offer these services, is a significant deterrent to standardization, there is no technological or operational reason why a single card cannot serve the multiple purposes of access control, credit card, driver's license, and so on. Further, there is no need for such a card to be any smarter than today's cards used for these individual purposes. If the card is used only as a machine-readable means of identifying a person, and if the security controls—such as time and space zones and card lockout—are contained within the data base of the system, and if a PIN is used to guard against lost and stolen card problems, then any magnetic-stripe (since magnetic-stripe cards are the standard credit and bank cards) card can serve as identification. The user might be given the choice of what card—American Express, Visa, MasterCard, Mobil Oil—to use in the system, depending upon what card he chooses not to leave home without. The American Bankers' Association standard for magnetic-stripe recording makes this kind of operation a practical possibility today, and a likely candidate to be in widespread use in five years or so.

Wireless Systems

Installation and wiring of an access control system, and indeed of any electronic security or other building automation system, is a major part of the cost of such a system. Further, the problem is even more costly to solve if the building is already built than if it is being newly designed. Wireless security, alarm, and fire systems will continue to become more popular, and the new technology of cellular telephone communications will raise some interesting new possibilities in the design of security systems.

Computer Security

Computer security is in its infancy, and the equipment, software, and techniques for computer and communications security which were described in Chapter 3 are only the beginning of what will ultimately be provided. Access control means for computer terminals and personal computers will become routine features of this equipment in the not-too-distant future.

Physical Attribute Systems

Physical attribute systems will soon begin to be accepted as viable by users and security planners. It will also begin to be recognized that, similar to the method of encoding a card in a card access system, the security of a personal attribute system does not depend a great deal on which attribute the system is based upon, so long as the total system (for example, attribute-plus-card or PIN) is properly designed. Despite a continuing trend of reduced prices, despite an improved faith in the technology, and because of the adequate security provided by less exotic systems, these systems will continue to be viewed as top-of-the-line and justifiable only in particular situations, for most of the next decade.

Proximity Systems

Proximity systems have, within the past several years, captured a significant share of the access control market for the first time. Combined with the new capabilities conferred by the availability of increasingly intelligent devices at increasingly lower costs, we can expect that more applications will be solved by these access control systems in which the access card does not have to be inserted into a reader.

ARTICLE IDENTIFICATION AND SURVEILLANCE SYSTEMS

We have alluded in earlier chapters to Electronic Article Surveillance systems (EAS) because of their usefulness as one kind of alarm system. In discussing the future, it is appropriate that we devote a bit more attention to these systems, because we foresee both a current similarity and a future melding of the technologies and products used for personal identification (and therefore access control) and those used for article identification and surveillance.

Article Identification

The longstanding method of article identification has been the bar code, in its simplest, visible form. The Postal Service has sprayed it onto our letters and packages so that they can be tracked and routed (although they have since gone to a magnetic spray-on), manufacturers of goods have affixed bar codes to their packages so that inventory accounting can be quickly accomplished, and consumer products, such as groceries, now have bar codes affixed so that pricing (and, as a byproduct, inventory control and re-ordering) can be done without human transcription and its consequent cost and error. The bar code continues to be used in all but a few percent of article identification applications.

Up until very recently, bar codes could be read only from very close proximity, by passing them through a reader (impractical with large or irregular packages), or in close proximity to a reader (as on a conveyer belt passing by a reading station), or using a hand-held wand which was manually wiped over the code. Within the past half a dozen years, readers have been developed that can read the codes from distances of up to several feet, whether the code is upside down or backwards; these readers utilize laser optical systems.

Electronic Article Surveillance

On the security side of article identification, EAS, the problem has always been, not to identify a particular article or kind of product, but to detect if any article is removed from a premises, and to do so from a distance, without the necessity of inserting the identifying tag into a reader, an action few shoplifters are willing to perform. EAS tags, therefore, have always been "screamers," which sound an alarm whenever they are moved into an interrogating RF field. Now some EAS manufacturers are examining means of obtaining more than one bit of information from the EAS tag; for example, to have it scream a different signal when the shoplifter is attacking it with a pair of wire cutters in the fitting room.

Meanwhile, on the article identification side, vendors and users are exploring means of identification which have the same information content (that is, number of code bits) as bar codes but do not need to be visible for scanning, and these means usually revolve around some RF interrogation-response system very similar to those described in Chapter 7 as proximity access control systems.

Common Direction of Movement

Three industries currently serving three different markets, and mainly comprised of three different sets of vendors, are moving from three different directions towards a common point. The EAS people, who have always been in the RF business, are moving to add more bits to their RF transmissions. The EAI people, who have always been in the optical-reading business with plenty of bits, are moving to use RF transmissions without sacrificing any bits. And the access control people, who have been in the magnetic-in-contact reading business with plenty of bits, are increasingly moving to RF, proximity, techniques, also without being willing to sacrifice any bits.

It does not require Nostradamus, the Oracle of Delphi, or Merlin to predict that these three industries will one day comprise a single identification business sector served by a single set of vendors. In fact, some of these vendors in each of the three areas are already beginning to make overtures toward crossing-over.

THE FUTURE OF ALARM SYSTEMS

Since we devoted a considerable portion of Chapter 1 to presenting the fundamentals of alarm systems, since alarm systems are an important part of any total security system, and since the proper relationship between the alarm system and the access control system is vital to the proper functioning of the access control system itself, it is appropriate that we also view the trends in alarm systems, equipment, and technology.

Sensors

Continued evolutionary improvements in the quality and reliability of present types of alarm sensors and their electronics, along with reductions in their cost, will continue as a result of incremental improvements in materials, technology, and manufacturing techniques. This has already led to the introduction of dual sensors (known as "verified technology" in the alarm business) that incorporate two kinds of sensors linked in a single package. For example, there are new sensors for space protection which incorporate both an ultrasonic (or in some cases microwave) sensor and an infrared sensor; both of these sensors must detect an intruder in order for an alarm to be sounded, thus helping to overcome the false-alarm tendencies of each individual technique. This is a convenient and much less costly method of providing one kind of the multiple-and-combination systems previously discussed. (Note, however, that if both sensors must agree that an intrusion has taken place, this causes the concomitant risk that no alarm will ever be sounded if either sensor fails: there is still no free lunch.)

Ultimately, the increasing capability and the decreasing cost of microcomputer electronics will make possible an intelligent sensor that is capable of evaluating a potential intrusion more thoroughly before sounding an alarm (for example, for an infrared sensor, determining the difference between a warm body and a gust of warm air) and of being more accurately supervised by its central control (for example, by the exchange of digitally-coded messages). This intelligence will also allow greater combinational use of sensors and the interpretation of sequences of detected events (triggering of a portal alarm followed by triggering of a space alarm indicates that someone entered the room, whereas either alone may be a false alarm).

Communications

For those facilities using commercial central station monitoring services, and for those who must communicate alarm signals among separate buildings which are not contained within a single captive perimeter, the greatest coming technological change will be in the method of communicating the signals. The alarm industry relied for many decades on directly strung wire (in Holmes' day, the wires were strung from roof-to-roof as the installer wished, without necessarily having consulted the building owner) owned by the telephone company. The telephone company is no longer interested in obtaining revenues from only one customer per wire, since modern multiplexing technology allows the wire to be shared by many customers; further, there is neither enough copper nor enough room under the streets for everyone to have his own wire *ad infinitum*.

Multiplex systems and direct dial using conventional telephone lines are widely used, but at the risk of greater exposure to outside influences and telephone wire outages than a direct wire. Radio systems have captured a number of customers in recent years, but they have thus far proven sufficiently unreliable that nearly all systems are operated redundantly with another communications technique such as direct dial. This is not necessarily bad news since, as we have observed before, the combination of two simple systems can frequently provide greater security than one sophisticated system.

The telephone company's new offering is derived-channel, in which the normal telephone lines carry low-frequency signals that do not interfere with the normal operation of the telephone, nor does the telephone interfere with the low-frequency signals. They provide a direct path of communication independent of whether the telephone is in use, but they do require that the telephone line is in place. Other methods being promoted are cable-TV lines, communication over cellular radio facilities using the interband gaps, and direct communication using satellite channels that would be owned by the central station. It will be a decade or so before the winning technology emerges, but it has always proven risky to bet against the telephone company.

THE FUTURE OF CLOSED-CIRCUIT TELEVISION SYSTEMS

CCTV is an integral part of a total security system and must function smoothly in conjunction with the access control system—and, indeed, CCTV is considered by some market research firms to be a part of the access control industry.

The future of CCTV will be affected substantially by improvements in technology, but there is also much room for improvement in the way the existing tools are utilized, and in designing systems which have the appropriate synergy with those other important elements of the total security system, the alarm system and the access control system. We foresee, for example, a growing number of mixed film CCTV systems which take advantage of both the immediacy of CCTV operation and the inexpensive permanence of film. We also expect to see more creative use of slo-scan TV in appropriate combination with regular cameras and recorders, and integrated with the alarm electronics.

Solid-State Devices

On the technology side, the solid-state electronic revolution, which has within a decade totally transformed both the computer business and the consumer electronics business, is now spreading to encompass business areas that offer smaller volume markets than those early targets. Solid-state cameras already exist, and there is no reason to believe that they will not gradually equal and then surpass both the performance and cost of vacuum-tube-technology cameras over the course of the next five years, just as solid-state electronics has done in the other applications areas. This will result in smaller and lighter weight cameras which are more reliable, rugged, and cheaper, consume less power, and are more easily concealable.

On the receiving end, a similar sequence of events will occur with monitors as the venerable vacuum tube is supplanted by one of several technologies, both solid-state and other tube-types, which have been touted for a decade as the breakthrough to the true flat-panel display (a TV screen not much thicker than the picture on the wall). However, despite prodigious amounts of both research and development and public relations to date, we do not expect that there will be a reasonably priced production-model flat-panel display with performance approaching that of current tubes, before the mid-1990s.

Control Electronics

In control electronics, many new options are appearing and will continue to appear, fueled by both the continuing advances in solid-state electronics and the creativity of electronic security system designers. Control electronics may be packaged into the camera module, thus distributing the system intelligence so that all decisions need not be made at a central computer and transmitted to the camera. Alarm sensors will be integrated with cameras, so that the camera is activated only after an alarm, or a predetermined sequence of alarms, is detected. And CCTV system controls will more and more become an integral part of the total central control system for the total security system, rather than being freestanding sub-systems which are integrated at the system level, as is now usually the case.

Communications

In the area of communications, there is currently a considerable upheaval afoot in the technology of communicating alarm signals over medium and long distances, but this has less effect upon CCTV monitoring systems than it does upon the regular alarm system business. Where there is need for transmission of CCTV signals over these distances—for example, there are central monitoring services which monitor CCTV pictures rather than alarm signals—private microwave transmission systems are usually used. Within a building, which is the usual distance requirement for CCTV transmissions, we expect a trend towards the "data highway," a kind of local area network using a broadband carrier such as coaxial cable or fiber optics, to simultaneously carry a multiplicity of CCTV, alarm, and voice signals. Technologically, this data highway could also carry other signals such as facsimile, computer data, and the like, but there are new security risks created if the security communications system is made available to other users; therefore, a separate system for the security signals is appropriate.

Slo-Scan CCTV

Slo-scan CCTV is a perfectly adequate technique for many security purposes, and it is presently considerably under-utilized. It is an economical means of picture-transmission-only, since it can utilize ordinary wires instead of coaxial cable, which can cost from two to ten times as much. We expect to see more creative use of slo-scan in security systems, in appropriate combination with regular cameras and recorders, and integral alarm electronics.

Color TV

Color CCTV offers a benefit in security monitoring in that it adds information that can aid in identification of a criminal, but this benefit has seldom been perceived to be especially valuable in real security-budget dollars. As the cost of color CCTV systems begins to more closely approach that of monochrome, we expect a significant switchover and a substantially greater share of the applications to be using color equipment.

THE FUTURE OF COMPUTER AND COMMUNICATIONS SECURITY

Computer and communications security can be correctly considered to be an emerging product area, despite the fact that products for these purposes have been offered for many years; cryptographic encoding and decoding boxes, for example, were offered by half a dozen vendors in the early 1970s, but few users noticed and even fewer bought, and only one of those vendors survives to participate in the current serious market. The DES (IBM's Data Encryption Standard) was introduced in 1970 and is still embroiled in controversy; one set of opponents claim that the security which the DES provides is not worth the cost, and another set contends that its 56-bit key does not provide enough security. Physical access control devices have been around for over twenty years, but have been offered connected to terminals and computers since only the mid-1980s. Passwords have been used for access to the computer system for twenty years, but callback devices and passwords within modems are of recent vintage. Only auditing software, which may be the most effective security measure of all, is a venerable and proven product which has been available and in productive use for a dozen years.

Since we are now experiencing initial product offerings to this marketplace, we can safely predict that as a general trend these primitive products will be tested, accepted, rejected, and altered, and that from them in the 1990s will come the second generation of products which will endure for a longer time. It is also safe to predict that the leading vendors of the second generation of products will be a different group from those whose products are now leading the way: it has historically been the fate of the technological pioneer to blaze the trail and to leave his bones bleaching in the wilderness, while the promised land is reached by those well-funded and well-marketed plodders who follow.

Out of the current melee, we foresee a number of specific developments that will shape the future of computer and communications security products and their vendors.

Cryptographics: Easier and Cheaper

There are currently approximately two dozen vendors offering a variety of products that utilize a variety of cryptographic techniques. In general, the users do not understand the technology of the products, and are unconvinced that the disease is sufficiently serious to be worth the cost of curing it. We expect that methods and products will become standardized—the DES is certainly the most prominent current candidate to become the basis for a standard that could embody a variety of levels of security. We expect that costs will be reduced due to standardization, the increased volume of products sold, and most importantly, due to the fact that cryptographic facilities will be offered as built-in options with computing systems, rather than as third-party add-ons which they are now. We expect increased user acceptance, not due to increased user understanding of the technology, but due to the relatively small incremental cost of adding encryption.

Personal Computer Security

The need to solve the security problems attendant to the personal computer has become widely recognized only during this past year, even though many of us have cried into the wilderness for the past several years. A few physical access control products began to come into the market in 1985, and we expect a profusion of such offerings as the traditional access control vendor community recognizes this new opportunity: these products will be useful for traditional computer terminals as well. File encryption software, audit trail, and activity-logging packages will also be helpful, and these are now economically feasible since the personal computer now has as much memory and computing power as did a full-scale computer less than a decade ago. Networking and electronic mail security in the form of communications access control packages will follow by 1990.

Integrated Products

Currently, vendors of security products are a separate group from vendors of computers and communications products, so that, for example, one must purchase a computer from one vendor, a modem from another, and an encryption device for the communications line from yet a third vendor. Integration of cryptographic capability into the modem and integration of both into the computer will result in fewer distinct products, with greater capability, being offered by fewer vendors at lower cost. Some of this is already beginning to occur.

Entry of the Computer Manufacturers

With the exception of IBM, the list of vendors of computer and communications security products is notable for the absence of all of the vendors of computer systems and equipment. The future will clearly be the opposite. The current technology being pioneered by a group of entrepreneurs will be absorbed by the major manufacturers and into the computer systems, to be offered as optional equipment and features just as color terminals and payroll software are today.

Index